WEALTH

WEALTH

How the World's High-Net-Worth Grow,
Sustain and Manage Their Fortunes

Associates of
Merrill Lynch and Capgemini

John Wiley & Sons Canada, Ltd.

Library and Archives Canada Cataloguing in Publication Data

Wealth : how the world's high-net-worth grow, sustain and manage their fortunes / by associates of Merrill Lynch and Capgemini.

Includes index.
ISBN 978-0-470-15303-1

1. Finance, Personal. 2. Wealth. 3. Investments. 4. Rich people—Finance, Personal. I. Merrill Lynch & Co. (1973-) II. Capgemini (Firm)

HG179.W3945 2008   332.024'01   C2008-900607-0

Production Credits
Cover design: Michael Freeland
Interior text design: Adrian So
Printer: Friesens

John Wiley & Sons Canada, Ltd.
6045 Freemont Blvd.
Mississauga, Ontario
L5R 4J3

Printed in Canada

1 2 3 4 5 FP 12 11 10 09 08

To Our Clients and Our Colleagues

CONTENTS

Acknowledgments   xiii

**Foreword: Our Eight Convictions about the
Future of Wealth Management**   xvii

Taking Full Advantage of a Wealth of Opportunities   xix

Appreciating What a Difference a Decade Makes   xx

Leveraging Holistic Wealth Management to
Meet the Demands of the Maserati Investor Class   xxv

Recognizing "Asset Allocation" as Simply
Code for "Risk Management"   xxviii

Preparing for Increased Dependence on
Alternative Investments   xxviii

Witnessing the Rise of International Investing   xxix

Exploring the Emergence of Generational Wealth Issues   xxx

Changing the Rules and Roles of Philanthropy   xxxi

Looking to the Future of Wealth Management   xxxii

Chapter 1: The Evolution of Wealth Management   1

Preparing the Next Generation   1

Transitioning from a Transaction-Based
Industry to Wealth Management   6

Advocating the Triple-A Wealth Management Strategy   8

Placing a Renewed Focus on the Wealthy   10

The Changing Role of the Financial Advisor   11

Improving the Advisor–Client Dialogue   15

Understanding the HNWI Advantage:
How the Wealthy Manage to Enjoy Robust
Returns during Good Times and Bad   19

Describing the State of the World's Wealth   21

Prime Drivers of HNWI Wealth   24

Looking Forward   31

**Chapter 2: Global Trends and What
        They Mean for International Investing**   33

Coining the Term "Emerging Markets"   33

Globalization's Growing Impact on
High-Net-Worth Individuals   37

China: An Emerging Market for Foreign Investment   44

India: A Growing Major Economic Force   49

The European Union: The World's
Largest Integrated Economy   54

United States: Lost Luster   56

Latin America: A Growing Regional Economy   58

Globalization Promotes Local Investing   61

Radical Changes Impact Investment Opportunities   63

International Markets' Success Is Forcing U.S.
Investors to Rethink Their Domestic Focus   65

Emerging Markets Become Mainstream   68

Beyond Emerging Markets Lies the Final Frontier   69

**Chapter 3: Technology's Critical
    Role in Wealth Management**   75

Dawning of the Digital Age   75

Dispelling Five Myths of Online Private Banking   77

  Myth #1: Most private banking clients are not
  sufficiently Internet-savvy for online banking.   78

  Myth #2: An advisor-based business like private banking
  can only be distributed through high-touch channels.   80

  Myth #3: Because of concerns about security
  and confidentiality, private clients will never
  fully adopt the Internet channel.   82

  Myth #4: Financial advisors don't benefit from
  the increased transparency that online private
  banking provides clients.   83

  Myth #5: Online channel implementation requires
  major IT investments by the private banks with little
  return and little ability to pass costs on to clients.   84

Examining the Three Faces of Information Technology   85

  Client Facing   86

  Provider Facing   87

  Advisor Facing   88

Assessing the Role of Technology in the
Advisor–Client Relationship: A Cautionary Tale   89

Outsourcing Functions: The Joys and Perils   94

  Virtual Service Networks   94

  Service-Oriented Architecture   95

Melding Information Technology and Culture   96

Chapter 4: Holistic Wealth Management   99

Moving Beyond Investments to a
Broader Range of Services   99

Expecting More Extensive Financial Advice   106

Using Debt to Build Wealth   109

Defining the Role of Family Offices
within Wealth Management   112

Expecting Clear Reporting   114

Demanding Privacy   117

Chapter 5: The Doctrine of Asset Allocation   121

Enhancing Returns with Modern Portfolio Theory (MPT)   121

Uncovering the Preferred Asset Allocations
of the Wealthy and Ultra-Wealthy   125

Moving Beyond Modern Portfolio Theory   130

Commenting Expertly on Asset Allocation   135

Chapter 6: Alternative Investment Strategies   139

The Appeal of Alternative Investments   139

Structured Products for Individuals   145

Developing New Products by Listening to Investors   150

Grabbing Headlines: Hedge Funds and Private Equity   152

Hedge Funds   153

Private Equity   156

Facing the Challenges Ahead   160

Chapter 7: Family Matters 163

Fostering Financial Literacy, HNW Style 163

Partaking in Values Retreats 170

Enabling the Next Generation of
Wealthy through Peer Networking 172

Preparing for Great Wealth Transfer 174

Creating a Wealth Transfer Plan 174

Recognizing Regional Diversity 177

Appreciating Gender Differences 179

Preserving the Family Legacy 181

Chapter 8: The New Philanthropy: Proactive Involvement 183

Giving with Purpose 183

Philanthropy Lessons from One
of Great Britain's Wealthiest Men 184

Committing Funds and Demanding Accountability 187

Comparing Regional Differences 188

Global Trend 1: The Rise of Venture Philanthropy 189

Global Trend 2: Giving While Living 193

Taking Tax Consequences into Account 195

Making a Difference with Family
Foundations and Donor-Advised Funds 198

Witnessing a Decline in Giving? 202

Expressing Optimism for HNWIs' Grandchildren 203

Chapter 9: The Future of Holistic Wealth Management   207

    Creating Conditions to Build and Preserve Wealth
    for the Future—the Michael Lee-Chin Way   207

    Identifying Future Trends to Take into Consideration   213

    Increasing Wealth Across the Globe   214

    Easing the Stress of Intergenerational Wealth Transfer   218

    Trending Toward Open Architecture and Unbiased Advice 220

Index   223

ACKNOWLEDGMENTS

While the idea for *WEALTH* was inspired by the tenth anniversary of the *World Wealth Report*, it quickly took on a life of its own. This deeply collaborative effort has evolved over the past two years to, we hope, provide a richer view of the world of wealth.

First and foremost, we would like to thank the management of Merrill Lynch and Capgemini for their support in agreeing to support this effort amidst multiple priorities, as well as the many thought leaders who graciously agreed to share their views, insights and lessons learned about wealth and its preservation. Of these, we are particularly grateful for the expertise and guidance of Bob McCann, Vice Chairman and President of Global Wealth Management at Merrill Lynch, and Bertrand Lavayssière, Managing Director of Global Financial Services for the Capgemini Group. If not for their steadfast support and deep industry knowledge, the storyline could not have matured.

Secondly, we would like to thank the management of Merrill Lynch and Capgemini for their support in agreeing to support this effort amidst multiple priorities, as well as the many executives at both firms who invested considerable time and effort in reflecting and commenting on the points of view expressed in this book. The ability of both organizations to reach out to a global network of economists, academics and experts in the field for validation and support was a key factor in broadening the scope of the work.

Thirdly, Capgemini and Merrill Lynch would like to thank Michael Sisk of Hamilton, Bridges Media Inc., for the numerous interviews he conducted across the globe, and for his skilled organization of the many stories and ensuing research into a commendable first draft. In the process of guiding our manuscript to completion, Stephen Fenichell of Merrill Lynch's Executive Communications group provided color, texture and a narrative framework, in addition to conducting further interviews and research.

We would also like to extend our sincere appreciation to Petrina Dolby of secor Consulting for her insight, creativity and tenacity in overseeing this complex and collaborative process.

On the Capgemini team, we would like to acknowledge the key contributions of William Sullivan, Manager of Capgemini's Global Wealth Management Center of Excellence, for his leadership in the book's development; Scott Becchi, Karen Cohen, Chris Gant, Andres Guibert, Bob McGraw, Patrick Neuwirth, Eric Rajendra, Stephen Ray, Ileana van der Linde, Liz Witt, and Alan Young from Capgemini's Financial Services practice for providing industry insights and expertise; and Capgemini's Strategic Research Group for providing research and in-depth market analysis. We would also like to thank Capgemini's Group management for supporting this endeavor.

At Merrill Lynch, Erik Hendrickson, Michael O'Looney and Tricia Nestfield provided industry perspective and oversight of the editorial and research process.

We would additionally like to recognize the contributions of a number of senior executives at Merrill Lynch, including: Stacy Allred, Sameer Aurora, John Barrett, Nancy Bello, Richard Bernstein, Stephen Bodurtha, Candace Browning, Darcie Burk, August Cenname, Daniel Dunn, John Hogarty, Richard Jones, Karen Klein, Joseph Lam, Albert Lee, Rahul Malhotra, Patricia McLaughlin, Marcus Mitchell, Alyssa Moeder, former CEO Stan O'Neal, Paula Polito, David Ratcliffe, Diane Schueneman, Raj Sharma, Dan Sontag, Ed Specter, Michael Sullivan, Tom Sweeney, Victor Tan, John Thiel, Kevin Waldron, and Ken Winch.

We would like to express our appreciation to our colleagues at Wiley for adeptly steering *WEALTH* through the publishing process and for their collective commitment to editorial excellence. A special thank you goes to Karen Milner, Elizabeth McCurdy, Pamela Vokey, Peter Knapp and Lucas Wilk.

Finally, we have benefited enormously from the many industry authorities and clients who have been so generous with their time in granting extensive interviews for this book. Namely: Antoine van Agtmael of Emerging Markets Management, LLC, Patricia Angus of Shelterwood Financial Services, Jacques Attali of PlaNet Finance, Edward Bernard and James A.C. Kennedy of T. Rowe Price, Dr. James Canton, Jon Carroll of Family Office Metrics, Charles Collier of Harvard University, Larry Fink and Ralph Schlosstein of BlackRock, Doug Freeman and Lee Hausner of IFF Advsiors, Gerald Cavendish Grosvenor, The Duke of Westminster, Gregory Johnson of Franklin Templeton Investments, Michael Lee-Chin of AIC Investments, James Rothenberg of Capital Research and Management, Michael Saadie of ANZ Private Bank, Dr. Lee Shau Kee of Henderson Land Development, Charlie Simonyi, Domhnal Slattery of International Aviation Management Group, Dr. Paul Tiffany of The Wharton School of Business of the University of Pennsylvania and of the Haas School of Business of the University of California, Berkeley, and Dr. Cheng Yu-Tung of New World Development.

Our Eight Convictions about the Future of Wealth Management

By Bertrand Lavayssière, Managing Director of Global
Financial Services for the Capgemini Group and Bob
McCann, Vice Chairman and President of Global Wealth
Management at Merrill Lynch & Co.

The world is witnessing the greatest period of wealth accumulation
in history. Never before have so many people from so many different
regions of the earth become so wealthy in so short a period of time.
And never before have so many opportunities existed to create new
wealth, both as the natural outcome of new ideas and the product of
existing capital appropriately and prudently leveraged. Due to the
downfall of the Berlin Wall in 1989, coupled with the concomitant
rise of global capitalism and globally integrated capital markets, the
twenty-first century presents an unprecedented opportunity for innovative and entrepreneurial spirits to profit from these long-term
secular trends. This will continue to fuel the concentration and
consolidation of wealth at the unprecedented velocity witnessed
over the past decade. Although economic disruptions and volatility can by no means be relegated to history, we firmly believe that
the future of global capitalism is bright. In support of this belief,
we have documented and validated eight convictions, which we are

convinced will continue to shape the world of wealth as it evolves in the twenty-first century.

Eight Firmly Held Convictions Regarding the Future of Wealth Management

Based on our collective experience, extensive research and dozens of interviews conducted specifically for this book, we have developed eight firmly held convictions regarding the future of wealth management. We will illustrate all eight throughout the book by using detailed examples and case studies. We will demonstrate the myriad ways by which wealthy investors and their financial advisors, as well as the broader community of aggressive and informed investors worldwide, can materially benefit from the wide universe of wealth creation opportunities before us.

1. The global economy and investment focus for high-net-worth individuals is evolving from a two-pole world dominated by Europe and North America to a multi-polar world including Asia and the Middle East.

2. This multi-polar evolution will accelerate as an unprecedented wave of wealth transfer occurs, putting assets into the hands of a younger, more internationally focused, technologically savvy generation.

3. Diversification of investments across different investment vehicles, asset classes and geographies will be the key to consistent and, at times, superior performance.

4. New investment products will continue to arrive at a rapid pace, accompanied by rapid obsolescence and product cycles. As in the past, early adopters may benefit substantially before a new product is commoditized and returns inevitably revert to the mean.

5. Investor sophistication—the ability to understand these new products, to invest in them and to compare them—will depend on a mixture of cutting-edge technology, information and expertise.

6. Investors will have an increasing responsibility to stay informed and educated. They must be ready to engage and question their financial advisors about wealth management strategies. They must participate in the dialogue.

7. Family education around financial issues will become increasingly important to demystify money, create family unity and prepare children to be good stewards of capital—whether through investments or philanthropy.

8. Business ownership will remain the main driver of wealth creation. Business owners will increasingly demand that advisors manage their wealth as professionally as they manage their own businesses, prompting advisors to offer an ever-broader and deeper range of financial products and services to the wealthy and ultra-wealthy.

TAKING FULL ADVANTAGE OF A WEALTH OF OPPORTUNITIES

The recent growth of global wealth prompts an obvious question: How can the wealthy (and those of us who aspire to join them) and their families maximize their returns, commensurate with their risk appetite, in a rational and measured way that permits them to sleep at night while achieving their increasingly complex financial and personal goals? The purpose of this book is to provide some insightful working responses to this question. Not only are we convinced that the current era promises an unprecedented opportunity for abundance, but that all of us can share in the seemingly limitless prosperity of our era.

While the various topics treated herein may be of keenest interest to present and aspiring possessors of wealth, the rapidly increasing population of financial advisors and their associates will find much to provoke their interest and stimulate discussion of the ever-shifting landscape of wealth management. While we can by no means guarantee that we will address every question posed by professionals, we can offer assurances that most of the broader dimensions of this holistic wealth management process have been covered.

When Capgemini and Merrill Lynch published their first *World Wealth Report* in 1997, the goal of the project was modest and simple: to compile and distribute a discrete set of data points, conclusions and insights describing an explosively expanding class of individuals whom we dubbed HNWIs ("high-net-worth individuals"),[1] individuals with more than US$1 million in financial assets—and about whom the financial services industry of the time knew astonishingly little.

We could not have known then that this project would inadvertently give birth to the now commonly used acronym, HNWI (pronounced by the cognoscenti as "HUNWEE") which would be destined to take pride of its place in the popular parlance of the burgeoning wealth management industry. As we began more closely to observe, track and interpret the distinctive needs and behaviors of these individuals, we identified an even more rarefied class of investors with financial assets in excess of US$30 million, which we subsequently called ultra-HNWIs (ultra-high-net-worth individuals)[2] who exhibited behaviors more institutional-like than the "average" HNWI.

APPRECIATING WHAT A DIFFERENCE A DECADE MAKES

The world of wealth described in that first seven-page report was positively quaint by today's standards. In 1996, the number of dollar millionaires had just topped six million; ten years later the ranks of the wealthy had swelled to nearly ten million. In 1996, the pool of assets controlled by the wealthy stood at approximately US$17 trillion. By 2007, that number had surged to US$37 trillion.

---

1. HNWIs are defined as individuals with US$1 million in investible assets, excluding their primary residence.

2. Ultra-HNWIs are defined as individuals with US$30 million in investible assets, excluding their primary residence.

The approximately twenty trillion dollars in newly accrued assets accumulated by the wealthy and ultra-wealthy over the past decade represents not only a trend toward ever-greater wealth consolidation and concentration, but also its accelerating globalization. In 1996, the most dynamic regional wealth generators worldwide were in Asia and Latin America, although all the emerging markets were shortly to be significantly if briefly disturbed by the onset of economic contagion from Asia and its fallout. This included the disruptive default on Russian sovereign debt, which first raised its ugly head in the summer of 1997.

We also documented a trend by which many of the world's wealthiest individuals and families were abandoning traditional private banking havens in Switzerland in favor of offshore centers in the Caribbean. Additionally, we identified a behavioral pattern that has since accelerated, as the wealthy and ultra-wealthy diversified their portfolios to embrace a number of then-radical and exotic investment strategies, loosely grouped under the generic term "alternative investments."

Whether those alternative investments included taking the plunge into frontier emerging markets, making a proprietary private equity placement, or perhaps purchasing one or more holdings from a rapidly expanding menu of comparatively exotic structured financial instruments and vehicles,[3] the penchant of the wealthy and ultra-wealthy to seek enhanced performance closely mirrored an increased appetite for measured and structured risk—i.e., alternative investments—on the part of institutional investors. By late 2007 and 2008, however, the global credit crunch threatens to cast many of the rosy scenarios underlying these pooled assets into question.

---

3. The Committee on the Global Financial System (CGFS) provided the following definition of structured finance in its January 2005 report, *The Role of Ratings in Structured Finance: Issues and Implications*: "Structured finance instruments can be defined through three key characteristics: (1) pooling of assets (either cash-based or synthetically created); (2) tranching of liabilities that are backed by the asset pool (this property differentiates structured finance from traditional "pass-through" securitisations); (3) de-linking of the credit risk of the collateral asset pool from the credit risk of the originator, usually through use of a finite-lived, standalone special purpose vehicle (SPV)."

A brief history and synopsis of the ten-year trends can be found in Figure 0.1.

Figure 0.1 – *World Wealth Report* Spotlight Sections, 1996–2007

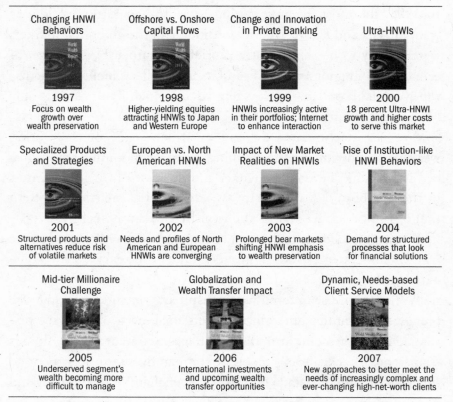

Changing HNWI Behaviors	Offshore vs. Onshore Capital Flows	Change and Innovation in Private Banking	Ultra-HNWIs
1997	**1998**	**1999**	**2000**
Focus on wealth growth over wealth preservation	Higher-yielding equities attracting HNWIs to Japan and Western Europe	HNWIs increasingly active in their portfolios; Internet to enhance interaction	18 percent Ultra-HNWI growth and higher costs to serve this market

Specialized Products and Strategies	European vs. North American HNWIs	Impact of New Market Realities on HNWIs	Rise of Institution-like HNWI Behaviors
2001	**2002**	**2003**	**2004**
Structured products and alternatives reduce risk of volatile markets	Needs and profiles of North American and European HNWIs are converging	Prolonged bear markets shifting HNWI emphasis to wealth preservation	Demand for structured processes that look for financial solutions

Mid-tier Millionaire Challenge	Globalization and Wealth Transfer Impact	Dynamic, Needs-based Client Service Models
2005	**2006**	**2007**
Underserved segment's wealth becoming more difficult to manage	International investments and upcoming wealth transfer opportunities	New approaches to better meet the needs of increasingly complex and ever-changing high-net-worth clients

From 1997 to 2007, the number of HNWIs grew at an annual rate of 7.6 percent, from nearly six million to nearly ten million. At the same time, their financial assets surged at an annual rate of 8 percent, to US$37.2 trillion from US$16.6 trillion. In 2006, for the first time, the Forbes 400 was composed strictly of billionaires. HNWIs, who tend to be older than the general population and hover somewhere on the cusp of traditional retirement age, have been saving and spending in their lifetimes according to patterns and strategies quite different from the wealth accumulation and preservation strategies employed by their parents. What is more, as these wealthy individuals pass their assets on to their children, they will in all likelihood usher in a new generation, armed with a different mindset and approach, which is likely to give rise to yet newer forms of investment methods and strategies. The profound social and economic implications of what is predicted to be the largest intergenerational transfer of wealth in history will be discussed at length in later chapters. This growth over the past decade is broken down into an annual timeline in Figure 0.2 below.

Figure 0.2 – *World Wealth Report* Scorecard, 1996–2006

HNWI Global	1996	1997	1998	1999	2000	2001	2002	2003	2004	2005	2006
Financial Wealth (US$ trillions)	16.6	19.1	21.6	25.5	27.0	26.2	26.7	28.3	30.7	33.4	37.2
Number of HNWIs (millions)	4.5	5.2	5.9	7.0	7.2	7.1	7.3	7.7	8.2	8.8	9.5

Source: Capgemini Lorenz Curve Model; Capgemini/Merrill Lynch 2007 *World Wealth Report*

Running concurrently with these long-term economic and demographic trends has been the overarching phenomenon of globalization, coupled with the advent of sophisticated technologies that have integrated the world's capital markets while fostering the creation of a steady stream of complex financial instruments. If two decades ago the financial services industry resembled a mom-and-pop sidewalk food stand offering a mere handful of plain-vanilla entrees on its menu—stocks, bonds and mutual funds—today's financial marketplace more closely evokes a full-service restaurant located inside a five-star hotel, replete with smiling and eminently capable maîtres d'hôtel and a concierge prepared to meet—and ideally anticipate—every conceivable need, articulated or not, of the discerning investor.

The popularity of structured instruments—including collateralized debt obligations and other forms of asset-backed securities, some of which courted controversy and even outright incredulity during the credit crunch of 2007—is clearly responsible for a significant proportion of the new wealth spawned within the first decade of the twenty-first century. Yet broader access to these high-performance and often high-risk vehicles (the Porsches and Maseratis of the financial world) has not come without cost or anxiety. The sheer complexity of such instruments demands a level of expertise to fully comprehend and navigate through their exotic universe and has only increased the value of expert guidance and advice to baffled yet justifiably intrigued clients. Many of today's structured products require advanced math degrees not only to create, but even to comprehend.[4] The global nature of these investments also means that numerous tax and regulatory jurisdictions may come into play, further enhancing the chances that expert guidance in the field will be required by clients and advisors alike when engaging with a wide variety of products.

Just as the *World Wealth Report* colorfully accomplished over the past decade, this book will trace the evolution of the financial services industry, from its comparatively humble beginnings as a straightforward purveyor of stocks, bonds, mutual funds and garden-variety investment advice to the affluent masses, to a globally distributed group of high-level custom-shops or boutiques, frequently contained within and supported by global financial powerhouses, and offering a staggering array of products and services precisely targeted at the wealthiest of wealthy individuals and households. We will also provide guidance on the strategies and insights developed by many HNWIs to take full advantage of the plethora of often exotic products and services on the menu.

---

4. Among the most commonly formulated structured finance instruments:
   - *Asset-backed securities* (ABS) are bonds or notes based on pools of assets, or collateralized by the cash flows from a specified pool of underlying assets.
   - *Mortgage-backed securities* (MBS) are asset-backed securities whose cash flows are backed by the principal and interest payments of a set of mortgage loans.
   - *Collateralized debt obligations* (CDOs) consolidate a group of fixed income assets such as high-yield debt or asset-backed securities into a pool, which is then divided into various tranches.
   - *Collateralized mortgage obligations* (CMOs) are CDOs backed primarily by mortgages.
   - *Collateralized bond obligations* (CBOs) are CDOs backed primarily by corporate bonds.
   - *Collateralized loan obligations* (CLOs) are CDOs backed primarily by leveraged bank loans.
   - *Credit derivatives* are contracts to transfer the risk of the total return on a credit asset falling below an agreed level, without transfer of the underlying asset.

As we noted a decade ago, the traditional world of the obsequiously discreet and low-key private banker was even then fading fast into a dusty past. "Private banks can no longer expect to receive handsome fees for providing old-fashioned trust and investment management services merely to protect assets from inflation or domestic taxation." Clients then, as now, "are becoming increasingly sophisticated and demanding...and expect not only outstanding service but consistent strong performance, active wealth management, and a multi-market investment strategy."[5]

Family offices and multi-family offices that provide tailored advice to an exclusive and limited network of families, relatives and friends have continued to proliferate in the HNW universe. Financial services boutiques (many located within larger institutions) that strive to maintain the high-touch intimacy of the traditional private bank have continued to thrive. Several of the largest financial institutions have been quite aggressive in preserving the best of the private-banking tradition by carving out private banks within their larger wealth management divisions, while supplementing the skill sets of their high-production private bankers with expertise drawn from the broad array of activities conducted by the firm.

LEVERAGING HOLISTIC WEALTH MANAGEMENT TO MEET THE DEMANDS OF THE MASERATI INVESTOR CLASS

Wealthy and ultra-wealthy investors' perennially urgent demand for convenient and comprehensive access to markets and information has given rise to a dazzlingly broad range of bespoke products and asset classes. The most avid consumers of these new asset classes consist primarily of a new client class we have labeled "active performance-driven investors." While once upon a time the average wealthy investor might have sought out a private banker for his or her

---

5. 1997 *World Wealth Report*, Capgemini/Merrill Lynch.

high-end investment advice—probably the same private banking house that served his or her parents or grandparents—today's more versatile, knowledgeable and empowered HNWIs are inclined to take a broader view of their entire financial picture. This broader view has in turn ushered in an era of financial service in which a comparatively small number of firms with a global footprint are prepared to combine the intimacy of a financial boutique with the intellectual capital of a financial powerhouse.

Active performance-driven investors require returns backdated into the past and thrusting far into the future, encompassing asset allocation, risk management, credit, tax strategies, insurance, estate planning, college planning, financial education and philanthropy—not to mention the occasional provision of a sought-after ballet ticket, entree to an intimate lecture by a world-class financial expert, or possibly even a financial boot camp for their children so they are more fully grounded in legacy issues and the ins and outs of intra-generational wealth transfer.

When a HNWI turns to a wealth manager in our era, he or she invariably demands to know about and perhaps even fully understand the identity of the newest exotic investment vehicle being offered, much as the same discerning consumer might prefer to acquire a custom-made designer suit as opposed to a mass-production item pulled straight off the rack. Whether it is the most secure risk management tactic, the latest estate tax strategy, or the best way to structure a charitable foundation in accordance with local tax law, the inherent complexity of managing wealth in this day and age demands a genuinely holistic approach.

Particularly for many of the more recently minted HNWIs, as well as for entrepreneurs so often busy building their businesses that they lack the time or inclination to dwell on wealth management issues, it is critical to grasp the fact that a more holistic wealth management view offers the surest path to wealth for the broadest class of discerning investors. For advisors, it pays to know that HNWIs will increasingly expect this breadth of service. For large banks, with complex global structures, it has become all the more urgent to break down silos and integrate across lines of business and geographies to provide the holistic service HNWIs need and will expect.

In our chapter on investor sophistication, we examine the remarkable strides in financial literacy among HNWIs, arguably driven by three factors:

1. The enormous amount of information available via the Internet, which allows HNWIs to educate themselves more easily than ever before;

2. Globalization, which has forcibly broadened HNWIs' investment views;

3. Steadily increasing household liquidity. Through initial public offerings and private equity buyouts, entrepreneurial HNWIs, or those with a family business, may suddenly find themselves with tens or even hundreds of millions of dollars on hand, which they must wisely allocate across asset classes and geographies.

A key finding here is that as HNWIs become more engaged than ever before in their investments, they are less and less self-directed. HNWIs will continue to require and value the high-level expertise and sophistication that a good financial advisor can bring to the table. That may be good news for advisors, but it also means that HNWIs are relentlessly raising the bar of expectations for them. They fully expect their financial advisor to understand and explain how products fit into the overall portfolio. Or, depending upon the product or instrument in question, they expect their advisor to be in a position to call upon the right expert to add their specialized knowledge to the relationship—a synergy that private banks cradled within global financial institutions and offering a wide array of products and services excel at delivering.

To ensure the highest level of service, HNWIs need to be active participants in a dynamic dialogue between client and advisor. Investors cannot be passive bystanders to the management of their wealth. Advisors, for their part, need to know how to encourage and stimulate this dialogue so that goals may be clearly understood and expectations managed on both sides. The wealth of opportunities available today mean that one's net worth should be viewed as a means to achieve life goals, in addition to being a potential revenue stream.

RECOGNIZING "ASSET ALLOCATION" AS SIMPLY CODE FOR "RISK MANAGEMENT"

"Asset allocation" is, in fact, code for "risk management." HNWIs and their advisors should use asset allocation as a tool to achieve acceptable risk levels. If conducted correctly, unexpectedly high returns are as much a warning sign that risk levels are out of sync as low returns. While concerns about achieving high returns are perfectly understandable, rest assured that the rules of investing are suspended for no one and that unexpectedly high returns will very likely over time lead to unexpected volatility and losses. According to the "wealth allocation framework" designed by Ashvin Chhabra, former head of wealth management strategies and analytics at Merrill Lynch—now at the Institute of Advanced Studies at Princeton—HNWIs and their advisors should move beyond modern portfolio theory, today the basis of virtually all investment strategies, and put *risk allocation* ahead of *asset allocation*.

PREPARING FOR INCREASED DEPENDENCE ON ALTERNATIVE INVESTMENTS

We delve deeply into the heady issue of alternative asset classes, including hedge funds, private equity, derivatives of all stripes and even investments of passion such as art or yachts. All are playing an increasingly critical role in the ongoing quest for diversification of assets and concomitant mitigation of risk. Collectively, alternative assets have shifted from a minor component of the average HNWI investment portfolio ten years ago to roughly 25 percent today; in addition, this multifaceted asset class has become a veritable wellspring of financial innovation and high returns for clients and advisors alike. While financial advisors must ensure that their clients have been provided with access to the best thinking around these innovative products, attaining diversity through an appropriate distribution of risk across multiple alternative asset classes remains the key to consistent and even superior performance. HNWIs who fail to demand educated access to these asset classes are, by definition, failing to optimize their returns in the current environment.

WITNESSING THE RISE OF INTERNATIONAL INVESTING

The rise of international investing is the natural outgrowth of globalization and the free flow of capital it encourages. This international flavor in investing has been adopted by a large percentage of investors globally. An exception has been North American investors, who have not taken full advantage of the growth and benefits international diversification has to offer. They have historically invested the least overseas, certainly by comparison to their European and Asian counterparts, thanks to the deep and stable U.S. market. This provincial strategy has until recently served them fairly well, but as exotic frontier markets including Vietnam, Dubai and Brazil continue to mature, such reluctance to invest overseas will limit potential returns. Overall, international investing will continue to grow and play a more significant role in investor portfolios, including those in North America as has been highlighted in the *WWRs* over the past three years.

In the meantime, emerging markets are attracting local investment on a scale never seen before. In Asia and the Middle East, where local wealth frequently flowed without question to Europe and North America, more capital is staying onshore. We see local HNWIs as canaries in the coal mine, with their increasing participation in their own markets and economies a powerful validation of the growing internationalization of capital (and of returns), which every wealthy individual or household worldwide should strongly consider emulating.

EXPLORING THE EMERGENCE OF GENERATIONAL WEALTH ISSUES

We zero in on the trends around educating children and multiple generations about wealth. Not long ago, parents could, if they chose, keep most of the details of their fortune hidden from children. Many did this not for the purpose of deception but out of a not unreasonable fear that if the full scope of their fortunes were known they would demotivate their children and create passive "trust funders"— children who sponge off their inherited wealth and never develop into fully formed adults who contribute to society.

Today's parents no longer have the luxury of nondisclosure— even if they think they still do. Information age tools, such as the Internet, and greater mandated disclosure by players in increasingly transparent financial markets mean that children are able to find out plenty about their family fortunes in the absence of parental consent. According to the most sophisticated advisors in this area, it is generally advisable to talk directly with these children about wealth, the responsibility it brings, and commonly held expectations about what they must accomplish with their lives than to leave offspring to a guessing game that might help to foster precisely the problems that most parents would prefer to avoid.

At educational seminars and "financial boot camps" sponsored by advisors such as Merrill Lynch, psychologists specializing in money and family dynamics increasingly play an invaluable role in helping wealthy families face the complex issues around great wealth—as will be discussed in greater detail in Chapters 1 and 3. These formal events have become critical for families engaged in preserving, protecting and passing on their wealth to future generations since, upon each generational transfer, HNW families must work harder to keep the family's portfolio from splintering into insignificance.

CHANGING THE RULES AND ROLES OF PHILANTHROPY

We identify and explore two major trends on the philanthropic scene: "venture philanthropy" and "giving while living." Today's millionaires—many with strong entrepreneurial bents—are working to change the rules of philanthropy by bringing corporate world discipline to philanthropic pursuits: they set specific goals and timelines, track and measure results, tie future funding to meeting certain milestones and, whenever possible, aim for profitability and self-sustainability. Today's entrepreneurially inclined philanthropists like to encourage entrepreneurship in their grant recipients, not handouts. In 2006, eBay co-founder Pierre Omidyar donated US$100 million to his alma mater, Tufts University, while stipulating that the funds be used exclusively to make micro loans to people in poor countries looking to start a business.

"Giving while living" has been provided a recent boost by Bill Gates, who in 2006 stepped down from his day-to-day duties at Microsoft to devote more time to the Bill and Melinda Gates Foundation, which focuses on global health and education. Just a few weeks after Gates made his announcement Warren Buffett declared that he would donate US$31 billion to the Foundation. The carefully considered decision on the part of the two wealthiest men in the world to tie their fortunes together—even posthumously—propelled philanthropy and its latest trends to the front pages of media outlets worldwide. For the less well-heeled, "giving while living" is being reinforced by the rise of donor-advised funds, which firms can set up with an initial contribution of no more than a few thousand dollars. Not only do donors enjoy the satisfaction of seeing their donations at work while still alive, but they can also keep tabs on their charities.

LOOKING TO THE FUTURE OF WEALTH MANAGEMENT

We wrap up with a look into the future. And we predict that the same drivers at work today—demographics, globalization and technology—will continue to propel and shape wealth management for decades to come. And they will do so in ways not necessarily obvious. For instance, the aging of HNWIs is generally expected to mean a wave of retirement and the need to implement "decumulation" or distribution strategies to manage cash flow over a thirty-year span of leisure. But how many HNWIs will truly retire? And how late might they push the age of that retirement? Dr. James Canton, CEO of the Institute for Global Futures and author of *The Extreme Future*, contends that many of today's HNWIs will continue to accumulate wealth well beyond the age that past generations retired.[6]

This is just one example of the twists and turns wealth management will take over the coming decades. For instance, what is the future of globalization? While it is likely to remain a powerful force, it is not without its vulnerabilities. Dr. Paul Tiffany, an adjunct associate professor of management at the Wharton School of the University of Pennsylvania, has observed the rise of more anti-trade legislation across the globe over the last four years than the previous twenty-five. The perceived inequalities created by China's managed currency will need to be corrected, he argues, or developed countries may pull back on free trade. Meanwhile, technology innovation and development continues apace in this space. Will we ever witness the rise of a truly integrated global electronic stock market? The political and regula-

---

6. Interview with the authors.

tory hurdles are certainly not insignificant or even fully understood at this stage, but such a development lies certainly within the realm of imagination, not to mention technological feasibility.[7]

Despite the fact that this book plainly focuses on wealth management strategies employed by the wealthy, we firmly believe the messages here are deeply relevant for a broader community of investors. Our reasoning is simple: the wealthy are trendsetters. By watching how they put their money to use, one gets a valuable insight and feeling for what investments will become popular and more widely available in the future. A case in point is how hedge funds and private equity investments have steadily moved downstream from HNWIs into the mainstream of strategies open to the mass affluent. Such forward-looking insight tends to be particularly valuable since HNW investment strategies tend to outperform those routinely employed by other categories of investors. The rich do, on average, get richer—and do so faster than other investors—because their purchasing power and their access to the best thinking and innovative products gives them an advantage, an advantage that we hope to confer through the knowledge embodied in this book.

As you can see in Figure 0.3, the higher the net worth, the faster wealth accumulates, with UHNWI's accounting for 1 percent of HNWI population, yet holding 35 percent of HNWI wealth.

For the broader investment community, the most persuasive argument for studying how HNWIs manage their wealth is to spot early trends and best practices that can help *everyone* with investable assets achieve superior results and returns—manifestly a pressing concern for many of us in an era when defined benefit plans are fast disappearing and even average-income investors must manage their retirement investments more aggressively. For HNWIs, learning best practices from each other has long been a proven and valuable strategy.

---

7. Interview with the authors.

Figure 0.3 – Number of HNWIs and Growth, 2004–2006

		Number of Individuals (000s)	% Growth[1]	% Total Wealth	
Ultra High Net Worth	$30 million	95.0 (1.0%)	11.3	35.1	2005–2006
		85.4 (1.0%)	10.2	33.6	2004–2005
"Mid-tier Millionaire"	$5 million to $30 million	881.7 (9.3%)	9.4	22.7	2005–2006
		803.6 (9.2%)	8.4	23.0	2004–2005
"Millionaire Next Door"	$1 million to $5 million	8,515.9 (89.7%)	8.2	42.2	2005–2006
		7,853.5 (89.8%)	6.2	43.4	2004–2005

Source: Capgemini Lorenz Curve Model; Capgemini/Merrill Lynch 2007 *World Wealth Report*
1. Figures from Bahrain and Qatar are not included in the growth calculation as both countries were added in the 2007 *WWR* and reflected in the 2006 HNWI population and wealth figures only—effect on growth at the global level is insignificant; numbers do not add up to 100 percent due to rounding.

This traditionally spontaneous practice—of which the most common variant is most likely the swapping of hot stock tips within the confines of private club locker rooms—has been increasingly systematized and reinforced in recent years by the establishment of peer networks such as TIGER 21. Co-founded by wealth investors Michael Sonnenfeldt, Richard Lavin and Tommy Gallagher, the New York-based TIGER 21 (*The Investment Group for Enhanced Returns in the 21st Century*) requires members to possess in excess of US$10 million in investible assets and relies upon candid peer review and sharing to enhance members' already sophisticated personal wealth management tools and strategies. Other similar groups, including the Institute for Private Investors and the Met Circle, offer comparable peer counseling to wealthy investors.

The highly touted success of such groups should not, however, lead us to assume that all innovation comes from the top. In some cases, valuable acumen and advice can "trickle up" to HNWIs from the entrepreneurial middle class. For example, much of the impetus and trial-and-error innovation around real-time, on-line trading of currencies and securities, and even the push for e-IPOs over the past decade, has come from middle-income "mass-affluent" investors who enthusiastically capitalized on decreasing transaction costs in the rapidly evolving open electronic marketplaces. Their ability to seize control of hitherto esoteric investing techniques and break into new markets without the direct use of any financial advisor made many HNWIs sit up and take notice, and led them to eschew the occasionally conventional guidance they were passively receiving from their advisors.

It is important for all of us who are intrigued and possibly even fascinated by the fast-changing face of wealth management to keep up with the latest trends whether generated from above or below. That said, it is also necessary to bear in mind that the nature, timing or origination of valuable new ideas is not easy to predict. Smart investors will always keep their ears to the ground and be constantly prepared to act with prudence and judgment. Our overriding objective is to provide you with some of the insights and guidance that the wealthiest individuals and most talented investment advisors currently enjoy so that no matter what your current net worth, you will find yourself in a position to take charge of and prudently safeguard your own financial future.

—Bertrand and Bob

CHAPTER 1

The Evolution of Wealth Management

PREPARING THE NEXT GENERATION

Judged strictly by outward appearances, the twenty-odd twenty-somethings gathered at the Steinberg Conference Center at the Wharton School are indistinguishable from the grad students passionately debating the pros and cons of conducting business in Africa in Conference Room A, or collectively salivating over the bounties bestowed by the judicious deployment of Investment Logarithms in Conference Room B. Among the nineteen males and seven females (median age: twenty-five) dutifully taking notes at the afternoon session are the generationally and demographically predictable percentage of skin piercings in locations other than the ear (4), hair dyed in primary colors other than blonde (3), two-ply V-necked cashmere sweaters in a dazzling array of designer colors (6) and non-native accents (2). In fact, the only commonly shared trait separating this group from any other attending conferences at Wharton is rather discrete: the approximate average net worth of the participants' parents was easily north of US$100 million. Or as the folks at MasterCard put it, "Priceless."

Welcome to Merrill Lynch's Financial Boot Camp, a high-touch, high-focus financial literacy program offered exclusively to the off-spring of ultra-high-net-worth (UHNW) clients around the globe by the firm's Global Wealth Management division "designed to give the next generation a higher level of understanding and comfort with money," according to its mission statement. "The agenda not only targets the hard financial concepts but also addresses the softer issues associated with family wealth." This is a fine example of how the wealth management industry has developed into one of the most sought after segments in financial services—it is no longer simply based on transactions with well-established clients, but has begun to focus on investing in relationships that will be of value in the future.

Expertly honing in on a few of the softer issues, Beverly Hills psychologist Lee Hausner (author of *Children of Paradise*, "a comprehensive parenting guide for financially advantaged families [that] offers a clear nine-step program for affluent parents to improve their skills and inspire healthy values in their children") kicks off the session by breezily drilling her raw recruits on the broader implications for human relations of the uneasy conversations on the ever-emotionally-charged subject of money that the wealthy frequently have with their non-wealthy peers.

Now a partner at IFF Advisors, a California-based consulting firm "created to enhance the human, intellectual, social and financial capitals" of its clients, "empowering them to do the right things by doing things right" with their money, Dr. Hausner candidly confronts such hot-button topics as that hardy perennial of the celebrity tabloids, the prenuptial agreement, followed by the awkwardness associated with requests for repayment of casually extended personal loans to non-wealthy "friends," and the bizarre hesitation so many people (wealthy and non-wealthy alike) seem to feel about challenging glaring overcharges on restaurant checks, for fear of being made to look cheap. But by far the keenest source point of tension, which drew the highest volume of knowing nods and winces from the crowd, is Dr. Hausner's scalding treatment of the topic "Speaking with Significant Others When Fiscal Unequals." The gist of Dr. Hausner's advice is that when the wealthy enter into relationships

(God forbid marriage) with those from less privileged backgrounds, difficulties may well ensue that could make that staple of late-night talk show humor, the prenup, seem like the soundest investment the family could make since it bought big into Google at US$120.

In many wealthy families, particularly those in which the family fortune has been earned not inherited, some degree of confusion may reign regarding the question of how best to talk to the offspring about the money they're likely to inherit as opposed to earn…because every self-made entrepreneur or corporate executive who goes on to reproduce is destined to rear not fellow scrappy pull-oneself-up-by-the-bootstraps types but children of privilege—or as Dr. Hausner would prefer to have it, "paradise." With the notable caveat, of course, that there's often trouble in paradise.

"In less affluent families," Hausner cautions, "money is often more about context than subtext. Kids constantly hear their parents argue about money. They're told that the family can't afford this or that, whether it's a trip to Walt Disney World or a college education. In high-net-worth (HNW) families, the kids might see the glossy brochures on the dining room table describing the next high-end vacation, or see the grand estate with the ten cars parked in the garage. But despite the visibility of that wealth, those same families often prefer to treat money as if it's taboo—a topic off-limits to honest discussion."

As Bertrand and Bob observe in the Foreword, the pace of global wealth creation has been remarkable—if not downright startling—over the past decade, which goes a long way toward explaining why wealth management issues have become so top of mind from New York to London to Mumbai to Beijing. Naturally, these established and newly minted millionaires want to know how to stay ahead—making wealth management so topical. But the mass affluent—emerging everywhere from the United States, Europe and increasingly the far-flung corners of the world—are paying attention to what works and what doesn't. They wisely want to learn from other successes and mistakes. They want a shot at joining the club. And they want a shot at doing what the wealthy have done since time immemorial—preserving and protecting their wealth for the next generation and even generations beyond. For that to take place, the next generation has to be educated about the perils and minefields of money—hence the financial boot camps conducted at Wharton and elsewhere globally.

In the here and now of the twenty-first century, wealth management firms of any size and scope are aggressively stepping into the breach, spying an opportunity to strengthen the advisor-client bond with the family by offering financial education for offspring as a natural adjunct to estate planning, philanthropic advice, alternative investments or exclusive access to an event starring a noted author, an invitation to a museum gallery on a closed day, tickets to the theater or a concert, a fly fishing outing on a noble estate in Scotland, or a round of golf at St. Andrews or Pebble Beach.

And if that all sounds like a far cry from Merrill Lynch's humble origins, well, welcome to the brave new world dominated by the wealthy and ultra-wealthy—the natural outcome of the stunning success of global capitalism in concentrating and consolidating family, personal and household wealth worldwide. In an era of galloping financial surplus, many firms have been obliged to adopt an outlook and skill set more commonly associated with private bankers domiciled in Switzerland, Luxembourg or other tax havens. They must transform into firms intensely focused on meeting the needs of the wealthy and ultra-wealthy in all their variability and complexity. As Merrill Lynch's Private Banking and Investment Group promisingly proclaims, "Substantial wealth is different. It deserves substantially different care."

Clearly such services are not typically available to the HNWI or the average investor, yet many of the lessons learned and applied herein can be adapted to multiple environments. For example, when anticipating the advent of a pending intergenerational wealth transfer, clearly communicate your expectations for the next generation, and seek to ensure that the next generation grasps and internalizes what tools and skills will be required to meet those expectations. Getting the next generation more deeply involved in actively thinking about and managing whatever level of wealth they aspire to or already possess can only be a positive development for all concerned.

Taking It from Wall Street to Main Street to Rodeo Drive

The securities industry in the United States in the early decades of the twentieth century was so scandalously under-regulated that most Americans, not without cause, saw little reason to distinguish between the purchase of corporate securities—stocks or bonds—and spending a long boozy night at a casino.

One of Wall Street's most rigidly held traditional precepts at the time was that it was ungentlemanly for brokers to advertise. Charlie Merrill, the son of a prosperous doctor who had suffered an irreversible financial setback after being badly beaten during a holdup near his home in Jacksonville, Florida, was one of the first to break from tradition by garnering his first clients by sending out a soberly written letter to a select list of New York physicians, offering them the chance to consider the purchase of a few promising shares in firms whose attractiveness he outlined in a low-key fashion. Merrill's conviction that a core value would be the provision of accurate and timely information to clients—a common practice fifty years later—was decades ahead of its time.

In 1915, Merrill and his partner, Edward Lynch, established a retail organization distinguished by the embrace of a pervasive philosophy that today would go by the name of "transparency." Merrill personally coached every new recruit to avoid overselling clients on specific securities, particularly if they offered a rapid speculative route to profit. "A salesman deserves no credit for any sale made on the strength of exaggerated statements," Merrill insisted in a widely circulated internal memo.

Not long before the 1929 stock market crash that he predicted, Merrill placed a US$5 million bet on the long-term future of the securities industry by purchasing a controlling share in E.A. Pierce & Co., the largest "wire-house" in the country. The overarching vision was to create a nationwide chain of brokerage houses, linked by telephone and telegraph wire, that would serve the financial needs of America's burgeoning middle class in the same way that the Safeway supermarket chain—Merrill's largest single personal investment—met its biological requirements.

At a two-day managerial conference held at New York's Waldorf Astoria hotel in April 1940, Merrill outraged his audience by suggesting that the lofty financial services industry had much to learn from the lowly food industry. "When a customer comes into a Safeway," he insisted, "she is entitled to buy with confidence, [knowing] that she will get full value at the lowest possible price." Brokerage or investment banking customers of the *new* Merrill Lynch should expect nothing more and nothing less. "We must bring Wall Street to Main Street," Merrill charged persuasively, "and we must use the efficient, mass merchandising methods of the chain store to do it!"

Financial writer Martin Mayer would eulogize Merrill's crowning achievement as having coaxed the broad public into the financial markets "not as lambs to be fleeced but as partners in the benefits."[1]

TRANSITIONING FROM A TRANSACTION-BASED INDUSTRY TO WEALTH MANAGEMENT

From its inception in 1915 by Charles Merrill and Edward Lynch, the firm of Merrill Lynch pioneered the transformation of the financial services industry from an enterprise based on the processing of individual transactions to a fee-based wealth management enterprise. A key figure in this evolution was Donald Regan, an ex-Marine World War II veteran and Harvard graduate who became CEO of Merrill Lynch in 1971 (and would go on to serve as Treasury Secretary under President Reagan).

Along with a number of his senior executives, Regan pushed for the scrapping of the regulated commission rates that for decades had kept Wall Street profits artificially high while providing a nearly

---

1. Martin Mayer, *Wall Street: Men and Money* (New York: Harper, 1955).

insurmountable barrier to entry for "average investors." He further challenged the traditional ways of the Street by taking the firm public in 1972, insisting that Wall Street firms that championed the sales of securities by publicly owned firms should practice what they preached and go public themselves.

But the chief insight that crowned the Regan era was his realization that trading and brokerage not just on Wall Street but around the world would soon be extensively automated. The long-term impact of technology on the brokerage business, he forecast, would be the erosion of the traditional source of profit for retail financial firms: high commissions on individual and block trades. In light of this realization, Regan launched Merrill Lynch Asset Management, a pioneering attempt to redefine the fundamental purpose of a traditional brokerage firm into an organization specializing in wealth management.

In the wake of wide-ranging deregulation at the national level, the overarching question posed by Regan's grand strategy was, what was the future of the financial services industry? Regan's key contribution was to promote the continuing conversion of the industry from a gentleman's club catering to the needs of the old money elite into a convenience-based service model dedicated to vastly improving the lives and financial security of the mass affluent. What would become industry practice within a few decades was—like Merrill's own innovations—rather radical for its time.

Paramount among the mass-market tools that Merrill Lynch developed to engineer this pronounced and profound shift of emphasis was the CMA (Cash Management Account), a first in the industry. The product of a creative collaboration between Merrill Lynch's wealth management business and a team of academics at Stanford's Research Institute, the CMA combined a checking account with a money market account, a brokerage account and a credit card account—a potent combination providing an extraordinarily convenient streamlining of services in an era before ATMs, PCs, and even handheld calculators. Having a CMA meant that for the first time, brokerage customers intending to buy and sell stocks no longer had to physically write checks and ensure that they were physically delivered to their brokers, who would then deposit the checks in their brokerage houses. The brokers would in turn track purchases of individual securities by actual stock certificates and check stubs, which clients were obliged to physically store in safety deposit boxes at their banks or brokerage houses.

Critics hotly denounced the CMA as a sneak attack on the Glass-Steagall Act, the Depression Era U.S. law that maintained a strict separation between the banking and securities industries. But the CMA had been scrupulously designed to pass muster with the relevant regulatory authorities and by 1977 the Federal Reserve Board, the Justice Department and the SEC had all given the green light for its rollout. As for the death of Glass-Steagall, although it survived for another two decades, the critics were spot on. When Citibank CEO Walter Wriston was asked in 1979 to describe the financial institution of the future, he replied without hesitation: "Don Regan already runs it—and it's called Merrill Lynch."[2]

ADVOCATING THE TRIPLE-A WEALTH MANAGEMENT STRATEGY

From the point of view of both firm and consumer, the CMA was a highly effective tool for managing the purchase and tracking of securities transactions. But its larger implication for the industry (and for its clients) was that it spearheaded a broad-based philosophical shift on the part of the entire industry away from a transaction-based to a fee-based foundation. John L. "Launny" Steffens, Merrill's Consumer Markets division chief at the time, publicly proclaimed that "profitability—both for our clients and for the firm—can no longer hinge on day-to-day transactions." He passionately advocated

---

2. "Don Regan: For Rhyme and Reason," William R. Doerner, *Time*, January 21, 1985.

a "Triple-A" strategic approach to managing the new broker-client relationship, which was comprised of a tripod supported by the following three legs:

1. Asset gathering;

2. Asset allocation;

3. Asset management.

"We believe long-term relationship building is best achieved by consultative selling," Steffens contended, describing the ideal broker-client relationship as one in which the financial firm would assist its clients across a broad spectrum of financial activities, including setting aside funds for education and retirement, establishing trusts, long-term health care financing and even estate planning services—a collaborative process that would bring in expertise provided by attorneys and certified public accountants. The mechanics of the CMA, coupled with the Triple-A approach to investment counseling, ushered in the era of holistic wealth management (HWM).

Asset gathering provided the foundation of this new approach. It emphasized placing the entirety of a client's assets under one roof as the only practical means to tackle the multiple challenges faced by clients attempting to get a grip on their financial lives in their totality. The newly enshrined doctrine of asset allocation—the rational distribution of a client's total pool of investible assets, to be treated in greater depth in a later chapter—could only be effectively implemented through comprehensive client profiling and extensive consultation.

Asset allocation called for a client's assets to be rationally allocated among a broad range of savings, investment and insurance instruments, including liabilities and debts such as mortgages and other loans. On the investment side, an appropriate mix of equities, fixed income securities, credit derivatives and mutual funds was understood to compose the ideally balanced portfolio.

The third leg of the Triple-A tripod, asset management, was frequently farmed out under the new dispensation to a select group of outside money managers deemed capable of providing the highly specialized expertise needed to match an investment strategy with a carefully prepared client risk profile, which Merrill Lynch dubbed "The Financial Foundation."

PLACING A RENEWED FOCUS ON THE WEALTHY

By the dawn of the new millennium, an estimated seven million people worldwide held liquid financial assets exceeding US$1 million, according to the 2000 *WWR*. More than a million new people had joined that exclusive club in 1999, and their financial assets worldwide had increased in that single year by 18 percent to over US$25.5 trillion. Global stock markets expanded by 37 percent in 1999, with Asian stock markets shooting up an astonishing 70 percent, boosting the wealth of high-net-worth households in Asia.

At the close of the twentieth century, the United States was leading the world "in the creation of younger active HNWIs (high-net-worth individuals) likely to have created their wealth in the technology sector as the digital economy takes hold," the 2000 *WWR* advised. Unbeknownst to the report's authors, the tech boom and the world's stock markets were destined to suffer a sharp decline toward the end of the following year. Yet the long-term trends of wealth creation and consolidation set off by the abrupt collapse of socialism, the advent of global capitalism and the liberalization of capital markets in virtually every nation and continent on earth were bound to continue and even accelerate unabated into the new century.

Global, full-service financial services firms began to systematically segment the mass affluent and the affluent from the wealthy and the ultra-wealthy. Merrill Lynch's dividing lines slightly diverged from those adopted by the *WWR*. "Mass-affluent" clients with less than

US$250,000 of investible assets would find the majority of their needs efficiently served by calling a newly established Financial Advisory Center. At the upper demographic ranges, the firm's private banking services were expanded and reinvigorated by the establishment of a dedicated Private Banking and Investment Group (PBIG).

To those inclined to decry this client segmentation strategy as representing the abandonment of Merrill's historic mission of taking "Wall Street to Main Street," supporters of the new system responded that the world had changed over the eighty-five years since the firm's establishment in 1915. By the dawn of the twenty-first century, the HNWIs ("Hunwees"), whose customs and aspirations were being avidly documented in the *WWR*, were transforming the financial services industry as decisively as the rise of the mass-affluent class had changed the game during the twentieth century.

The world's financial industry was evolving and adapting to this changing landscape by becoming an industry in which the most basic transactions were increasingly frictionless and cost-free, and where the true differentiating factors and mark of excellence would be the degree to which firms were able to engage with their wealthiest and most sophisticated clients at the broadest, deepest and even most profound and emotionally intimate levels. The leading edge of the global financial services industry had become, for better or worse, the high-net-worth wealth management industry.

THE CHANGING ROLE OF THE FINANCIAL ADVISOR

It didn't take long for independently minded financial advisors (FAs) to be faced with discount brokers like Fidelity and Schwab offering block trades at US$29 a pop on the Internet, calling the entire proposition of the traditional full-service brokerage firm into question.

The overriding question became whether firms with bloated brokerage arms could survive a hitherto unimaginable degree of automation. At a time when so many of the business's traditional functions were rapidly becoming commoditized, what value-add was being provided?

What differentiated full-service financial firms like Merrill Lynch from the low-cost competition were several things: the quality of that advisor-client relationship combined (particularly at the higher end of the scale) with the ability of a huge firm with a global footprint to deliver to clients access to expertise in a variety of investment instruments, vehicles, strategies, methods and philosophies that few of the boutique firms could ever hope to match.

In a 2000 speech to the Securities Industry Association,[3] Stan O'Neal, who headed Merrill Lynch's Global Private Client Group at the time and who would go on to become CEO from 2002 to 2007, observed that the industry was "in a period of wealth creation such as the world has never seen." In light of that development, he argued that financial services firms were obliged to grow their share of the high-net-worth market or see the fattest piece of the pie go to their competitors.

Most shocking of all, especially to the healthy number of traditionally minded brokers sitting in the audience, was O'Neal's blunt statement that "we do not even consider ourselves to be in the retail securities business anymore. We're in the wealth management business."

But rather than congratulate the other leaders of Merrill Lynch on being the "Christopher Columbuses" of the financial services industry, O'Neal frankly acknowledged that "we're all engaged in the process of trying to figure out what it is that will distinguish us in the eyes of the wealthy investor." The firm's wealthiest clients were being underserved—not because their financial advisors were doing something wrong, but because the firm as a whole had not developed a rational system to segment clients according not just to their

---

3. Since renamed the Securities Industry and Financial Markets Association (SIFMA).

net worth but their actual needs, goals, objectives and aspirations as stated in their client risk profiles, which were subject to frequent re-balancing, typically on an annual basis. The real job of an FA must be to do the best possible job of identifying and meeting these increasingly complex and sophisticated client needs by utilizing the entire intellectual capital of the firm. This was an extraordinary transition for not only FAs, but also for HNWIs.

Bullish Times for Financial Advisors

In early 2007, *Money* magazine named "financial advisor" the third best job in America. "As company pensions die out and Americans increasingly have to manage their own retirement savings, financial planning is no longer only for the rich. With Gen X-ers entering their peak earning years and boomers nearing retirement, business will get better still." As individuals receiving these services, we need to also keep in mind that the advisors we work with should be able to instill in us the confidence that they enjoy their jobs, value their clients and are able to protect us from some naïve decisions we might otherwise make.

In Singapore, which is rapidly becoming a hub of wealth management, there are currently about two thousand financial advisors. But according to a survey by the Singapore-based Calamander Group, the immediate demand is for twenty-five hundred with the need expected to rise to five thousand to six thousand in five years. As a result, the government and local bankers are putting on a full court press to recruit and train people. This indicates that in Asia, individuals are realizing the benefit and are reaching out to professionals for advice.[4]

Michael Saadie, managing director for Asia and former head of the private bank at ANZ Bank (also known as The Australia and New Zealand Banking Group and the fourth largest bank in Australia) observes that identifying, attracting and retaining talent is one of his top priorities—not to mention *the* paramount issue that keeps him and his colleagues awake at night. Growth in wealth management in his country and the rest of Asia is putting enormous

---

4. "Singapore Makes a Pitch to Draw the Wealthy," Wayne Arnold, *The New York Times*, April 26, 2007.

personnel strains on firms across the region. The Singapore government is going so far as training people from other professions to become private bankers. Through the recently created Singapore Wealth Management Institute, the government offers year-long masters programs and a two-month course to retrain anyone, from curtain salesmen to pianists and to sewage engineers, to become financial advisors and planners.

Of course, becoming a productive FA takes more than a good mind for numbers. It takes an understanding of etiquette, cultural taboos, attention to client details, and an ability to make connections with people. Joseph Lam, a wealth advisor in Merrill Lynch's Hong Kong office, vividly recalls his entry-level job at Goldman Sachs. One of his first big assignments? Get everyone's lunch orders—and don't get any of them wrong, or else.

At first it might seem like a way to serve a bit of humble pie to a newcomer (and perhaps it was) but Mr. Lam saw it differently. He got to speak to everyone on the floor, including the most senior people. And even if it was just to take a lunch order, he made a small, first connection.

Connections, insists Mr. Lam, are vital to being a successful financial advisor. As FA to two of the most highly respected billionaires in Hong Kong, Dr. Lee Shau-Kee and Dr. Cheng Yu-Tung, Mr. Lam encourages young FAs to get out from behind their desks, take a walk, get a cup of coffee, clear their minds, find ways to expand their social horizons and work closely with senior managers. In fact, our research for this book has led us to believe that a general rule for all clients is that they need to feel that they know their FAs, and be confident that they are not simply a voice on the phone. They need to feel that they are a personality with specific needs. If this is not the case, you (the client) do not have the right FA for long-term success, regardless of the economic climate.

According to Lam, the most important thing is for clients to like you, "because people like to do business with people they like." This, he insists, cannot be faked. "An advisor must truly care about the client to win their friendship. Don't pitch to them every time you see them. Sometimes just have some soup and listen to what is on their mind, financial issues or not."

That sentiment is echoed by Victor Tan, Market Director of Merrill Lynch's global wealth management division in Hong Kong. "Be genuine. Be who you are." This is essential, he says, because personal authenticity is the best way to truly differentiate oneself. "It can be surprisingly easy to get a first meeting with even the wealthiest prospective clients because they are always on the lookout for new talent. They welcome new faces. They want to talk to people," Mr. Tan says. The hard part "is establishing your identity in that meeting and getting a second [meeting]." As a client on the receiving end of these interactions, we also need to ensure that we listen and realize that the individuals we are dealing with as advisors need to understand us as best they can to enable them to help us most effectively.

IMPROVING THE ADVISOR–CLIENT DIALOGUE

The defining benchmark for determining the quality of any wealth management service is the quality of the dialogue between wealth manager and HNWI, contends Bertrand Lavayssière, Capgemini's managing director for Global Financial Services. The construction of a productive and often subtle dialogue between a client and his or her financial advisor is the name of the game. "When it's your money, you—the client—*must* have an opinion. *You need to be part of the dialogue.*" According to Lavayssière, "If wealth is managed passively and with limited or no dialogue with advisors or specialists who possess in-depth knowledge of your situation, many opportunities are missed and assets are often placed at greater risk."

At Merrill Lynch, Private Wealth Advisors (PWAs) are required to trim client rosters to a few dozen choice individuals and households in order to maintain their PWA designation. Those individuals and households would preferably be those possessing the highest net worth and the most complex financial needs, those prone to participate and collaborate with their advisors in establishing a financial framework and clearly articulating their goals and objectives, so that their FA can devise strategies tailor-made to achieve them.

The primary value-add of the FA–client relationship is inevitably defined by the nature and substance of the dialogue between them, coupled with the support services that a firm can provide to take the resulting profile and design a bespoke portfolio to consistently meet those objectives. Prior to entering into a relationship with a financial advisor, a few well proven success strategies can enhance virtually any client's selection process.

Finding Your Holistic Wealth Advisor: A Punch List

Because establishing an open dialogue is the key to forging a productive relationship between a financial advisor and a client, consider the introductory meeting as the onset of that dialogue. What should you ask? How do you find an advisor that best fits your personal profile?

Many of us are sometimes overwhelmed when we meet with financial advisors and discuss our needs—we may not always be as inquisitive as we should be when selecting who should manage our portfolios, possibly because we are concerned that we will not understand the answer, we don't know what questions to ask, or we don't know how to measure their performance. We certainly behave differently when selecting a realtor, who—like a financial advisor—may be responsible for helping us to make some of the most important investments decisions of our life.

Here are a few key questions to ask and areas to probe when making decisions related to financial advisors. And here is a list of ten areas that individuals and families should consider to not merely evaluate a potential FA, but also to become more actively involved in the dialogue regarding the management of their assets.

1. Source of FA's Name: HNWIs typically learn about financial advisors through personal referrals. Lawyers, accountants, colleagues and other service professionals tend to be in a position to recommend an individual, team or firm. Referrals can also come through friends and family members. The advantage of a personal referral is that the referrer already knows something about your needs and interests and also about the firm they are referring you to, and you have common ground to start a conversation.

2. Background check—training, licensing and certification: Most, if not all, financial advisors have undergone an extensive training program. Some may style themselves as financial planners, others as financial advisors, still others as wealth managers or private bankers. Most established professionals in the majority of countries, including the United States, are accredited by a variety of reputable professional organizations, including the National Association of Personal Financial Advisors (NAPFA), the Financial Planning Association (FPA) or the American Institute of Certified Public Accountants (AICPA). Similarly, in the U.K. clients should look for firms they deal with to be FSA (Financial Services Authority) authorized. If the advisor is not registered with a government agency, that should raise a red flag.[5]

3. Established investment philosophy and strategy: Whether looking for aggressive growth or to protect your assets, you should establish a set of personal goals and objectives beforehand and compare this to the philosophy of the financial advisor you are interviewing. Good financial advisors will work closely with you to develop a strategy appropriate to achieving your personal lifestyle and financial goals. Similarly, a financial advisor's interests should be aligned to your personal interests: How aligned are the firm's interests to yours as a client? Are the firm's financial advisors rewarded in a way that will encourage them to work more in your interests than those of the firm? What is their total remuneration based on? Which metrics have the most weight in determining their remuneration—the money they bring into the bank, investment performance, or maybe customer satisfaction/retention? Asking this last question will tell you a lot about how the firm sees its clients. The way FAs are measured for remuneration tends to drive their behavior.

---

5. All financial advisors and planners in the United States are obliged to register with either the Securities and Exchange Commission or the securities agency in the state of their primary place of business. Depending upon jurisdiction, advisors may be designated certified financial planners (CFPs), chartered financial consultant (ChFCc), NAPFA-registered financial advisors, or certified public accountants/personal financial specialists (CPAs/PFSs). The Central Registration Depository (CRD) maintains a database that contains information on brokers, their representatives and the firms they work for. Background information is also available from the Financial Industry Regulation Authority (FINRA) and/or state securities regulators.

4. Range of activities undertaken and products and services offered: You should also check what other activities or services are conducted by the institution you are entrusting your money to. Is private wealth management a large part of what they do? Are they committed to it (and to you) for the long term? What is the turnover rate of advisors in the firm? Will your FA keep changing, leading to discontinuity in your relationship with the institution? Some attention should be given when assessing the products and services offered. As this book will highlight, the investment planning and financial advice field is crowded and fragmented, running the gamut from single-proprietor consultants and planners to discount brokerage houses that conduct the bulk of their interaction with clients online. HNWIs typically demand and enjoy a high level of service, with the most rarefied model being a family office that attends to clients' any and every need, from travel arrangements to speaking engagements to estate planning and other legacy issues.

   The distinguishing factor between firms is the advisor's capacity to determine the optimal mix of products and services that will fit your particular goals and objectives and then deliver on that strategy. Does the firm or individual offer a truly holistic approach? If so, can they explain this in greater detail? Additionally, as the wealth management industry becomes more global and more complex, you should ensure your advisor is aware of and able to navigate global markets or have access to this information in a form that can be readily and easily shared and understood.

5. Fee structure and other charges: What are the fees you will be charged? How are these calculated? What percentage is the FA prepared to put at risk against investment performance? How do the fees reduce as the sum you entrust to your FA increases? Typically, you will be quoted an annual fee that is levied as a percentage of your entire portfolio. Ask your FA to explain what the fee includes. Also ask what it does not cover and what any additional charges might be. If you are investing for the long term, a difference of a few basis points in fees for a similar product/service could materially affect the long-term value of your investments.

6. Support in creating a legacy: Find out if a prospective financial advisor is willing to discuss how he or she intends to assist you in transferring not just your assets but also your moral framework and values to the next generation and beyond.

7. Frequency and discipline of the review process, timeliness of reporting and sophistication of technology tools: How does your prospective financial advisor intend to help you reset your strategy and objectives in light of changing circumstances? Almost as important is how timely and accurate the individual's, team's or firm's reporting process claims to be. How sophisticated is the technological platform used by the advisor and how seamlessly is a client able to access that network?

8. Access to leading money managers: Is the FA going to handle the details of asset allocation him or herself or will this activity be handled by outside investment advisors? Where will your money be invested—in the firm's own funds or in third party funds?

9. Target client profile: What is the FA's typical client profile? Do you and your family or household fit it? What is the tenure of these clients?

10. Communication of performance: What performance benchmarks will the advisor employ to measure progress against meeting goals and objectives? How will these be communicated to you? Most professionals shy away from promising specific performance objectives. A common caveat is that if a prospective advisor starts laying out specific parameters or expected rates of return, regard such promises with the degree of skepticism they deserve.

UNDERSTANDING THE HNWI ADVANTAGE: HOW THE WEALTHY MANAGE TO ENJOY ROBUST RETURNS DURING GOOD TIMES AND BAD

The main reasons that the industry has shifted to servicing the needs and demands of wealthy and ultra-wealthy clients are extensively documented in the *WWR*s. The overarching fact is that even during down periods when market returns tend to be dismal, returns enjoyed by the wealthy are generally quite robust. The wealthy tend to be beneficiaries of a virtuous cycle in which access to superior information, expertise and service from FAs and money managers further fuels the process of wealth aggregation and accumulation that produced their wealth in the first place. Even during the sharp slowdown of 2004–2005, when rising oil prices, inflationary pressures and monetary tightening took their toll on the world economy, the ranks of the ultra-wealthy continued to climb by 6.1 percent, while their total financial assets grew 8.5 percent.

Figure 1.1 – Primary Source of Wealth, Regional Breakdown, 2006

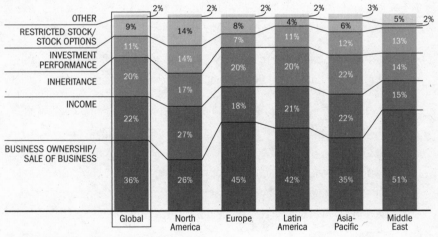

Source: Capgemini/Merrill Lynch Relationship Manager Survey, 2007.

When studying wealth, it pays to consider where the wealth comes from. According to the 2007 *WWR*, 36 percent of the world's millionaires derive their wealth from the ownership or sale of a business, 22 percent from income, 20 percent from inheritance, 11 percent from investments, 9 percent from restricted stock and stock options and 2 percent from elsewhere.

Take a good look at those numbers, particularly the 11 percent figure for investments. This figure tells us that HNWIs are typically talented at *not* relying on global economic prosperity to expand their financial holdings through dividends and capital appreciation—which helps in turn to explain why HNWIs' returns consistently beat market averages.

Across the industry, investment advisors have discovered that investment challenges and demands vary dramatically according to how a client's wealth was originally generated. In the case of inherited wealth, it's often found that much of the client's total assets have been invested for the long term, in stocks or real estate. Those clients shifting out of legacy investments could, as a result, suffer significant tax consequences from certain transactions. For those with inherited wealth, flexibility of style and strategy is in some cases reduced. Wealth earners, by contrast, tend to enjoy considerably greater flexibility and tend to be more creative and open to investment mandates.

Entrepreneurs, particularly those who have enjoyed a huge windfall from the sale of a business, often require an investment strategy designed to put a lump sum of funds to work at a single point in time, projecting needs five and ten years out from the present. Income earners, on the other hand, enjoy the luxury of constructing portfolios over time through stable cash flows, which means their time horizons may prove flexible. For all three major sources of wealth—income, business and inheritance—the destination is typically the same, yet the route varies.

DESCRIBING THE STATE
OF THE WORLD'S WEALTH

While it's a comparatively simple matter to identify global trends in wealth *accumulation*, there remain strong regional differences in *sources* of wealth origination. In Europe, business ownership, or the sale of a business, was the number one source of wealth, at 45 percent, while income, which is much more heavily taxed than in the United States, accounts for a mere 26 percent.

In North America, income accounts for 27 percent of wealth—higher than anywhere else in the world. In the United States in 2005, the number of HNWIs and the value of their assets grew at twice the rate of the domestic economy—driven largely by substantial gains in real income that have far outpaced gains at lower income levels. According to the Center on Budget and Policy Priorities, the poorest fifth of US taxpayers have seen a 6 percent growth in income ($900) over the 25 years prior to 2005, adjusted for inflation. Meanwhile, the top 1 percent saw their incomes jump 228 percent over the same period.[6]

In the United States, where GDP and stock market returns have proven remarkably steady but hardly dramatic, this growing income gap and concentration of wealth is magnified by a long-term trend of scaling back the progressive income tax. As recently as 1980, the progressive income tax imposed a 70 percent tax rate on income above a certain level. That rate has been halved. Also, new compensation strategies—such as restricted stock and stock options, which are not widely available to the population at large—have helped HNWIs accumulate greater wealth at a faster pace than the economy at large.

A study recently conducted by the Massachusetts Institute of Technology's Sloan School of Management found that 75 percent of chief executives culled from a sample of one hundred publicly traded companies enjoyed an average net worth of US$25 million in 2004, mainly from stock and options in their companies. That was up from 31 percent in 1989, adjusted for inflation. In 2005, CEOs in the United States earned 231 times what an average hourly worker at their company earned, up from forty-two times in 1980.

---

6. "Income Inequality Hits Record Levels," Arloc Sherman, Center on Budget and Policy Priorities, December 14, 2007.

All over the world, earned wealth is expanding more rapidly than inherited wealth. Income plays the largest role in wealth accumulation in North America, but in every other region of the world, save the Middle East, business ownership creates the majority of wealth. As recently as 2001, according to the 2007 *WWR*, 21 percent of North American wealth was inherited, compared to 17 percent in 2006, and 37 percent of European wealth was inherited, compared to 20 percent in 2006.

Figure 1.2 – Percentage Breakdown in HNWI Assets by Region, 2005–2008F

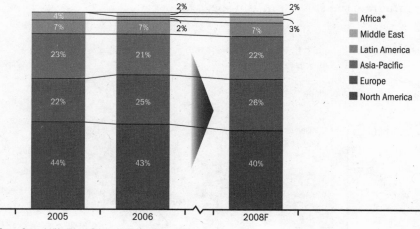

Source: Capgemini/Merrill Lynch Ralationship Manager Survey, 2007.
* In 2005, investments in Africa were less than 0.4%.

Because of rapidly growing income among HNWIs in the United States, and a flurry of entrepreneurship in Asia, Russia and Eastern Europe as those societies embrace free markets, the global trend is toward earned wealth in general. (The diminished role of inheritance in wealth creation is due in no small part to the fact that there is no wealth to be inherited in former communist countries, where all the businesses were state owned.) If this trend continues, and all evidence suggests that it will, we can expect to see an ever-growing number of wealth earners joining the ranks of the world's HNWIs.

If the way wealth is accumulated varies in each region, it's no wonder that the pace of HNWI growth and asset accumulation also varies by region. North America and Europe are home to most of the world's HNWIs, about 6.1 million of the world's 9.5 million. But these regions grew the slowest in 2006. The Middle East, Latin America and Asia-Pacific all outpaced the more developed nations in minting new millionaires. Africa, albeit working off a tiny base, saw the biggest jump—a 12.5 percent increase. And the same trends hold true for the accumulation of financial assets, which occurred most rapidly in Africa, the Middle East and Latin America, while wealth grew the slowest in Europe.

Figure 1.3 – HNWIs' Wealth by Region, in Dollars and Percentage Growth, 2004–2006

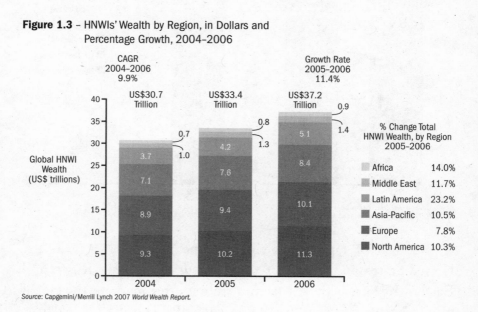

Source: Capgemini/Merrill Lynch 2007 *World Wealth Report.*

PRIME DRIVERS OF HNWI WEALTH

Gains in local GDP and regional stock exchanges accounted for much of the disparity in HNWIs' wealth growth. In 2006, real GDP grew worldwide to 5.4 percent, compared with 5.0 percent gains posted in 2005. The accelerating growth of real GDP was partially driven by consistent performance of the world's most mature economies. While U.S. GDP growth in 2006 was relatively constant at 3.3 percent in 2006, compared to 3.2 percent in 2005, European economies saw slightly accelerated growth—Germany (from 0.9 percent to 2.3 percent), U.K. (from 1.9 percent to 2.7 percent) and France (from 1.2 percent to 2.0 percent).

However, emerging markets continued to outperform the rest of the world. In general, the reason for the disparity is that emerging markets continue to play a moderate game of "catch up" with major markets. Financial gains were particularly strong in Latin America, Eastern Europe, Asia-Pacific, Africa and the Middle East, where certain countries enjoyed real GDP growth rates that outperformed the global average of 5.4 percent. This trend was particularly noticeable in Brazil, Russia, India and China, four countries that are often grouped together because of their vast sizes and referred to as the "BRIC" nations. In 2006, China and India, for example, sustained real GDP growth rates of 10.5 percent and 8.8 percent, respectively, among the highest of any economy in the world.

Figure 1.4 - Real GDP Growth, 2004–2006

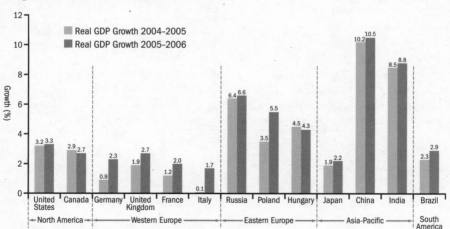

Source: Capgemini/Merrill Lynch 2007 *World Wealth Report.*

Meanwhile, the other macro driver of wealth accumulation—market capitalization—handsomely rewarded those invested in regional stock exchanges. The S&P 500 in the United States bounced back with a 13.6 percent return in 2006, compared to 3.0 percent in 2005. Markets in Europe, Asia-Pacific and Latin America delivered even stronger returns, after record gains in these geographies in 2005 enticed foreign investors to invest even more heavily in these markets in 2006.

In Europe in 2006, markets rose in response to corporate restructurings, technology investments and a range of cost-cutting moves. In Germany, the DAX gained 22.0 percent for the year, albeit a decline from the 27.1 percent gains posted in 2005. France's CAC 40 and the London FTSE 100, too, were up by 17.5 percent and 10.7 percent respectively for the year. In Russia, the RTS Index saw a 70.7 percent return in 2006.

Figure 1.5 - Stock Market Returns, 2006

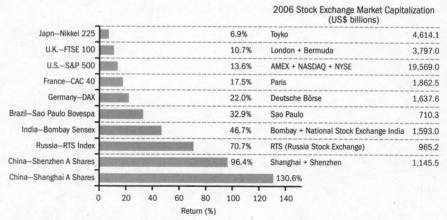

Source: Capgemini/Merrill Lynch 2007 *World Wealth Report.*

Asia-Pacific markets—with the exception of Japan—remained particularly strong in 2006. The Shanghai/Shenzhen market capitalization grew by 220.6 percent in 2006, mainly on the strength of Initial Public Offerings (IPOs). Also, smaller Asian markets, including Indonesia and the Philippines, did well in 2006, where Dow Jones Indexes returned 62.0 percent and 49.5 percent, respectively, on the back of strong economic fundamentals. Overall, we see HNWIs being interested in opportunities around the globe and moving quickly to take advantage of them.

Such outsized returns not only mint new local millionaires, they are drawing HNWIs' investment from other parts of the world. More than ever before, HNWIs are moving their investments across international borders and the reason is clear—for HNWIs to stay ahead, they must have an international outlook. Of course, these outsized gains cannot continue indefinitely, but there's a sense among HNWIs and their advisors that many emerging markets have turned a corner, and confidence is growing that these far-flung economies are stable.

A hallmark of today's global economic expansion is the way emerging markets are reinforcing each other's expansion—a phenomenon most evident in China and in other commodity-rich emerging markets around the globe. China, with its abundance of cheap skilled labor, has rapidly become the factory to the world, and some experts expect its economy to surpass that of the United States by 2030. With the cash it's generating from manufacturing, it has the power to invest overseas—and it is doing just that. Some investment is flowing into the real estate markets of Hong Kong and Singapore, but China's main focus has been to secure the raw materials necessary to keep its voracious economic engine humming. It's doing this on many fronts, everything from, literally, building bridges and other infrastructure in Thailand and Myanmar to forging close relationships with Chile and Brazil to lining up allies in Africa.

Meanwhile, the more stable and democratic countries in Latin America are only too happy to have another large trading partner to counterbalance the sway that the United States has long had in the region. For them, China represents a gigantic hedge against the

United States, and may at long last permit the region to escape the boom-and-bust cycle that has dogged it for decades. This stability helps in the accumulation of wealth in this region. Brazil, Mexico and Venezuela, in particular, all profited from the worldwide surge in oil prices, buttressing Latin American growth in 2005.

Commodities, particularly energy, have been the primary drivers of the Russian economy. The RTS Index rode to historic highs on the backs of its two primary exports—oil and natural gas. The number of HNWIs in the country jumped by 15.5 percent and the accumulation of assets was even higher. These kinds of results lend credence to a report earlier this decade by Goldman Sachs that projects that by 2040, the BRIC nations will leapfrog the G7 nations in terms of total output. In fact, the BRIC nations grew faster than expected from 2003 to 2005. Morgan Stanley's emerging markets index is up 171 percent since the end of 2002, while its BRIC index has surged 262 percent.

If China is the factory of the world, India has become the outsourcing capital of the world. It too has a growing thirst for energy and other commodities. Its educational system—though not uniformly excellent—churns out hundreds of thousands of skilled workers every year; what's more, the widespread use of English, its status as a relatively stable democracy, its familiarity with capitalism (though not a wholly free market), the comparatively low wages, even the time difference with developed nations (India works while North America and Europe sleeps) are factors in India's success. None of this would have been possible, of course, had India not consciously decided ten years ago to begin dismantling the protectionist economic policies in place since its independence.

Elsewhere in the world the emerging market firmament is the Middle East, which accounts for nearly 65 percent of the world's oil reserves. It continues to benefit enormously from the large industrialized nations' ongoing and deepening dependence on fossil fuel—not to mention the growing thirst of India and China, the latter of which has rapidly become the number two consumer of oil after the United States; rising prices continued to drive oil export revenues skyward in the Middle East and one need look no further to understand its economic success.

In emerging markets where exchange rates are allowed to freely float—China's yuan being the notable exception though progress is being made—the local currencies generally gained strength during the past decade of relative stability since the destabilizing Asian Contagion of 1997–98. This has been the case in commodity-rich nations such as Mexico, Brazil and Canada. The increased value of the local currencies boosts the wealth of local HNWIs, and it has another salubrious effect: a strong currency engenders confidence in the local economy, increasing reinvestment by local HNWIs, which in turn helps reinforce the economy. In a post-oil boom, for instance, oil revenue generated in the Middle East from sales to developed countries made a round trip. With no place to confidently invest at home, Middle Eastern HNWIs sent their investments overseas—mostly back to Europe and North America.

The Cost of Living Extremely Well

How much one earns is only half the picture when framing someone's financial well-being; the other half is how much one spends. It's no easy matter to accumulate wealth, no matter how impressive the financial returns, if your cost of living is spiraling upward. Quite simply, the "admission and maintenance charges" to a life of privilege cannot be overlooked when discussing the state of wealth. The exception is, of course, those who are the richest in the world, such as Oracle's co-founder, Lawrence Ellison, according to economist Christopher Carroll at Johns Hopkins University. In his article "Why Do the Rich Save So Much?"[7] Carroll estimates that with Ellison's net worth in 2006 at US$16 billion and at a 10 percent annual

7. Carroll, Christopher "Why Do the Rich Save So Much?"; published in *Does Atlas Shrug: The Economic Consequences of Rating the Rich.* Harvard University Press, 2000; ed. Joel B. Slemrod.

rate of return, he would need to spend more than US$30 million a week just to stop accumulating more money than he already has, as well as eat into the US$16 billion.

To get a handle on costs, *Forbes* has been tracking the price of a basket of luxury goods since 1976 with its Cost of Living Extremely Well Index (CLEWI). While the old saying "if you have to ask, you can't afford it" might still be true, this index is instructive nonetheless. It turns out that HNWIs' financial returns—which generally beat the market average—had better continue to outperform. HNWIs' cost of living is escalating much faster than the average consumer's. Since inception, the value of the *Forbes* basket of forty-odd luxury goods—which includes everything from a sable coat to a yacht to a catered dinner for forty—has grown more than 700 percent, roughly twice the rate of the Consumer Price Index (CPI).

For a period in the nineteen nineties, the CLEWI and CPI rose at about the same rate, but since then the CLEWI has consistently risen faster than the CPI and 2006 was no different, with the average cost of such items as caviar, a thoroughbred yearling and a psychiatrist increasing 7 percent compared to the CPI's 4 percent rise. The history of the CLEWI does show a cyclical pattern to these costs, accelerating and decelerating over stretches of time, but it certainly never dips below the CPI.

For a more detailed look at HNWIs' costs, the *WWR* began tracking prices on a regional basis to ascertain relative purchasing power in Asia-Pacific, Europe and North America. If you were a HNWI, where would you get the best and worst deals? Like *Forbes*, the *WWR* also uses a basket of luxury items, including five-star hotel rooms, spa visits and boarding school tuitions. Turns out the Europeans bore the highest cost of maintaining a wealthy lifestyle. Europeans are lagging the rest of the world in their population growth and asset accumulation, and now European HNWIs are shelling out more to live the same lifestyle as other HNWIs! HNWIs in Asia-Pacific, meanwhile, have the lowest cost of living of the HNWIs.

LOOKING FORWARD

All of the above would certainly appear to add up to a healthy global environment for growing wealth in the coming decade. Only during one year out of the last decade—2000—has the number of HNWIs and their assets actually declined. This success has not, as in the past, been largely limited to the developed nations. A hallmark of the past decade is that wealth has grown faster in the emerging markets than the developed ones, creating a more globally dispersed population of HNWIs.

In both emerging and developed markets, the rules of investing are the same. In order to stay ahead of the game, the wealthy and those who aspire to join their ranks must bear in mind the four pillars of wealth management:

1. Time horizon;

2. Risk tolerance;

3. Liquidity needs;

4. Performance expectations.

Practicing disciplined wealth management means, first and foremost, protecting and growing the wealth of an individual or family. Although it might sound simple, regardless of strategy, maintaining an effective long-term focus on all four pillars of wealth management requires negotiating cascading layers of complexity. Wealth management is inherently multidimensional, taking into account everything from the health care costs of a grandparent, to tax strategies for the head of the household, to college savings for the children. Disciplined wealth management also must account for the fact all four of these pillars continuously change over time, requiring the frequent updating and refinement of even the best-laid wealth management plans. This remains the irrefutable reality for all wealthy clients, prospective wealthy clients and aspiring wealthy clients—and of course their financial advisors, from Bar Harbor to Singapore.

CHAPTER 2

Global Trends and What They Mean for International Investing

COINING THE TERM "EMERGING MARKETS"

One unseasonably warm day in September 1981, a young, Dutch-born banker employed by the International Finance Corporation (IFC, the private sector arm of The World Bank) stood sweating at a lectern in an auditorium at the Salomon Brothers headquarters in New York. He was preparing to pitch a rather zany idea he and a few colleagues had recently dreamed up for what they were calling a "Third World Equity Fund."

During a stint at Banker's Trust in the mid-seventies, Antoine van Agtmael, a graduate of the Netherlands School of Economics with a master's degree in Russian and Eastern European Studies from Yale, had fallen madly in love with the frequently turbulent and often lackluster economies of what was then referred to as the "Third World." Many years later, he vividly recalled the indignant reaction he induced from a senior executive at that major money-center bank when he asked for his opinion of the prospect of recycling petrodollars overseas. "There are *no* markets outside the U.S.!" the senior banker had thundered while pulling wrathfully on his bright crimson suspenders.

Although van Agtmael realized that the senior executive was not literally correct in his assessment, the man's provincialism accurately mirrored the investment landscape of the seventies and early eighties, when not just North Americans but just about every investor on earth displayed a strong propensity for investing in their own local markets, if for no other reason that for even the wealthiest individuals to invest in markets beyond their own jurisdiction was logistically and practically next to impossible, not to mention prohibitively costly.

The young banker had every reason to anxiously reflect on that unsettling moment of six years before as he leaned into his lectern to launch his presentation to prospective investors, a thesis premised on the decidedly unconventional proposition that—as he later put it—"our data demonstrated a real possibility of making real money in [what would come to be called] emerging markets, despite their admitted volatility."[1]

"Developing countries, we argued, enjoyed higher economic growth rates and boasted a rich set of hitherto-ignored promising companies. We persuasively demonstrated that investing in a basket of companies and countries would provide the diversification required to mitigate the risk of investing in individual stocks and countries."

Judging from the faces in the crowd of thirty-odd fund managers staring up at him as he spoke, van Agtmael sensed "that some were clearly intrigued, others were skeptical, and that just possibly we might win over one or two confirmed skeptics to our cause." At the conclusion of van Agtmael's presentation, a well-respected senior investment banker, Francis Finlay of JPMorgan, helpfully observed, "This is a very interesting idea you've got there, young man, but you will *never* sell it using the name 'Third World Equity Fund'!"

Briefly crestfallen, van Agtmael nevertheless recognized that the man had a point. The term "Third World," with its vaguely derisive tone that strongly evoked "flimsy polyester, cheap toys, rampant corruption, Soviet-style tractors, and flooded rice paddies," was

---

1. Antoine van Agtmael, *The Emerging Markets Century: How a New Breed of World-Class Companies Is Overtaking the World* (Free Press, 2007).

hardly likely to induce any great sense of confidence in the traditionally conservative community of international bankers and brokers.

Over the course of the following weekend, the aspiring international fund manager racked his brain for a more uplifting alternative
label. Just before his self-imposed deadline of Monday morning, he
conceived of a term that struck him as "more positive and invigorat-
ing" and that was destined to become the preferred nomenclature for
this fledging field for the next several decades: *emerging markets.*

Having experienced a classic eureka moment, van Agtmael
sat down at his desk on Monday morning and dashed off a memo
mandating that he and his colleagues henceforth refer to their forthcoming vehicle as The Emerging Markets Fund. The first index they
were working on that tracked the performance of "Third World"
firms would be promoted as the IFC Emerging Markets Index. Although it took a few years of hard work and artful persuasion to pull
the deal off, IFC did in fact introduce its pioneering Emerging Markets Growth Fund (managed by Capital Investment, Inc.) in the
mid-eighties. Fortunately not just for van Agtmael but for the world
at large, this first fund of its kind was healthily subscribed to by an
intrepid group of institutional investors from around the world who
over time did very well by their initial investments—thank you.

Not long thereafter, another pioneering international investor,
the British-born Sir John Templeton, hired Mark Mobius, a Long
Island-born, Hong Kong-based pioneer expert in Asian and Latin
American investing, to head up the Templeton Emerging Markets
Fund, later subsumed into the family of funds offered by Franklin
Templeton. Both van Agtmael's own firm, established with a group
of colleagues from The World Bank, and Mobius's Templeton
Emerging Markets Fund began to solicit subscribers shortly before
the stock market crash of October 1987—anything but an auspi-
cious time to entice new investors with exotic strategies.

Yet the most significant geopolitical phenomenon of the latter
part of the twentieth century—the downfall of the Berlin Wall and

concomitant collapse of communism two years later in 1989—led to a radical revision and liberation of capital markets, not just in Eastern Europe and the former Soviet Bloc but also in Asia and Latin America. The resulting unleashing of capitalistic energy and vitality throughout the nineties, spurred by often controversial and in some cases corrupt privatizations of government-controlled firms, became a driving force behind the most powerful economic trend the world had yet seen: globalization.

Despite a series of traumatic international crises in the nineties, including the Mexican peso devaluation of 1994 and the Asian Contagion of 1997 (which started in Thailand with the devaluation of the *bhat* but quickly spread to all the emerging markets, ultimately leading to Russia's default on its sovereign debt), the fundamental premise of emerging-markets investing—that "developing countries…enjoyed higher economic growth rates and boasted a rich set of promising companies," as van Agtmael opined—was a rich promise destined to be fulfilled exponentially over the coming decades.

"In 1988," van Agtmael recalled, "when we launched our first fund, there were just twenty companies in emerging markets with sales of over US$1 billion… By 2005, there were thirty-eight companies in the emerging markets with sales of over US$10 billion, and 270 with sales of over US$1 billion."[2] By midway through the first decade of the twenty-first century, a significant number of emerging-markets-based multinationals—including Samsung Electronics and Hyundai of South Korea, iron-ore producer CVRD of Brazil, energy producer Gazprom of Russia and synthetic fuel producer Sasol of South Africa, to name just a few—had attained positions of global dominance as the leading producers in their industries.

While the stunning rise to economic prominence and prowess of India and China (following the equally remarkable growth of the

---

2. Ibid, 31.

Asian tigers, including Taiwan, Korea, Thailand and Singapore) easily garnered the highest volume of anxious headlines in the North American and northern European press, the reality is that the advent of the "emerging-markets century" had fundamentally altered the investment equation for mass-affluent and high-net-worth individuals and households worldwide.

Another defining moment for the newly globalized century came about in 2007, when Carlos Slim Helu, who built a massive empire out of the privatization of Mexican telecom giant Telmex, was hailed as the world's richest man, moving up from the number three position he'd held on the *Forbes* list and smartly surpassing both Buffett and Gates.

GLOBALIZATION'S GROWING IMPACT ON HIGH-NET-WORTH INDIVIDUALS

As Larry Fink, chairman and CEO of asset management giant BlackRock—now owned in part[3] by Merrill Lynch—puts it: "Globalization has been *the* transformational theme of the past six years in investing." The International Monetary Fund (IMF) defines globalization as "the growing economic interdependence of countries worldwide through increasing volume and variety of cross-border transactions in goods and services, free international capital flows, and more rapid and widespread diffusion of technology." Typically, this broad phenomenon is broken down into a cluster of discrete facets, just about every one of which powerfully influences the investment complexities, decisions and opportunities facing wealthy individuals today.

• Industrial globalization—the rise and expansion of multinational enterprises;

---

3. Although subject to change in accordance with share price fluctuations, Merrill Lynch in 2008 owned just under 50 percent or less than controlling interest in BlackRock.

- Financial globalization—the emergence of worldwide financial markets and better access to external financing for corporate, national and sub-national borrowers;

- Political globalization—the spread of political spheres of interest to regions and countries outside the neighborhood of purely political (state and non-state) actors;

- Informational globalization—the increase in information flows between geographically remote locations;

- Cultural globalization—the growth of cross-cultural contacts.

As Bertrand Lavayssière and Bob McCann pointed out in the foreword to this book, the world is irreversibly evolving from a two-pole into a multi-polar world, with Asia, Latin America and the Middle East emerging alongside North America and Europe. This broad-based phenomenon, in which nations formerly below the radar of capital markets are now drawing serious investment from developed countries, is largely due to the fact that so much of the incalculable wealth being produced and accumulated in Asia, Latin America and Eastern Europe is now being reinvested in the exploding emerging markets, reversing a longstanding trend in those countries to experience the dwindling of assets that goes along with capital flight.

Not only patriotic or nationalistic impulses prompt so many wealthy emerging-markets-based investors to keep their assets at home. It's also the fact that a gradual "decoupling" of the Asian and Latin American economies from their counterparts in North America and Western Europe has substantially reduced the risk of investing in Asia and other emerging markets, while brightening the unprecedented opportunity of attaining growth rates unparalleled by any other region on earth.[4]

---

4. Proponents of "decoupling" observed the credit crunch of 2007–2008 in the hopes of confirmation of their theory, but as of press time the global jury was still out.

According to Mr. van Agtmael, one of the primary reasons that emerging markets have soared so dramatically in recent years is that wealthy investors located inside those markets altered their perception of the risk of investing closer to home. "Traditionally," he points out, "you saw significant volumes of capital inflow into emerging-markets countries based on workers' remittances sent back by immigrants home to their families. Historically, you also saw emerging markets' entrepreneurs and wealthy households—many of whom owned their own businesses—investing in the more developed markets out of an interest in diversification, because they and their financial advisors understood that so much of their assets were tied up in their own businesses that it made sense to invest some significant portion of their liquid capital offshore."

Emerging markets' entrepreneurs from Asia and Latin America were also enthusiastic depositors in the famously discreet tax havens of Switzerland, Luxembourg, the Isle of Man and other low-tax jurisdictions. "The common phenomenon of capital flight was nothing but simply rational economic behavior in its day," van Agtmael contends. "But at some point, as the risk premium shifted, all that began to change."[5]

Even in the wake of the integration of global capital markets, a "certain lingering prejudice prevented many wealthy individuals and investors in emerging markets from grasping the fact that their own economies were doing so well." It took a while for the lesson to sink in even among the savviest investors that, for example, infrastructural spending by emerging markets' governments was spurring a wave of internal investment leading to rapidly expanding economies. Transparency on the part of corporations aspiring to tap the international capital markets improved the investment profile of many firms that had hitherto operated according to the loosey-goosey rules of "crony capitalism."

5. Interview with the authors.

September 11th and its aftermath, which prompted a rising xenophobia among some American investors and the American public, has played a role, van Agtmael says, in influencing emerging markets' investors to keep their money at home. "Particularly in the Middle East, many wealthy individuals and investors feel that their funds and assets are no longer welcome in the U.S. Nowadays, they're more inclined than ever to invest in their own regions, which they regard as in many ways safer, more solid and offering a higher rate of return than the former safe haven of the U.S."[6] By 2008, declining asset prices in the U.S. touched off a wave of foreign investment in the U.S., with newly emergent Sovereign Wealth Products (SWPs) leading the way in infusing capital into the world's largest economy at a rate unrivaled in modern memory.

The global trend toward economic liberation has been intertwined with advances in information technology (documented in Chapter 3), enhanced by the greater ease of transportation of goods, funds, people and, most importantly, ideas since the downfall of the Berlin Wall in 1989. It is a classic positive feedback loop, producing the net effect of a world that is ever more tightly knit.

Not all leaders and people, of course, enthusiastically embrace globalization. While its proponents credit the phenomenon with being an engine of commerce that brings an improved standard of living to developing countries and additional wealth to developed nations alike, its detractors argue that globalization is a latter-day form of corporate imperialism that tramples human rights in developing countries, destroys their local ecologies and steamrolls indigenous traditions through cultural assimilation. At the same time, foes of globalization maintain that it erodes the living standards of blue-collar workers in developed countries, whose jobs are shipped overseas, thus exacerbating the already widening gap between the rich and the poor. What proponents consider commerce and prosperity, detractors regard as plundering and profiteering.

---

6. Van Agtmael interview with the authors.

James Rothenberg, chairman and principal executive officer of Capital Research and Management Co. (a principal subsidiary of the Capital Group Companies, and an investment adviser to the American Funds Group), observes that "globalization is a powerful force. But capitalism, while it may lift all boats, also creates enormous disparities." Mr. Rothenberg, who has held his current position since 1994, points to "the rise of populism and socialism associated with leaders like Venezuela's Hugo Chavez. Will you see actual rebellion or revolts driven by populism? You do have to worry about that. Globalization may not be reversible, but it will have bumps along the way. I don't want anyone to believe that the trend is a 45 degree uninterrupted up line."[7]

It should not go unnoticed that more than 87,000 *officially acknowledged* riots and demonstrations broke out in China in 2005, nearly all of them connected to the state's seizure of farmland for development. Protectionist forces in the United States and European Union (EU) are acting more assertively against cheap Chinese imports, demanding trade barriers and basing their actions on an argument that China has unfairly exploited its natural competitive advantages by means of currency manipulation. Ultimately, globalization benefits from the participation of as many as possible, so addressing local concerns is not merely an act of goodwill, it's a prudent strategy to avoid a globalization backlash.

Jacques Attali, an academically trained economist, former French presidential advisor, the first president of the London-based European Bank for Reconstruction and Development and today the president of PlaNet Finance, plays his own private part in promoting globalization (and preventing the possibly forthcoming populist backlash against it) by offering financial assistance to micro-lending programs around the world. Muhammad Yunus of Bangladesh, awarded the Nobel Peace Prize in 2006 for his pioneering microfinance work at

---

7. Interview with the authors.

Grameen Bank, is co-president of the PlaNet Finance international advisory board. Attali points out that the last great wave of globalization concluded with the onset of World War I in August 1914. The year before, foreign trade accounted for 13 percent of the world's GDP, but from there foreign trade went into a prolonged reversal, from which it failed to fully recover for nearly eighty years. Not until 1991 did global trade attain its pre-World War I peak of 13 percent of GDP.

The reason? Two world wars and a cold war, which cordoned off much of the globe, as well as the fading sway of the world's nineteenth century superpower, England. Before World War I, Britain, with its global empire and naval prowess, kept world trade routes open. But as its might waned after World War I, countries began enacting trade barriers. By the thirties, many developing countries taxed imports by as much as 75 percent, virtually wiping out world trade.

"There is no reason to believe this kind of reversal cannot be repeated," Attali warns. "The risk is that there will be globalization of markets without a globalization of democracy and regulations." This, he contends, would further disenfranchise large swaths of the earth's population while discouraging more widespread participation in the global economy, further debilitating an economic system reliant on connectivity and participation. As mentioned earlier, globalization, like the Internet itself, derives its power from participation. The greater the number of people engaged in globalization, the more everyone involved benefits. As Attali observes, "What's the value of the Internet if you're the only one on it?"[8]

Yet nearly all economic observers would likely agree that the prevailing momentum today is propelling globalization irreversibly onward and upward. Most economies of the world are making an effort to open their borders and capture increased foreign and domestic investment in their economies. Still, the integration of

8. Interview with the authors.

capital markets is not without risk—risk on a global scale hitherto unimaginable.

"Thanks to globalization, systemic risks are everywhere," insists Edward Bernard, a vice chairman at T. Rowe Price. He cites "interest rate increases in Japan, depreciation of the U.S. dollar, an industrial accident in China, [and] a hedge fund meltdown" as all potential examples of systemic risk that might pose a shock to the international financial system—shocks against which, he contends, the vast majority of enthusiastic international investors have failed to prepare.[9] One way to prepare is to retain exposure to international markets while limiting risk, by investing in global blue-chip companies that sell their products in emerging markets. Another would be to maintain a prudent asset allocation that limits exposure to these more volatile markets to a set percentage of the portfolio, in much the same way that institutional investors practice portfolio risk management.

Larry Fink of BlackRock strikes a similarly cautionary note regarding the twin dangers of global systemic risk and investor complacency. "The biggest worry I have—and many of my contemporaries have—is that the market is not pricing in liquidity risk." Liquidity, generally defined as the ability of an entity to sell an asset quickly without substantially affecting its price, certainly seized up during the international credit crisis of 2007 and 2008. A wholesale "breakage in liquidity," according to Fink, was presaged by the fact that in early 2007 the market was pricing liquidity risk for emerging-market stocks as aggressively as it priced liquidity risk for Internet stocks in 1999, which was to say that there was virtually no risk.[10]

Not surprisingly, Fink's concerns regarding liquidity risk proved well grounded by the summer of that turbulent year. Investors alarmed by subprime fallout and reversals in other mainly developed markets could point to a number of danger signs erupting circa

---

9. Interview with the authors.

10. Interview with the authors.

2006, including the collapse of the US$9.2 billion U.S.-based hedge fund Amaranth Advisors, which lost US$6.5 billion in less than a month and had to shut down because its sophisticated algorithms and risk modeling did not predict a crash in natural gas prices entering the fall heating season.

The Thai government rattled markets later in that year by announcing capital controls on foreign investments in stocks, bonds and commercial paper, which, while eventually reversed, shook the confidence of international investors and evoked memories of the Asian Contagion of ten years before. Russia, for its part, which had defaulted on its debt in 1997, flexed its newfound energy-rich muscles by strong-arming Royal Dutch Shell into turning over a majority stake in a US$20 billion natural gas project in the Far East. As for China and India, while both economies continued to expand at dizzying rates, many observers cautioned that such rates were unsustainable and would at some point decline—perhaps precipitously.

Caveats notwithstanding, the fact is that HNWIs from both developing and developed markets have little choice but to invest in emerging markets to maintain earnings that meet today's enhanced expectations. The aging populations in Europe and North America, in particular, have plenty of money to invest, and they and their advisors must seek above-average returns to fund decades-long retirements.

CHINA: AN EMERGING MARKET FOR FOREIGN INVESTMENT

Just twenty-five years or so ago, Chinese leader Deng Xiaoping famously said—perhaps apocryphally—"to get rich is glorious," unleashing market forces that challenged socialist orthodoxy and ultimately turned it on its head in the most populous nation on earth. According to *Forbes*, it took fewer than twenty years for China to mint its first billionaires—the Liu brothers, founders of the Hope Group, who made the famous *Forbes* list in 2001. The fact that Deng's declaration occurred just before the rise of globalization is no coincidence; China's headlong participation in the world economy has been a primary driver of the phenomenon.

Since the nineties, the government of China has almost exclusively focused on foreign trade and exports as its chosen vehicle for attaining economic growth, gradually opening its market to foreign investment by creating special economic zones where investment laws are relaxed in order to attract foreign capital. The result has been a six-fold increase in GDP since 1978, with an average annual GDP rate of 9.4 percent for the past 25 years. By the end of 2005, China had become the world's fourth largest economy by exchange rate and the second largest in the world after the United States by purchasing power parity.

All this has propelled China, the former economic basket case, from an agrarian, inward-looking society to one enthusiastically embracing technology and all that the twenty-first century promises. Consider this: In 1995, there were virtually no cell phone users among the country's population. By 2005, there were 400 million subscribers and China had become the number one consumer market for mobile phones in the world.

The Chinese economy is still far from completely open and transparent, yet even its staunchest critics are inclined to concede that considerable progress is being made. China is attempting to harmonize the system of taxes and duties it imposes on enterprises, domestic and foreign alike; in many industries where the old system in which personal "connections" were necessary to conduct business, crony capitalism is diminishing. On the downside, bankruptcy rules, intellectual property rights and ownership rules remain murky or nonexistent. The rules governing foreign ownership of businesses, for instance, vary from industry to industry. In the retail industry, firms such as Wal-Mart, Best Buy and Tesco have been permitted to purchase significant stakes in Chinese companies since the start of 2005, but the foreign banks are more hamstrung by government fear and fiat.

The Chinese fixed exchange rate has also been a sore point with trading partners. Here, too, a decision in 2005 to move to a floating peg, allowing the Chinese renminbi to move against the U.S. dollar in a narrow "trading band," represents a form of progress. But Merrill Lynch's CEO in Taiwan, Albert Lee, seriously doubts that China will permit a fully floating currency any sooner than 2010, because to do so would endanger many exports by making them more expensive. Not only do exporters account for a third of the economy, but they employ ninety million people and operate on razor-thin margins. A drop in sales could force millions out of work. And in a country where millions of people are leaving their farms each year to work in the cities and factories, that could spell disaster. "They need to keep a tight lid on it; they can't just let it go," Lee insists.

One major policy change that Lee does expect to see by 2010 is the granting of permission by the Chinese government to the country's citizens to invest directly offshore, something they can't do today. China tends to prefer a gradual approach in its economic reforms. According to Lee, the Chinese government is likely to go this route when it comes to loosening capital controls. He looks to Taiwan as a possible model. In 1985, Taiwan first allowed citizens to move investments overseas. The amount started at US$100,000 and has gradually ratcheted up until today a Taiwanese citizen can move US$5 million out of the country. Given the vast wealth creation occurring in China, the prospect that some capital will start moving offshore is a tantalizing one, both for the HNWIs who live in China as well as for financial institutions, which could offer these HNWIs a whole new array of products and services. It's also an encouraging prospect for globalization itself, since the free flow of capital is one of its cornerstones.

The expectation that the Chinese market will one day be a huge market for wealth management services added some degree of urgency to a recent competition among more than one hundred financial firms to win a mandate from the Chinese government to invest money on behalf of its US$28.5 billion social security fund. The deal is relatively small in terms of money management, so the ten firms eventually chosen are clearly eyeing future opportunities. China is a society of savers, with an estimated US$2 trillion to US$3 trillion in bank accounts, while the mutual fund industry remains small, roughly the size of the U.S. mutual fund industry in the late seventies.

A New Approach to Wealth Management: Private Banking in Asia

Born and educated in Taiwan, Albert Lee obtained a law degree there and attended a graduate program in finance at the University of Illinois at Urbana-Champaign before practicing law with a prominent firm in Taipei. After joining Citibank's Taiwan office as a management trainee, he rose to department head and branch manager of the institutional finance division before joining Merrill Lynch in 1991 as a private banker in Taiwan.

"Merrill's banking license at that time was strictly advisory," Lee recalls. "This was the early stage of wealth management in this virgin territory. The Taiwanese government was concerned about granting too much influence to foreign wealth managers. In Taiwan and elsewhere in Asia, there was virtually no concept of private banking." As the regulatory environment gradually loosened up in Taiwan, by 2001 Lee was managing three Merrill Lynch branches there and had over a hundred FAs in Taiwan and Singapore reporting to him.

A year later, Lee transferred to Merrill's Hong Kong office as chief of its Global Private Client division for the entire Pacific Rim. "Wealth management as a separate entity scarcely existed at that time," Lee contends brightly. "I witnessed"—and personally participated in—"the development of private banking in Asia."

As a discipline, wealth management was still immature compared to the more developed markets in Europe and the United States, according to Lee. "There remained a casino mentality in some of the stock markets in Asia, which remain highly volatile." By Lee's account, when he started out in the business in the early nineties, Merrill's major competitor in private wealth management in the Pacific Rim was Citibank, with

JPMorgan running a distant second. "Merrill was still largely perceived by many high-net-worth individuals," he modestly says, "as mainly staffed by stock jockeys."

Lee made it his mission to "raise the image of Merrill in Asia." This was not only a matter of attracting top clients; it was a matter of attracting top talent. "In Hong Kong we were successful at building up our image even in an immature market. Yet for some years, it was difficult to recruit FAs from Citi, JPMorgan or Morgan Stanley because so many expressed a disinterest in joining what they regarded as a 'stock brokerage firm' as opposed to a 'private wealth manager.'"

Under Lee all that was destined to change. "Client behavior evolved dramatically during the final decade of the twentieth century. Alternative investments, including hedge funds, private equity, other direct investment opportunities and a variety of more sophisticated synthetic, structured and derivative products, really took off during that time. The economic development of China created a dramatic wealth effect throughout the region."

On the private wealth management side, "If a client was still stock picking, we would attempt to convert the client to the gospel of asset allocation. Some clients would respond, 'Don't tell me about asset allocation. I've got some money with you that I want you to play with and give me a high return.' And as long as the client understands the risk and rewards involved, we will adapt to that client's personal style. Yet others were intrigued by this asset allocation idea, and determined to check out this new mantra."

At the same time, during the tech boom of the late nineties, Lee observed significant changes in client behavior. "I noticed in Taiwan, Hong Kong, Singapore and the Philippines a sharply increased appetite for derivative products." Today, Lee—who was recently appointed CEO for Merrill Lynch in Taiwan—is keen on the fact that "at last count we have 280 billionaires in our region. Every financial firm is pitching product to these clients. Clients are no longer satisfied with our just picking stocks. In general clients are getting smarter, which is another way of saying that the FAs are doing a better job of educating them about new opportunities in the markets."

In the Pacific Rim, Merrill's latest thrust is its Private Banking and Investment Group, a joint venture between its Global Wealth Management (GWM) retail division and its Global Markets and Investment Banking Group (GMI). As Lee describes it, "FAs draw on the specialized knowledge and product specialists within GMI while GMI gains access to the deeper and more personal relationships enjoyed by GPC and the FAs."

INDIA: A GROWING MAJOR ECONOMIC FORCE

China's giant neighbor, India, is another growing power in Asia, and the liberalization of its capital markets has also played a significant role in the pace of the region's globalization. With a GDP of US$719.8 billion in 2005, India has become the world's twelfth-largest economy and the second-fastest growing major economy in the world, with a GDP growth rate of 8.8 percent as of 2006. It boasts the world's third-largest GDP of US$4.042 trillion as measured by purchasing power parity (PPP).

Since its independence in 1947, India has mostly followed a socialist-inspired approach to its economy, with strict government control over private sector participation, foreign trade and foreign direct investment. But since the early nineties, India has gradually opened up its markets through economic reforms by reducing government controls on foreign trade and investment. The privatization of publicly owned industries and the opening up of certain sectors to private and foreign interests has proceeded slowly amid the kind of political debate impossible in China. But as was the case with China, globalization has gathered momentum from its participation.

India and China: Two Powerful Trading Partners

Economic relations between India and China were strained for decades as the two jockeyed for economic advantage and tried to prove which of their nations was better equipped to sustain the high growth rates of the past several years. But lately the two are driving growth through stronger ties, and this is expected to continue.

At the heart of this historical tension are complex social and political differences. India is the world's largest democracy, with a mixed history of entrepreneurialism and state control. China is the world's largest communist state and now a cauldron of capitalist experimentation. There are large swaths of disputed territories in India's northeast, and while not as prone to violence as the India/Pakistan tussle over Kashmir, the feud does simmer.

But there are growing signs that the differences that have hindered trade between the two nations for many years are acting as trade stimulants, with each side poised to take advantage of its distinctive strengths and, ultimately, complementary differences—in China's case, a genius for manufacturing and computer hardware, and in India's, for services and software.

From 2001 to 2005, trading volume between India and China grew by more than 50 percent annually, reaching US$18.7 billion in 2005. By contrast, during the same period, India–U.S. trade grew by 18.7 percent annually. A further sign of recent progress: in July 2006, the Nathu La Pass—the former silk trade route between China and India—reopened after a forty-four-year closure, creating new overland trade opportunities to complement a trading relationship that has existed primarily by sea. Predictions that China will become India's largest trading partner in the near future seem highly credible.

The economic power inherent in this burgeoning relationship is likely to be a welcome hedge against some of the risks associated with being too reliant on the United States and EU, whose growth rates are expected to slow over the next several years. If India and China succeed in supporting each other's growth, the Asia-Pacific region may one day outgrow its dependence on the economic health of western countries and become self-sustaining.

Today, India's economy is increasingly diverse and encompasses agriculture, textiles, manufacturing and a multitude of services, including high-tech outsourcing. Although two-thirds of the Indian workforce still earns their livelihood directly or indirectly through agriculture, service is a growing sector and is playing an increasingly important role in India's economy. The advent of the digital age, and the large number of young and educated populace fluent in English, is gradually transforming India. India is a major exporter of highly skilled workers in software, financial services and engineering. And the country has quickly emerged as an important "back office" destination for global companies as they look to cut costs by outsourcing customer services and technical support. India continues to push the envelope, moving higher and higher up the ladder in the provision of more strategic and front office services.

Industrial policy reforms have substantially reduced licensing requirements, removed restrictions on expansion and facilitated easy access to foreign technology and foreign direct investment. India liberalized its foreign direct investment policies in 2005, allowing a 100 percent FDI (Foreign Direct Investment) stake in some ventures, such as the construction business, and reforms in the retail sectors are expected shortly.

Not only do these reforms pave the way for non-domestic HNWIs' investment in the Indian economy, they lay the groundwork for those in India's huge middle class, 300 million strong, to move up into the ranks of the wealthy. Reform significantly impacts a class of investor unique to India: Non-Resident Indians (NRIs). NRIs have in the past sent home more than US$20 billion a year to support family members. But due to a lack of good investment opportunities and irksome capital controls, NRIs tended not to invest directly in the Indian economy. Now that's changing as investment options burgeon and capital controls are expected to gradually lift. This new "financial connection" that will accompany the long-nurtured "cultural connection" is sure to create even more wealth on the subcontinent in the coming decades.

Non-Resident Indians Play a Unique Role in Wealth Accumulation in India

Non-Resident Indians (NRIs) are people of Indian origin or descent working or living outside of India—and their influence on the future wealth accumulation within India is likely to be significant. Even NRIs that left India more than a generation earlier have maintained strong cultural and economic links with India. In 2005, NRI deposits in the banking system totaled US$33 billion and remittances amounted to US$21.7 billion, representing approximately 3 percent of India's GDP and four times its foreign direct investment. From 2002 to 2005, NRIs acquired more than US$3.3 billion of shares on Indian stock exchanges.

Many NRIs are successful business owners in the textile, gem and jewelry, hospitality and trading industries, and are integral to the business communities in Hong Kong, Singapore, Indonesia, Thailand and Malaysia. Additionally, the NRI community contributes many skilled workers to the financial services, information technology and shipping industries. Because of their strong local business ties in their adopted region and the maintenance of ties with India, NRIs are particularly global in their outlook—both in terms of their business interests and personal investment opportunities.

According to the 2007 *WWR*, HNWIs in the Asia-Pacific region—numbering about 2.6 million—trade actively in both the local and international financial markets. As one Hong Kong NRI financial advisor commented, "Some of my NRIs are more knowledgeable about Hong Kong stock markets than [are] the local residents!" And due to the close-knit nature of the NRI community, NRIs openly share investment information with each other and provide excellent referrals for the wealth advisors lucky enough to work with them.

The professional NRI client segment offers some distinctive opportunities for specialist financial advisors. Because of currency convertibility restrictions, it makes sense for these Indians to retain some wealth offshore in foreign currency. Many hold Indian ADRs (American Depositary Receipts) or mutual funds, and some have gone through the process of registering for the Indian government's NRI Portfolio Investment Scheme, enabling them to trade in Indian domestic stocks from overseas. Business owners are inclined toward high-volume transactions, say advisors, and make bold opportunistic moves, such as margin trading.

At the same time, NRIs are highly demanding clients who are notorious for spreading their investments and comparing pricing across numerous wealth management advisors. From the standpoint of the financial advisor, therefore, NRI business owners make for difficult, but rewarding, clients. To this end, nearly all of the international private banks, along with many of the domestic Indian banks, have set up teams of financial advisors specializing in servicing NRIs.

In early 2007, a Goldman Sachs report[11] forecast that India could overtake Britain and boast the world's fifth-largest economy within a decade, as the country's growth accelerates apace. Moreover, contrary to the demographic profiles of many developed countries, India's workforce will remain young and robust; the massive retirement waves likely to stall growth in other regions of the world will not figure in the near futures of most Asia-Pacific markets, with the possible exception of Japan and China. As a result, India's HNWI population—along with the opportunities for accumulating wealth—is likely to expand significantly in the years to come. Investors might be well served to watch and determine how much of their portfolio they can allocate to similar vehicles based on the experience of India.

Merrill's Passage to India

For the first time, India has become the largest revenue contributor among Asia's emerging economies for Merrill Lynch, highlighting the country's increasing importance for global investment banks. A record flow of share offerings

---

11. "India's Rising Growth Potential," Global Economics Paper #152, economic research from the GS Institutional Portal; http://portal.gs.com.

and significant mergers and acquisitions, coupled with increasing principal investment by Merrill Lynch, meant that "India has finally become relevant to Merrill Lynch in revenue terms, not just regionally but globally," Patricia McLaughlin, Merrill's vice-chairman and managing director for investment banking in India proudly informed *The Financial Times* in August, 2007.

As global investment banks rushed in to create beachheads in India during the past few years to take advantage of a rapidly growing economy, mergers and acquisitions volume in India rose in 2006 to an unprecedented US$63.9 billion, more than double that of the same period the previous year, according to data firm Dealogic. A rise in new share issuance was responsible for investment banks underwriting a record US$23.3 billion of share sales in India within the first six months of 2006. Just five years earlier, by sharp contrast, Indian companies sold a comparatively paltry US$603 million worth of shares. In 2007, Merrill plunged even further into India's rapidly expanding real estate market, paying US$377 million for a 49 percent share in a portfolio of residential projects managed by DLF, the country's largest listed developer, in one of the largest deals of its type ever struck on the subcontinent.

THE EUROPEAN UNION: THE WORLD'S LARGEST INTEGRATED ECONOMY

The rise of China and India has grabbed so many headlines of late that it can be easy to gloss over the pivotal role that Europe has played in the evolution of globalization. The Maastricht Treaty, defining the guidelines for the EU in 1992 and following soon after the fall of the Berlin Wall, took a continent of more than two dozen countries and created a single market. In fact, it created the world's largest single market.

The EU consists of a customs union, a single currency managed by the European Central Bank (in 2008, fifteen of the twenty-seven member states are using the euro), and a set of policies to create a single market of more than 350 million customers. The Schengen Agreement abolished passport control for some member states, and customs checks were also abolished at many of the EU's internal borders, creating a single space of mobility where EU citizens can live, travel, work and invest.

The EU remains the world's largest integrated economy, with a 2005 GDP of US$13.5 trillion compared to US$12.5 trillion in the United States, according to the IMF. Enhanced trade and higher growth from the newest EU members of the former Eastern Bloc are helping to drive EU growth. Indeed, private banks are now grappling with how to service the emerging millionaires of Eastern Europe, a group that is growing very quickly, but whose private banking preferences are still largely unknown.

For all the strides that the EU has made during the past fifteen years, it faces significant long-term challenges. As briefly mentioned earlier, low birth rate and aging demographics are likely to weigh on economic growth, but so will EU policies that may make the continent a bit less competitive on the world stage. The EU is a highly regulated, highly taxed jurisdiction. Even the tax and privacy haven of Switzerland, which has not joined the EU, must pay some heed. Switzerland has agreed to levy a withholding tax (initially at 15 percent) to return on savings paid to the citizens of EU member states, which means that EU citizens cannot sidestep taxes as they once could.

In fact, EU rules may eventually topple Switzerland's place at the pinnacle of offshore banking; Singapore is poised to capture that honor, positioning itself as a tax-friendly alternative and aggressively courting emerging Asian HNWIs and HNWIs from the developed markets. That said, one should not overstate the plight of Switzerland, currently the third-largest center of wealth in the world. Even if overtaken by Singapore, Swiss banking is in no danger of disappearing. It continues to be a haven for Latin America and the Middle Eastern HNWIs, who remain unaffected by the tax rules imposed by the EU on its citizens.

Switzerland's dilemma in Europe represents the flip side of globalization for the developed world. If developing economies worry they will be plundered and assimilated by globalization, developed countries worry their standards (living/environmental/human rights) will be degraded and their leadership roles eroded. Liberalized markets are wonderful for financial markets and the creation of wealth, but the financial herd is merciless and unsentimental. HNWIs and their advisors will always look to move their assets to the most advantageous markets—as well they should. Taxes too high in Switzerland? Move money to Singapore. Wages too high in Germany? Move jobs to China. Regulatory and legal costs too high in the United States? Move operations to India.

UNITED STATES: LOST LUSTER

For another example of how globalization can put established powers back on their heels, look no further than New York City. In 2000, as the Internet boom peaked, 90 percent of foreign IPOs were issued in the United States. Six years later, those numbers were flipped; just 10 percent of foreign IPOs chose to list in the United States. The total number of foreign IPOs has fallen 75 percent, and more and more non-U.S. companies (and U.S. companies for that matter) are delisting through private equity and management buyouts.

Why? Two reasons are commonly cited. The first is linked to regulations enacted after the corporate scandals of Enron and WorldCom. Sarbanes-Oxley (SOX) added investor protections, but some say it went too far with overly burdensome audit requirements. Large companies spend millions per year on these rules; meanwhile, the attention of boards of directors is less on strategy and more on regulatory compliance. But SOX is not the only regulatory thorn in the side of the United States. In the U.S. there are at least ten federal, state and regulatory bodies governing the capital markets, with overlapping and sometimes competing jurisdictions. (Rather ironic since Americans often chide emerging markets for their labyrinthian bureaucracies and inefficient business environments.) The second reason often cited for the falloff in U.S. listings by foreign companies is U.S. tort law. In 2005, class action lawsuits cost American corporations US$9.6 billion, up from US$150 million in 1997. In fact, comparing the cost of litigation to GDP shows that the United States is clearly the most litigious society.

To the credit of the Securities and Exchange Commission, it's been willing to consider that some of these rules and regulations may have overshot the mark. In late 2006, for instance, it proposed softening the costly oversight rule for small companies. That's a good thing, because the message from global entrepreneurs and investors is clear: the United States must have a regulatory and legal regime that's in step with other financial centers, or it will lose even more market share.

Companies from developing countries, as they grow richer and their financial markets become better governed, have plenty of options besides the United States to raise money. It also doesn't help U.S. market share that investment banking fees attached to IPOs are higher in the States than either Asia or Europe. Russian firms can turn to the U.K., and China's and India's entrepreneurs can look to Hong Kong. Globalization of financial markets, to put it bluntly, makes a New York listing seem less necessary or brag worthy. Retail investors themselves, especially given that most hold stocks via mutual funds, care even less where a company is listed. Once again, this is the flip side of globalization. Once financial advisors outside the United States fully understand the U.S. business models and can compete with respect to service, regulatory issues, etc., competition for HNWIs could go global as long as the perception remains that service delivery was local.

Foreign investors' interest in North America has decreased in recent years to 43 percent from about 46 percent and is forecast to drop even further. In 2004, enthusiasm for North American investing dimmed due to the gains witnessed in other markets, and also another important development: HNWIs' confidence in the U.S. dollar began to crack. Huge deficits, the mounting cost of the war in Iraq (not to mention Afghanistan), and entitlements in the form of Social Security and Medicare that will eat up a greater percentage of the budget as baby boomers retire are all starting to weigh on the dollar. The dollar's further losses in 2006 added to the urgency with which some HNWIs began investigating other markets and considering how they will hedge their dollar exposure. BlackRock cofounder Ralph Schlosstein is forthright in his belief that HNWIs are more aware than ever that a fall in the dollar could impact their long-term standard of living.

In 2005, the Asia-Pacific region surpassed Europe as the second most popular destination for HNWI investments, accounting for 23 percent of total assets. A number of emerging economies with large growth prospects—such as China and India—combined with strong performance in the region's more mature markets—such as Singapore and Hong Kong—is likely to keep international interest focused on this part of the world for some time to come. Such numbers clearly buttress Mr. Lavayssière's observation that the world is evolving from a two-pole world to a multi-polar world. Asia-Pacific is that third pole; this triumvirate will drive the economic and political narrative of the twenty-first century.

LATIN AMERICA: A GROWING REGIONAL ECONOMY

Although Latin American markets have not enjoyed the explosive growth that Asian markets have experienced over the past ten years, the tangible effects of globalization remain strong nonetheless. The regional economy enjoyed a 5.3 percent growth rate in 2006, the third strong year in a row, and although countries such as Venezuela and Bolivia seem to be sliding toward socialist policies, many Central and South American countries are embracing globalization.

Take Brazil, which saw its HNWI population grow 10.1 percent in 2006, and its main stock exchange, the São Paulo Bovespa, jump 32.9 percent. Thanks to smart fiscal policies and a marked improvement in Brazil's current account, foreign exchange reserves, and balance of trade, the country has attracted foreign investment and grown the economy to the world's ninth-largest by purchasing power parity and eleventh largest—both according to early 2007 market exchange rates. It possesses large and well-developed agricultural, mining, manufacturing and service sectors, as well as a large labor pool.

With the increased economic stability provided by the Plano Real, Brazilian and multinational businesses have invested heavily in new equipment and technology, a large proportion of which has been purchased from North American enterprises. Many of its companies are regional and, increasingly, global powerhouses, such as Gerdau and CSN.

Brazil has not been without its ups and downs over the past decade, but it has successfully moved from a fixed to a floating real and, ahead of time in 2006, paid back IMF loans related to its currency devaluation. This has occurred while the country and others in the region, particularly Chile, have forged closer ties with China for its abundant raw materials.

Darcie Burk, head of Merrill Lynch's Wealth Management Latin American division and a twenty-year veteran at the firm, can distinctly recall a time not so long ago when traders "physically clipped the coupons on bonds" and "international investing was regarded as kind of a gray area—there was the U.S. and everywhere else, which was just this great empty white space on the map."

It was the pervasive influence of the doctrine of asset allocation within the firm that finally propelled international investing to its present prominence, Ms. Burk contends. "We started getting into providing hedge funds for our private clients," she recalls, "many of which were either headquartered overseas or heavily involved in international investments of various kinds, some of them rather exotic. A lot of hedge funds were also investing in sovereign debt immediately prior to the 1997 crash, so that taught all of us a number of lessons about risk reduction and client risk profiles."

The twin principles of asset allocation and diversification created a virtual mandate that every FA had to know something about international investing, which inevitably involved an engagement in emerging markets because those generally offered favorable rates of return. In recent years, the most dramatic change on the international investing front, according to Burk, is that "it's no longer about wealthy entrepreneurs parking their money safely offshore." These markets have spawned their own indigenous derivative products, which successfully mimic their originals in developed market economies.

"All of these compelling secular trends offer strong implications for the Latin American economy," Burk notes. "If the U.S. suffers a crash, China offers a little bit of a hedge due to decoupling. The entire region is stronger thanks to globalization."

Mexico's mortgage market offers another example of what's happening in Latin America today, and how fiscal policies have created enormous wealth and opportunities for domestic and non-domestic HNWIs. Ten years ago there was no mortgage market in Mexico to speak of. As a result, a person had to pay 100 percent for their home, which, not surprisingly, kept home ownership low. But by reining in inflation and successfully issuing sovereign debt, the country has developed one of the deepest local debt markets in Latin America. In 2003, it issued its first twenty-year peso-denominated bond, and in 2006 issued the first thirty-year bond. In 2005, it was estimated that non-Mexicans, in search of long-term, relatively safe, high-yielding investments, owned about 75 percent of the twenty-year notes.

A deep debt market has allowed the mortgage market to develop, since banks now have the confidence to lend over such long time horizons. People can now finance home purchases, and with low interest rates and President Vicente Fox's push for home ownership the Mexican housing market has heated up. That's good for the middle class in Mexico, which can now more readily access a more liquid real estate market.

GLOBALIZATION PROMOTES LOCAL INVESTING

Despite improvements brought by globalization, emerging markets clearly have political and financial risks greater than do developed markets. In the Middle East, for instance, regional business practices do not have the same standards of transparency and accounting as exist in the West, according to Hawkamah, a corporate governance institute. On the whole, however, these risks have lessened. That's partly because developing markets have improved monetary and legal policies, but also because the financial community is better at assessing financial risk and political risk, lessening the chance of a surprise.

The capability of global credit rating agencies to more reliably quantify risk—even high risk—has proven critical to stabilizing these markets and soothing investors; instead of panicking at the first sign of trouble and stampeding for the exits, investors who knew the risks going in to an investment are more likely to ride out trouble. Investors hate surprises, and the fewer surprises there are, thanks to rigorous due diligence, the more confident investors are and the more stable the whole system is. This should be the responsibility and role of the financial advisor, and individuals should demand clarity from their advisors on what the risks will be with these types of investments.

One of the interesting results of globalization and stability of markets has been the degree to which it has encouraged local HNWIs to invest in their local economies. By keeping inflation under control through smart monetary and fiscal policies, creating a legal system that guarantees rights of ownership and promoting free and transparent capital markets, developing countries not only attract investment from overseas investors, they convince homegrown HNWIs to invest in the local economy, helping to further the economic transformation.

This is already a well-established trend in the Middle East, where oil revenue that once automatically returned to Europe and

North America is being invested locally (though much of the oil wealth is still parked in safe government bonds issued by Western governments). Stock markets in Kuwait and Saudi Arabia have become viable, and Dubai is building a financial center—really a city within a city—with zero tax on income and profits, 100 percent foreign ownership rules, no foreign exchanges or repatriation of profits, and a regulatory regime akin to the U.K. and Australia.

HNWIs' growing confidence in their countries and regions is not limited to the oil-rich Middle East. Advisors note that business ownership and income accounts for 57 percent of wealth in Asia and 63 percent in Latin America, and that it's within Asia and Latin America that the lion's share of new wealth is being created. In places like South Korea, Taiwan and Singapore, the standard method of operation is to create wealth onshore, and then at certain points move wealth offshore to developing markets to preserve wealth and guard against the political and financial uncertainties that still exist in their markets. In India, a booming economy and galloping stock market (the Bombay Sensex returned 46.7 percent in 2006) give local HNWIs confidence to keep their money working in the Indian economy and not stealthily move money offshore. What's more, high domestic returns and a well-run financial market mean that once capital controls are lifted, as is expected over the next several years, HNWIs are less likely to suddenly shift huge amounts of capital out of the country.

This marks a radical change from ten years ago, when HNWIs in developing markets possessed few investment options in their home markets. In those days they coped with inflation, uncertain taxes, the threat of expropriation and poor wealth management service in their home market. They moved their money to developed markets for safety and to build their wealth. Those bad old days may be over in some developing markets, but not in all of them. Many HNWIs in Africa as well as certain Latin American and Asian countries still consider it wise to stash most assets offshore—and will continue to do so for years to come. Therefore, the ability to research and gather information on global markets can certainly help individual portfolios.

RADICAL CHANGES IMPACT INVESTMENT OPPORTUNITIES

Globalization and the mobility of capital it implies are having a radical impact on how HNWIs across the globe are investing. Free-moving capital means that investors are empowered to continually cross borders to find the best returns in an ever-increasing number of well-run, transparent financial markets. It also means they are free to depart those markets when financial discipline breaks down, or when another jurisdiction becomes comparatively more attractive. And, ironically, it also means that the best returns might be had by *not* sending investment overseas.

If HNWIs wish to use their wealth to accrue more wealth (and we assume that virtually all of them do), investment opportunities—no matter where they are—cannot be overlooked. HNWIs must open their eyes to the entire globe, shed the antiquated Cold War mindset of political and financial borders, and move their investments adroitly to pockets of growth around the world. This acumen will be necessary to build wealth and to maintain it; what's more, HNWIs and their advisors must work to hone their investment skills quickly. Speed is required to stay ahead of the next wave of investors, which will surely be moving more of their investments overseas soon.

Indeed, an aging population in the West concurrent with the decline of defined benefit pension plans portends a ferocious competition for investments that generate high returns and can fund long-term retirements. It's not a race anyone will care to lose—and settling for lesser returns in more mature economies will not sustain wealth and build a family legacy. HNWIs, if they are to remain HNWIs, must remain in tune with the changes and opportunities of globalization.

While there are certainly risks to globalization and investing in the economies new to free markets, the momentum is clearly toward globalization. As more and more markets around the world open themselves to capital, there will be a series of waves of new investment opportunities. For aspiring HNWIs, the best bet is to keep an eye on how and where the established HNWIs are allocating their capital and follow suit when possible, closing the gap and capturing as many of those early, often higher, returns as possible.

Understandably, some wealthy individuals and households will remain skittish about investing in overseas markets, particularly developing ones; but they should take comfort in the fact that the HNWIs from the emerging market themselves are increasingly confident about investing in their own economies thanks to reforms and opportunities brought about by globalization—and they are the ones in the best position to know what they're getting into. Foreign investors would be wise to scrutinize their investment and sentiment. This means that despite the increasing globalization and complexity, the basic fundamentals will remain:

• Understand your risk profile and appetite;

• Determine your "disposable income" level;

• Set floors and ceilings on exposure, upsides and downsides;

• Agree to set review and reallocation periods;

• Aggressively adhere to your plan.

This will become more and more important. Being aware of this and having the discipline will allow individuals to raise critical issues with their advisors.

As the international situation evolves, the challenge for advisors is to ensure that they are aware of and able to navigate global markets, or have access to this information and can readily and easily understand and share it. Many HNWIs who were interviewed stated that for them, this is now a key financial advisor selection criteria. This means that advisors need to be a steady hand in this tumultuous investment environment, and wealth management firms must also resist using globalization as a cover to treat all HNWIs the same. For instance, a firm cannot hope to succeed in India if it does not set up a truly local operation there, one that operates in the local time zone and designs services and products that fit the local culture. A financial institution operating at arm's length could miss the important nuances of how to manage the wealth of non-resident Indians and their families still in India.

To be successful, the financial advisor needs to fully comprehend the individual style of the investor, based on where the money originated (income versus business versus inheritance), and then overlay that with appropriate products and services. Concurrently, HNWIs need to be prepared to provide that information, which will then allow the advisor to build the most appropriate and compelling investment strategy for their investment needs.

INTERNATIONAL MARKETS' SUCCESS IS FORCING U.S. INVESTORS TO RETHINK THEIR DOMESTIC FOCUS

The increasing interest and allocation to international investments is occurring because of many of the same reasons as those driving alternative investments such as hedge funds and private equity: investors' growing familiarity with these markets, a hunt for yield and diversification. The dilemma for the HNWI is the same as well: greater risk. The following must be considered:

• How liquid will these investments be in a time of crisis?

• How well does the financial community understand the risks—political and economical—in all of these remote corners of the world where investments are now possible, often for the first time?

- And, even if the risks are fairly well understood, are HNWIs being properly rewarded for the risk they are taking, or is the rush of capital into new markets driving up prices and discounting the risks too much?

- Therefore: Should the fifty stocks on the Vietnamese stock exchange really be trading at a higher price-to-earnings multiple than the S&P 500—as was the case in early 2007?

Make no mistake, however, that while these questions must be asked and precautions taken, they cannot be used as a pretext for inaction. Smart investors continue to diversify their holdings as their confidence in less familiar markets grows, and this international approach is playing a larger role in their wealth creation strategy as markets outside North America and Europe rack up double-digit gains year after year. To keep up, other investors will be forced to follow suit and fundamentally shift the composition of their portfolios. The so-called "wheel of fortune" below highlights some of the rationale behind the drive toward an increasingly international view.

For HNWIs tempted to wait on the sidelines to see if international investing will fall out of favor, money managers stress that this new global investing approach is no flash in the pan. The smart money will continue to flow into international investments. "This is part of a permanent trend. The world has changed and the world view of investors is different today. Globalization is the biggest shift in history in terms of economic development; countries are participating that never have before," says Gregory Johnson, CEO of Franklin Templeton Investments, founded by his grandfather in 1947 and which today boasts US$465 billion of assets under management. Mr. Johnson's father, Charles Bartlett Johnson, serves as co-chairman of Franklin Resources, has an estimated net worth of US$4.3 billion and was ranked in 2006 by *Forbes* as the *147th richest person in the world.*[12]

---

12. Interview with the authors.

Figure 2.1 – Wealth Creation in Global Economies

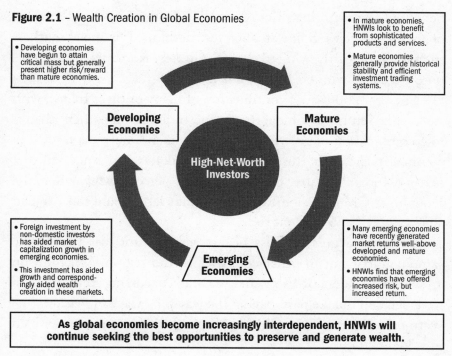

- In mature economies, HNWIs look to benefit from sophisticated products and services.
- Mature economies generally provide historical stability and efficient investment trading systems.

- Developing economies have begun to attain critical mass but generally present higher risk/reward than mature economies.

Developing Economies

Mature Economies

High-Net-Worth Investors

- Foreign investment by non-domestic investors has aided market capitalization growth in emerging economies.
- This investment has aided growth and correspondingly aided wealth creation in these markets.

Emerging Economies

- Many emerging economies have recently generated market returns well-above developed and mature economies.
- HNWIs find that emerging economies have offered increased risk, but increased return.

As global economies become increasingly interdependent, HNWIs will continue seeking the best opportunities to preserve and generate wealth.

Source: Capgemini analysis.

Market capitalizations and benchmark index performance have grown rapidly in Eastern European, Asian-Pacific and Latin American markets, driven by ongoing foreign investment and strong corporate profits. HNWIs have paid close attention and taken advantage. In 2006, emerging-market mutual funds worldwide saw a record US$22 billion of net new money, up from US$20 billion in 2005, according to Emerging Portfolio Fund Research. The Dow Jones World Stock Index—excluding U.S. equities—rose 88 percent from 2002 to 2005 and then tacked on another 23 percent in 2006.

In the Asia-Pacific region, stock market growth has remained consistently strong. The MSCI AC Asia-Pacific Index returned 21.0 percent in 2005, up from 14.1 percent in 2004. Similarly, commodity-producing nations such as Brazil, Mexico and Canada benefited from surging prices, as well as from a boost in the value of their currencies. Some smaller, less developed financial markets such as those of the United Arab Emirates, Romania and Singapore were also winners for HNWIs in 2005.

The year 2006 saw a continuation of many of these trends, with substantial returns in China, Russia and India, among others, thanks to a combination of growing domestic demand, overseas trade and commodity prices. In Russia, the benchmark RTS Index jumped 70.7 percent. India's Bombay Sensex rose 46.7 percent. Meanwhile, the Dow Jones China 88, a measure of China's largest and most traded stocks, scored a 97 percent rise.

To some degree, success begets success, not just within the same country, but in other countries in the region. Mr. Johnson argues that leaders of Vietnam see what's occurring in China and have decided to take part, paving the way for a wave of Western investment. The main Ho Chi Min Stock Index more than doubled in value in 2006.

EMERGING MARKETS BECOME MAINSTREAM

The overarching narrative in terms of HNWI international allocation is that investments in North America and Europe are expected to continue to decline over the next few years as HNWIs redeploy assets to the Asia-Pacific region and other emerging markets that outperform North America and Europe. This is virtually inevitable if HNWIs want to position their portfolios for the highest growth. In 2006, for instance, China notched another year of 10-percent-plus growth and is on track to surpass Germany in 2008 as the world's third-largest economy.

HNWIs' heightened interest in international investments, combined with their growing exposure to equities and alternative investments, are clear signs that the world's wealthiest individuals are not only becoming more sophisticated investors; they have also become somewhat more aggressive than in the past and seem even more determined to achieve returns that surpass market averages. The lesson for investors is that the global economy is not only altering real-time communications, but also the ways that money is managed and leveraged.

Indeed, the strong results in emerging and international markets—coupled with the capital flowing into them—have prompted some observers to argue that the emerging markets are "decoupling" from the United States, whose performance remained less robust—albeit respectable—in 2006 and became more severely challenged by the subprime mortgage crisis that dominated the final half of 2007 and continued to roil global markets well into 2008. Many formerly Third World countries are in better financial shape than in the past, with lower deficits, increased reserves and reduced dependence on exports to the United States. The rise of China and, increasingly India, has helped dilute the dependence of many emerging markets on the United States, particularly those that rely on exporting commodities.

How resilient these emerging economies would really be if U.S. consumer demand dried up, however, remains to be seen. This is one of the great unanswered questions going forward as the world is transformed by globalization.

BEYOND EMERGING MARKETS LIES THE FINAL FRONTIER

With so much money chasing investments in places like China and Russia, the more established emerging markets are starting to look mainstream. As investments become more widely available to the mass of investors and demand increases, returns often decline, which leads aggressive investors casting about for the next big thing. This formula has played out with hedge funds and other alternative investments, and now it looks like it's starting to occur with emerging markets as well. Indeed, some HNWIs and their advisors say returns in many emerging markets are declining at too fast a rate, leading them to worry that investors are getting lax about risk.

In pursuit of the highest yields, some HNWIs are looking beyond mere emerging markets to what are known as "frontier markets," where the potential risks and returns are both a magnitude higher than those of emerging markets. Frontier markets are tiny. With a total market capitalization of about US$40 billion, the whole sector is worth less than 20 percent of the current value of China's ICBC bank. They include countries such as Bangladesh, Côte d'Ivoire, Jamaica, Slovenia and many other countries in Africa, South Asia, Eastern Europe and the Caribbean.

The International Finance Corporation (IFC) first launched the S&P/IFC Frontier Index in the mid-nineties. The index measures the performance of stocks of twenty-two countries and has returned an average of 37 percent over the past five years, compared with an average 25 percent for the Morgan Stanley Emerging Markets Index.

Among the countries there are some big winners and big losers. Since March 2003, in dollar terms, the Ukraine has risen by 570 percent, Kenya by 279 percent and Bangladesh by 79 percent. In 2006, Namibia was the top performer by posting a 126 percent return, while Tunisia declined 8 percent. And Saudi Arabia's market plummeted a whopping 50 percent in 2006.

The Vietnam Stock Exchange, which was added to the S&P/IFC Frontier Index in 2006, doubled in value, due to commodity exports and a young, cheap workforce. Foreign investors spent US$123 million for Vietnamese stocks and by the end of 2006 owned about 31 percent of the market. Investors have raised US$1.8 billion to invest in Vietnam ahead of a privatization program next year, which will include eight US$1 billion listings, according to Nicholas Vardy, editor of *The Global Guru*.

For the past several years, investing in these countries has been the province of only the most sophisticated HNWIs but, right on cue, new "frontier funds" are now cropping up to take advantage of such attractive returns, giving more investors a chance to take part. Investment firms Hamilton Bradshaw and AKD Securities recently launched the first fund focused solely on Pakistan, while Investec is pushing the case for Africa and managers are talking up the prospects they're finding in Vietnam.

Many of the opportunities, for now, are open only to institutional investors, including a fund opened in December 2006 by Acadian Asset Management, which quickly raised US$200 million for a frontier markets fund based on the S&P/IFC Frontier Index. Meanwhile, Imara Asset Management's Imara African Opportunities Fund focuses primarily on Africa, excluding South Africa, attempting to tap Africa's wealth of natural resources and growing trade links with booming economies like China. But the minimum investment in the fund is US$100,000. A few mutual fund companies, including Franklin Templeton, Eaton Vance, T. Rowe Price and Fidelity Investments, offer limited frontier exposure through emerging-market mutual funds.

According to Merrill Lynch global emerging-markets equity strategist Michael Hartnett, frontier markets have outperformed both emerging and developed equity markets for several years, earning annualized returns—as measured by the S&P/IFC Frontier Index of 23.75 percent between 2000, when data first became available, and September 2007. Compared with a 12.42 percent rise for emerging markets, as measured by the MSCI Emerging Markets Index, and a 1.18 percent increase for the S&P 500 Index in the United States, both over the same period, frontier markets may display a compelling case for savvy and risk-tolerant investors.

The fundamental driver of their growth potential, Hartnett observes, is the global boom in basic commodities. In 2007, Dubai's stock market rose more than 37 percent, while Abu Dhabi's was up over 40 percent and Qatar's 35 percent. Even sub-Saharan Africa has been experiencing its strongest growth and lowest inflation in more than thirty years, according to the IMF.

On the downside, the challenges faced by these markets are fairly obvious and include not insignificant political uprisings, human rights and environmental issues, hyperinflation, and poor infra-structure that can make power, transportation and information intermittent. Some countries, like Bangladesh, are prone to natural disasters. Laws and regulations can be nonexistent or subject to the whims of local bureaucracies, making investor rights iffy at best.

On the plus side, frontier markets tend to be not closely cor-related to the economic winds in the developed countries, which mean they offer a degree of diversification to the intrepid investor with the risk appetite to go where others justifiably fear to tread. In fact, intrepid may be too subdued a word to describe the atti-tude required to plunge into these markets without losing several years' worth of sleep. Many of these stocks are highly illiquid, which makes them impractical for big mutual funds to participate in and more suitable for private pools of capital that can commit to these investments for the long term and need not worry about redemp-tions. Also, the markets themselves might gyrate radically, and the ultimate goal—that a frontier market becomes an emerging market and eventually a developed market—may in fact never occur. De-spite such hurdles, the S&P/IFC Frontier Index includes Bulgaria, Estonia, Latvia, Lithuania, Romania, Slovakia and Slovenia, some of which are looking decidedly more advanced than their frontier status might suggest.

An additional challenge with frontier markets is that they may be bid way up as investors rush in, even though experienced invest-ment pros say frontier markets are really only worthwhile if they are cheap and overlooked. A case in point: Vietnam, where shares on the Vietnam Stock Index traded at approximately twenty-six times estimated 2006 earnings, above the S&P 500's trailing price/earn-ings ratio of eighteen. As a result, HNWIs and their advisors need to be extraordinarily disciplined when dipping their toes into fron-tier markets and not be lured into taking on too much risk, chasing possibly phantom returns. Such lessons need to be given serious consideration by everyone—clients and advisors alike.

More than a quarter century after Antoine van Agtmael stood at that podium at the Salomon Brothers headquarters in New York, pitching his offbeat idea of an emerging-markets equities investment fund, emerging-market stocks still represent only about 10 percent of market capitalization worldwide. Yet the boundless potential of emerging markets' companies and economies is neatly encapsulated by the fact that taken together, the top one hundred companies from the world's fastest-growing economies are growing ten times faster than their U.S. counterparts, twenty-four times faster than Japan's and thirty-four times faster than Germany's, according to The Boston Consulting Group.

Few investors, regardless of risk tolerance or time horizon, can afford to ignore the fact that the total shareholder return of the MSCI Emerging Markets Index jumped 150 percent during the first six years of the twenty-first century, while the Standard & Poor's 500 Index declined over the same period. "It's astounding that so many people continue to remain oblivious to this new reality," van Agtmael contends.

This new reality is also one more accurately defined by the emergence of dozens of world-class companies, as opposed to world-class economies, according to Mr. van Agtmael. Too many Western investors continue to think about pulling off "country plays" while they should be focused—as they are with companies based in the more developed economies—on individual corporate performance.

As the world's capital markets become ever more closely linked because of the blessings of advancing technology, the global economy is becoming increasingly dominated by forward-looking firms, many based in the developing economies, which possess not just a global footprint but a global outlook. World-class firms like Taiwan's Hon Hai, the world's largest electronics contractor, which produces iPods for Apple; Mexico's Grupo Modelo (Corona beer); Samsung Electronics; or Mexico's Cemex, the largest producer of cement in the United States, are not just the blue chips of the future but the blue chips of today.

Five Tips for International Investing

1. **Go where the growth is:** With the growth of the HNWI population strongest in emerging markets (up 21 percent in Singapore, 20 percent in India, and more than 15 percent in Indonesia, Russia and the UAE[13]), much of the market action in those economies appears to be heavily influenced by higher levels of domestic investment, with inflows into emerging-markets funds from developed countries remaining relatively stable.

2. **Seek proper asset allocation and diversification:** Emerging-markets investors, wherever they may be domiciled, are gaining exposure to economies not traditionally tightly correlated with developed economies. Fans of the "decoupling theme" saw their pet theory stress-tested during the global turbulence caused by the credit collapse in the third quarter of 2007.

3. **Focus on world-class companies, not world-class economies:** India and China may be the national heroes, but maintaining one's focus on individual corporate success stories offers higher rewards than a more scattershot top-down investment approach.

4. **Don't forget frontier markets:** While highly volatile, frontier markets may be worth investigating provided that these targeted investments are undertaken in accordance with a professionally constructed, risk-balanced portfolio strategy.

5. **Embrace globalization; it's no flash in the pan:** To ignore the rewards of international investing would be comparable to refusing to invest in technology, media networking, or other significant social and geopolitical trends. Maintaining a provincial approach that avoids the perceived risk of "foreign" investments is no longer a practical option for investors seeking to maximize opportunities in the twenty-first century.

---

13. Merrill Lynch and Capgemini, 2007 *World Wealth Report.*

CHAPTER 3

Technology's Critical Role in Wealth Management

DAWNING OF THE DIGITAL AGE

In the 2006 *World Wealth Report*, two-thirds of wealth advisors responded to a survey question on technology that the quality and quantity of information available to clients was the most transformative trend in wealth management over the past decade. Forty percent contended that technology would continue to be the most powerful trend for the next ten years. Already, the velocity, volume and scope of information reaching today's investors have made them more sophisticated and demanding than their predecessors. Just as technology empowers wealthy clients and enables advisors to offer them superior service, technology increases the pressure on advisors to keep up with the furious pace of innovation and rapidly ratchets up investor expectations.

It would be difficult to overstate the impact of technology on the art and science of wealth management. Information technology puts sophisticated financial tools in the hands of the wealthy and their advisors. It provides an efficient and effective way for clients to communicate with their advisors as well as each other. The advent of information technology, in tandem with financial innovation in general, has been the primary driver of globalization, binding the world's markets closer together and enabling the nearly instantaneous transfer of information, ideas and liquid assets around the globe at a velocity that is historically unprecedented. ·

Access to aggregated account information (a single balance sheet across business lines and companies), is not merely desired but demanded by clients, not least by HNWIs. These now conventional expectations nonetheless sorely challenge the technology infrastructure of many a wealth advisory firm that has failed to invest the resources in cutting-edge IT. Yet it's a challenge they have no choice but to tackle. Today's U.S. and Europe-based financial firms must compete head-on with those based in Asia—and vice versa.

For clients, the primary benefits bestowed by technology are that they can simultaneously have access to the same up-to-date and sophisticated information as do their advisors and (presumably) the most informed market-makers. As information technology has steadily become more user-friendly, cost-effective and intuitive, the information gap between advisor and client has dramatically contracted. The closing of the information gap vastly improves the quality of the dialogue between client and advisor that lies at the heart of every productive investment relationship.

Charles Simonyi, former head of Microsoft's application software group (which oversaw the creation of Microsoft Word and Excel) and who now heads his own company, Intentional Software, observes that "because financial markets are entirely information-based, technology will drive the future of financial markets."[1] Proprietary databases and algorithms will one day become as valuable as capital and liquidity itself, he predicts. He cites as an example of the cutting edge of this trend the stunning success of Renaissance Technologies (Rentec), the quantitative hedge fund management company founded by former MIT math professor James Simons, whose flagship US$5 billion Medallion Fund has averaged 35 percent annual returns, after fees, from 1989 through 2007.[2]

1. Interview with the authors.

2. Thomas Landon, Jr.,"Pack Mentality Among Hedge Funds Fuels Market Volatilty," *New York Times*, August 13, 2007.

"The algorithms at their disposal have such incredible value that they truly take the place of capital," Simonyi contends. The Medallion Fund's remarkable yield allows it to charge clients a 5 percent management fee and a 44 percent incentive fee—generous even by hedge fund standards. The often daunting task of incorporating new technologies into the discipline of wealth management becomes even more pressing because many technologies considered novel today will not be considered worth talking about to the children of today's wealthy clients. Rapid technological obsolescence is simply a fact of modern corporate life. As younger generations become HNWIs in their own right, they are unlikely to display much patience for firms that have failed to seamlessly weave the most advanced technologies into the very fabric of their operations. "Technology is something invented after you were born," observes James A.C. Kennedy, CEO of financial firm T. Rowe Price. "For kids the Internet isn't a technology, it's an appliance. They couldn't imagine life without it because they've never had to."[3]

DISPELLING FIVE MYTHS
OF ONLINE PRIVATE BANKING

Despite the technology-fueled revolution around investor education and sophistication, it's hardly surprising that it's still possible to find advisors who believe that technology's place in wealth management is limited. The rationale seems to be that since private banking has thrive so long so successfully, it must be immune to the IT advances all around it. A corollary to this erroneous belief is that HNWIs aren't interested in technology, or that deploying technology will somehow put the wealth management firm itself at some kind of competitive disadvantage. This sentiment is particularly stubborn when it comes to shunning the Internet, which is quite simply a no-growth strategy for both the firm and, potentially, HNWIs. While it's

---

3. Interview with the authors.

true that any new and potentially costly IT strategy or deployment should not be undertaken lightly—especially when it touches the client as ubiquitously as the Internet does—too many advisors suffer from an abundance of caution when contemplating technology upgrades. Too many are fooled or seduced by what Capgemini has identified as the five myths of online private banking:

Myth #1: Most private banking clients are not sufficiently Internet-savvy for online banking.

We have extensively documented a widespread belief that wealthy investors are not sufficiently familiar with the Internet to move private banking online. Indeed, there is some basis for this misperception. Most wealthy clients in North America and Europe are in their late fifties, an age group that as a rule uses the Internet less frequently than younger demographics. (As recently as 2004, only 20 percent of Europeans between fifty-five and seventy-four had logged on within twelve months.) But the conclusion that many draw from this fact—that wealthy individuals are not good candidates for Internet banking services—is simply erroneous.

Conclusions based on crude demographics frequently miss critical details. Retail brokerage clients as a group are frequent and committed users of online communication. The typical advised client in 2005 spent nearly fourteen hours per week online, and more than half had a broadband connection. In fact, the wealthier the clients, the more active they tend to be online. In 2005, an affluent European was 73 percent more likely than a non-affluent counterpart to bank online at least weekly.

Nearly half of the affluent U.S. households conduct online stock research, with one in three HNWIs visiting financial provider sites and one in five trading stocks, mutual funds, options and bonds online. Indeed, for clients with actively managed portfolios, managing finances was the second most frequently performed online activity after emailing. HNWIs still demand ample telephone and face time with their advisors, but 56 percent require full Internet access to their portfolios and investment accounts as a prerequisite for client satisfaction—a figure that is surely to grow.

Figure 3.1 – Share of Investors Who Are Active Online, per Level of Wealth, United States, 2005

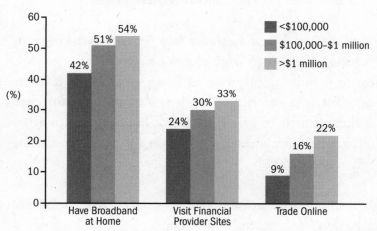

Sources: *Private Banker International,* May 31, 2005; *Private Banker International,* Apr. 27, 2004; Forrester research, "The affluent are the most active online investors," Sept. 2005; Forrester research, "How to boost online banking in Italy," Sept. 2004; Forrester research, "Europe's affluent rely on online finance," Feb. 2004.

Furthermore, the wealthier the client, the more they tend to factor websites into their overall satisfaction with their advisor. Forrester Research found that 58 percent of brokerage website visitors in the U.S. consider the quality of their brokerage firm's website extremely important to their satisfaction with the company as a whole.[4] Remarkably, the second-strongest predictor of high client satisfaction with their brokerage firm was how they viewed the firm's use of technology. And of course, when it comes to future generations, since younger people are by far the heaviest users of the Internet, their numbers will continue to grow as they age and turn into the next generation of HNWIs.

---

4. "How Mass Affluent Investors Use the Web," Tom Watson with Bill Doyle, Forrester Research, August 31, 2004.

Technology, in short, is critical to serving clients properly—and clients know it. In a fiercely competitive environment, where companies are looking for every conceivable advantage to retain and attract wealthy clients, the online channel must be embraced. Clients, in turn, would be wise to make the best use of the online channel as a means of optimizing communication with their advisor.

Myth #2: An advisor-based business like private banking can only be distributed through high-touch channels.

Private banking is quite rightly viewed as a people-based relationship business. But that description leads some observers to falsely assume that there is little to gain from providing clients with access to electronic channels. Frequent arguments against electronic channels and Web access include:

1. The high level of customization and personal service HNWIs expect can't be delivered through the Web;

2. Clients' complex financial situations require advanced services and products that cannot be delivered online;

3. The low frequency of transactions (compared to retail banking) makes an Internet channel too costly to maintain.

Yet as has been previously noted and well documented, HNWIs are increasingly intent on taking a more active role in the dialogue about their wealth. Whether this means they will or won't want to speak to their advisors on a daily basis is unknown, but it does mean that they require instantaneous real-time access to timely financial information. Ideally, a firm should be able to deliver this information and increase the touch points between the advisor and the clients to "extend the conversation," further proving the advisor's value as a trusted and accessible counselor. For example, a firm could design customized online investment alerts for deployment following every investor-advisor telephone conversation.

Of course, there are always going to be some tech-averse clients temperamentally inclined to avoid the online channel, preferring the intimacy of face-to-face meetings and phone calls. Personal preferences will perennially vary. Not all channels are suitable to all clients. But the fact is that by offering the broadest possible menu of channels, a bank can customize the mix to each client's specific needs and preferences, which will allow the bank to more accurately target services.

There will always be a significant difference between processing a stock purchase and providing estate planning services. To squeeze the maximum value from its distribution channels, private banks need to make low-value, low-touch distribution channels available for low-value and commoditized products and services such as stock purchases, while maintaining a high degree of flexibility to each investor's preferences in the event that they may want to perform, say, some estate planning online.

Figure 3.2 – Product Complexity and Value of Distribution Channel

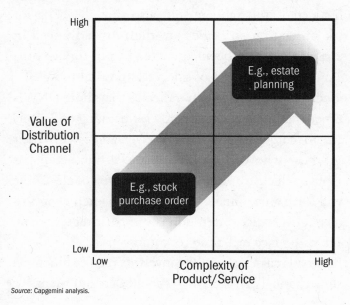

Source: Capgemini analysis.

Not only can the "low-touch" Web channels improve client satisfaction by offering more information and additional routes of communication with their advisor, they can materially assist banks to boost profits by increasing revenue while lowering costs. Revenue growth can be ascribed to higher client satisfaction and retention; shorter revenue cycles and increased cross-selling thanks to faster communication; and stronger client acquisition and lead generation. On the cost side, improved coordination between client servicing team members and processes yields cost efficiencies; and the cost of standard transactions is lower online than through any other channel.

Myth #3: Because of concerns about security and confidentiality, private clients will never fully adopt the Internet channel.

As the number of high-profile credit card security breaches in recent years highlight, security issues surrounding identify theft and online fraud must be adequately addressed if online banking stands any chance of truly attaining critical mass, particularly among the highest net-worth demographic. It's certainly clear that credit card fraud is the most sophisticated and frequent, but also that the behavior modeling and risk mitigation strategies are the most advanced in this area, as those of us who have been contacted by our service providers to validate purchases, location of sale, etc. know all too well.

Recently conducted primary research indicates that more HNWIs are using the Internet channel more frequently for banking and managing their wealth in conjunction with a conversation with their advisors. However, those who wish to keep financial transactions as "recordless" as possible will clearly look to avoid any type of electronic transaction that will leave an auditable trace. The ultra-rich clients of Swiss private banks, for instance, often don't even trust regular mail, relying instead on face-to-face real-time communication.

Regardless, the broad masses of wealthy investors require functional and reliable online channels; in fact, they should demand them. To meet their needs, providers are taking three broad measures to address security concerns: technological, educational/informational and legal.

On the technology front, private banks are developing more advanced functionality to tackle online security threats. In fact, in the United States, regulators mandate the use of two-factor authentication to provide a highly secure form of online access. (An ATM card with a chip and PIN that must be used in conjunction with the card is an example of two-factor authentication.) Elsewhere, firms are introducing the DigiTAG device, which generates a unique eight-digit security code to be used with a standard user ID and password to authorize access to online sites. Some banks offer their clients free downloads of anti-virus and anti-spam software, as well as free security checks for their personal computers. New initiatives are being announced regularly.

On the education/information front, private banks are educating their clients about security measures in order to boost client confidence in the Web channel. The challenge for private banks and advisors is to discuss security measures with clients without scaring them off or making the security measures appear too bothersome. Many firms are using visual clues to communicate security and confidentiality by using an email security zone with the retail banking client's first and last name as well as the last four digits of an ATM/debit card. This encourages users to look for personal clues to verify the information.

On the legal front, banks are educating customers on security best practices and explaining clearly what the bank's policies are in the event of fraud. Best practice examples include firms putting their "peace of mind" guarantee prominently on every Internet page, promising to compensate customers in the event of fraud.

Myth #4: Financial advisors don't benefit from the increased transparency that online private banking provides clients.

To avoid taking the leap into online banking, advisors often tell themselves that clients don't want full transparency and, even if they did, clients would not stand to benefit from such "uncontrolled" access to information. Aside from being self-serving and faulty, such reasoning blinds advisors to how increased transparency technology can help enhance their business.

Yes, pressures on advisors do increase with online banking and transparency. With constant real-time client access and with clients viewing and acting upon Web pages that provide them with details of their full financial portfolio, the advisor needs to provide more education about market conditions and the strategy and tactics of the investments, and be prepared to explain their decisions to the client. Clients should also be prepared to ask questions of their advisors versus solely accepting their advice.

Advisors also benefit. According to a 2006 Forrester Research study,[5] advisors who proactively encouraged usage of online channels had better financial results compared to advisors who didn't encourage online usage. They had 11 percent more clients, 50 percent more assets under management and 38 percent more annual revenue. Perhaps this is because such openness also reflects and promotes a level of trust between advisor and clients. Forrester further found that advisors who don't encourage site use are twice as likely to say that their clients don't trust them.

Myth #5: Online channel implementation requires major IT investments by the private banks with little return and little ability to pass costs on to clients.

The overriding concern at many firms is that systems designed to support online trading transactions are excessively complicated and costly due to compliance issues, fraud potential, and complex system integration between front-office and back-office systems. Certainly, no IT investment or upgrade is without cost, but firms may find that

---

5. "Full-Service Brokerages: Stop Neglecting the Net," *Outdated Web Sites Make You Increasingly Vulnerable to Direct Firms* "Affluent Investors Series" Forrester Research, September 13, 2006.

those costs are less than originally feared and may in some cases generate quicker returns than anticipated.

Through the use of middleware and service-oriented architecture (SOA; systems that enable software to work together and data to be shared), firms do not necessarily need to replace their entire existing infrastructure to implement additional functionalities. By leveraging existing technologies, private banks may increase the return from their technology investments. Many packages and platforms available today do not require as intense a customization as was necessary in the past to meet the needs of high-net-worth clients. For example, to enhance and enable superior online collaboration between clients and advisors, some firms are deploying a content management system to run their client portals and use financial planning tools or workstations for their advisors.

EXAMINING THE THREE FACES OF INFORMATION TECHNOLOGY

The universe of investing technology can be divided into three broad categories:

1. *Client* facing;

2. *Provider* facing;

3. *Advisor* facing.

While some technologies overlap, and some might not perfectly fit any of these categories, for the wealthy and ultra-wealthy it has become critical to know not only what tools a financial advisor is using, but also what tools are available that he or she may not be using, or at least not using to their fullest capacity. It's highly unlikely, however, that an advisor will volunteer that his firm is weighed down by legacy systems and is thus *not* adopting new technology, or is *not* providing the support he needs to do a better job. Wealthy and aspiring HNWIs need to educate themselves as to the gold standards of IT and press their advisors to either provide the very best or consider taking their business elsewhere. To improve their dialogue and their relationship, it's critical for HNWIs to talk with their advisors about the power of technology. If that subject remains in any way off-limits or taboo, the broader wealth management dialogue is likely to be stunted.

Client Facing

Many wealthy clients have financial terminals in their homes that provide them with access to a host of real-time, professional-grade data. They expect and frequently have instantaneous access not just to garden-variety financial news but to sophisticated portfolio modeling and rebalancing software as well. They typically demand, as a matter of course, an aggregated view of their accounts. And they assume that they will be able to peruse at their convenience these "family balance sheets" in the comfort of their own home offices so that they can pull up a private asset statement alongside a business's profit and loss statement. HNWIs feel that they have the right to an informed dialogue with their advisors about their investments and that if they don't have the ability to share data online with their advisors that their dialogue is not sufficiently well supported by the firm.

In order to ensure the highest level of service, clients expecting a technological capacity appropriate to their level need to do the following:

1. Ask their advisors if the firm is capable of offering the benefits of open architecture, which enables systems to access data from a variety of internal and external sources, as opposed to closed or proprietary architecture, which limits the offering to data provided by the firm's own analysts and experts.

2. Ask their advisors if the firm's technology platform is set up to enable continuous online reporting on every aspect of their portfolio.

3. Ask their advisors how the workflow of the practitioner or team is enabled by the firm's technological platform. How much does the advisor need to accomplish manually as opposed to being handled automatically by the system?

4. Get a clear sense of how sensitive the advisor is to their technological questions and concerns. This provides an indication of the degree to which the advisor comprehends and is available to leverage the available technology.

Provider Facing

To make client-facing tools live up to today's high expectations, wealth management providers need to invest heavily in their back-office technologies to integrate client information across channels in real time. Such "provider-facing" technologies allow an institution to communicate internally about each client. High-net-worth individuals typically don't display any great appetite for sifting through fifty roughly cobbled-together pages outlining their financial position. They quite reasonably expect, or should expect, software capable of telling them three primary things:

1. How am I doing?

2. Are there any deviations occurring from my financial plan?

3. If so, where, why and what's the strategy to realign back to my original plan?

An institution must seamlessly integrate its channels across product lines and geographies in order to retain any hope of providing precise answers to those deceptively simple questions. This goal, not surprisingly, creates huge operational and cultural challenges for some large institutions. Operationally, most legacy systems provide an *account* and not a *client* view, making the provision of a truly holistic "family balance sheet" difficult, unwieldy and challenging. Back-end data must be fully integrated. Turf wars must be tamped down and coordination spurred across every silo in the enterprise; to most capably serve the highest-end clients, a channel must be opened between the investment banking, private client, hedge fund and private equity operations. On the flip side, these challenges may provide a comparative competitive advantage to small and nimble firms capable of implementing new technologies more quickly and smoothly across the organization than their juggernaut brethren.

Advisor Facing

The most capable advisors are supported by the best technological tools. Institutions need to ensure that their advisors are provided with "advisor-facing technologies" designed to help them sort out and sift through the growing complexity of client accounts without exponentially increasing the administrative burden of servicing them. To give their advisors the ability to offer the best financial services to HNWIs, institutions must carefully evaluate the workstation needs for their advisors and the entire wealth management process. Some needs include:

- Intelligent alerts with dashboards that provide advisors with reminders/reasons to call their clients, data mining of relevant market portfolios and lifestyle alerts.

- Family and client insight with a comprehensive relationship view that provides an advisor with sufficient specific information on every relationship so that he or she can immediately answer common client questions such as How am I doing?

- Integrated wealth management that includes seamless integration of advice tools with client profiles and presentation builders.

- A product marketing catalog that matches clients' needs with relevant offers and delivers actionable product ideas to advisors.

• Client-review capabilities that deliver consolidated relationship-based reporting and reduce report-generation time, allowing advisors to conduct more frequent and enriched client assessments.

Not surprisingly, the root cause of many of the challenges besetting financial firms' IT departments is the back-end data at most institutions, which, as mentioned, typically offers an *account* but not a *client* view. Most global firms hoping to capture any reasonable percentage of the high-net-worth clientele have acknowledged the need to create more elegant solutions to the problem of creating the integrated "family balance sheet" views and reports that their wealthiest clients increasingly demand—and which most family offices (organizations of investment professionals that work exclusively for a single family or related cluster of families) are already equipped to provide.

A problem faced by many global institutions is that as new technologies continue to roll out, boutique shops and nimble start-ups, unburdened by the legacy issues affecting some large institutions, can adopt these newest technologies at comparatively low cost, to their competitive advantage.

ASSESSING THE ROLE OF TECHNOLOGY IN THE ADVISOR–CLIENT RELATIONSHIP: A CAUTIONARY TALE

At the beginning of the twenty-first century, few savvy business people could honestly disagree with the assessment offered by Microsoft CEO Bill Gates that "the Internet changes everything."[6] As Gates pointed out, "Now that customers can deal directly with manufacturers and service providers, there is little value added in simply transferring goods or information." As the phenomenon of "disintermediation"—i.e., the elimination of the middleman—threatened to profoundly disrupt just about every

---

6. Bill Gates, *Business @ the Speed of Thought: Succeeding in the Digital Economy* (Time Warner, 2000), 72.

service industry on the planet, E*TRADE Securities, which pioneered Internet stock brokerage in 1992, touched off a tidal wave that swept through the financial services universe. Meanwhile, Forrester Research accurately estimated that by the turn of the twenty-first century, fourteen million U.S. brokerage customers would be buying, selling and trading stocks, bonds, mutual funds and other securities online, accounting for as much as 20 percent of individual brokerage transactions.[7] Gates astutely analyzed the dilemma facing traditional financial services providers at the dawn of the twenty-first century:

> *These firms faced a fundamental strategy decision: Do you use technology to play the same game that e-traders play? And if you do that, how do you differentiate yourself from them? Or do you use technology to play to your traditional strengths—highly trained staff accustomed to managing long-term customer relationships? If you adopt the latter strategy, how can you use technology to be more efficient, and how can you turn the Internet's popularity to your advantage?[8]*

Perhaps not surprisingly, Merrill Lynch spied an opportunity to play to its traditional strength by using technology to support its "highly trained staff accustomed to managing long-term customer relationships" and created a highly-touted "FA-centric" system capable of managing the data flow required to develop, implement and monitor comprehensive financial plans for clients. The result was a desktop-PC-based proprietary system, Trusted Global Advisor (TGA), unveiled to great fanfare at an approximate cost of US$850 million.

Unfortunately, not long after TGA's rollout, more than a few frustrated FAs were complaining bitterly to management that the new

7. Ibid., 79.
8. Ibid., 80.

platform lacked any number of essential features they regarded as essential to compete in the brave, new digital age, particularly when going up against a new crop of upstart firms for whom the provision of state-of-the-art technology—including every conceivable bell and whistle—was a critical component of their value proposition.

Despite its technological sophistication, TGA failed to meet the needs of *its* clients—the FAs—who as a result did not feel supported to meet the needs of *their* clients. Neither was TGA particularly adept at integrating the FAs' workflow with that of the Client Associates (CAs), assistants to the FAs who handled the bulk of routine communications with clients.

The key to providing top-notch software and hardware support is to make sure that the user never has to tell a client, "I'll get back to you on that." FAs did not have online access to customers' monthly account statements or client correspondence. The paradigm shift that had to be executed—and quickly—was changing from a "product-centric" system to a "client-centric" system.

Merrill's second-generation, Internet-based Wealth Management Work Station is an example of the now-dominant IT paradigm of the wealth management industry: open architecture. Diane Schueneman, who developed the system as chief of Global Infrastructure Solutions, defines the term as follows: "As an end user, I'm going to take information from any source in an integrated fashion, in such a way that I really don't know or care whether the information is sourced internally or externally. That distinction should be invisible and immaterial to the end-user."

According to Capgemini's Bertrand Lavayssière, "It may sound surprising, but even today you will find long-established firms that either won't or *can't* perform the tasks necessary to achieve truly open architecture. Many firms continue to be reliant on an outmoded model that has the financial advisor pick stocks for you, and think about what is best for you, on his or her own terms, using proprietary systems and software."

The primary problem with closed architecture, as Merrill Lynch and its peers have discovered, is that FAs don't like it. The principal reason they don't like it is that it puts them at a strong disadvantage to their competitors empowered by open architecture. As Lavayssière asserts, "The key here is transforming the business from a traditional product-management business model to a relationship-based model. In such a business, customer interactions are handled holistically across the business. Ideal solutions assess the client's current position, help define the customer experience, determine the technical architectures required and how they can best be implemented across all viable channels to market."

When asked to describe how the advent of technology had transformed the advisor–client relationship, Lavayssière responds, "The first thing to keep in mind about technology is that the critical component is the nature of the person using it—that is, *the person facing the screen*. Many of the more sophisticated clients today will have their own planning and simulation tools on their desktops at home. This enables them and empowers them to develop a set of pretty strong opinions when they meet with their FAs. In some cases, they might test the FA's knowledge and capabilities against their own knowledge and capabilities. Some self-made wealthy individuals prefer, in many cases, to act as their own FAs."

The second thing to keep in mind, Lavayssière insists, is that "too much information *kills* information. Technology is only useful if it helps the advisor to perform his or her primary task, which is to cull through the universe of information to select what is most meaningful to meeting the needs of the client." One example of technology's enhanced role is in the realm of reporting: "What are we *actually* doing with those assets, not just today but yesterday and tomorrow? With all these new vehicles of increasing complexity, both advisors and clients need an accurate real-time snapshot of what the portfolio is *actually* doing. Even with the most up-to-date technology, it can be difficult to maintain a comprehensive view of the present, let alone the future."

Scott Becchi, vice president in Capgemini's North America Financial Services Businesses Unit, observes that "the ultimate goal is turning technology into an information system. I call it 'the personalization of pertinent facts.' This challenge increases exponentially when you have more demanding and knowledgeable clients who understand that their needs will best be met by 'uptiering' to the next category." By "uptiering," Becchi is referring to a phenomenon observed by Capgemini consultants by which clients in one demographic segment aspire to a level of service they know (or strongly suspect) is being offered to the segment above them. This is, of course, only human nature.

Chris Gant, head of Capgemini's Wealth Management practice in the U.K., contends that as the global phenomenon of wealth consolidation continues apace, an industry rooted in the discreet guidance traditionally provided to wealthy families by a small private bank in Luxembourg or Switzerland remains highly fragmented, with an estimated six thousand firms holding themselves forth as possessed of the expertise to run money for high-net-worth individuals and households. Of those, he maintains, only the relatively small handful committed to combining the capabilities of major players with a large global footprint with the intimacy and level of service provided by the traditional private bank will attain leadership positions in this fiercely competitive field.

The resulting polarization, Gant says, is largely driven by variations in technological capabilities, with regard to accuracy, timeliness of reporting and the provision of user-friendly aggregated data and actionable knowledge. Since the underlying purpose of technology is to enhance and support the dialogue between advisor and client, savvy clients should be on the lookout for firms willing to invest the substantial resources required to develop and maintain the most capable tech platforms—while educating end-users to keep in mind that technology should facilitate the human dialogue as opposed to restrain or replace it.

OUTSOURCING FUNCTIONS:
THE JOYS AND PERILS

In the face of competitive pressures to both retain clients and maintain high profit margins, firms must avoid becoming or being perceived as a distributor of routine commoditized products. Wealth advisors must provide value-added advice along with operational excellence, cutting-edge technologies, and broad product lines at competitive prices. For many firms this involves smart outsourcing of certain functions that will allow them to focus on delivering the products and services they do best and that differentiate them in the market.

Providers are taking a hard look at which IT activities to conduct themselves and which to outsource. Pure-play administrative specialists offer providers a way to outsource costly back-office tasks to organizations boasting the necessary global scale to keep costs down. This, in turn, permits advisors to offer wealthy clients competitively priced global products and services while freeing up their own time to concentrate on providing clients with the relationship management they deserve.

Virtual Service Networks and Service-Oriented Architecture are two examples of technology that enable multiple service suppliers to work closely and seamlessly with HNWIs.

Virtual Service Networks

The ongoing surge in global wealth reinforces the importance of serving the needs of "mid-tier millionaires"—corporate executive and small to mid-sized business owners with anywhere between US$5 million and US$30 million in investible assets. While such clients have every right to expect a level of service commensurate with their asset base, dedicated family investment offices are luxuries typically out of reach of any but the ultra-affluent US$100-million-plus households. For the rest of the HNW population, the industry has developed Virtual Service Networks (VSNs), which are virtual networks of financial, legal and accounting experts who collaborate via technology to deliver a level of service to clients roughly commensurate with family offices, at a fraction of the cost. We estimate that as many as 8 percent of the total HNWIs could potentially afford to tap into VSNs to obtain a cost-effective wealth advisory solution located somewhere between the more general private banking function and the full-scale family office.

Jon Carroll, co-founder of Family Office Metrics, a consultancy that provides business advice to family offices around business organization, management, operations and technology applications, observes that "a VSN allows the family to operate like a board of directors, and to maintain control over strategy and who they work with."[9] Despite the advantages, Mr. Carroll warns that even with a VSN, multi-family offices can find it costly and difficult to offer the kind of carefully personalized service seen in the single family office setting. This is a major issue, he says, since "relatively" lower bands of wealth always want the same service as those above them—a phenomenon we have described as "up-tiering."

Service-Oriented Architecture

The latest innovation in this field—a development in some respects more ambitious than the VSN—is Service-Oriented Architecture (SOA), which permits firms to establish a framework that supports multi-channel advisor and client-service strategies. OASIS (the Organization for the Advancement of Structured Information Standards) defines SOA as:

> *A paradigm for organizing and utilizing distributed capabilities that may be under the control of different ownership domains. It provides a uniform means to offer, discover, interact with and use capabilities to produce desired effects consistent with measurable preconditions and expectations.[10]*

---

9. Interview with the authors.

10. "Service Oriented Architecture (SOA) and Specialized Messaging Patterns," Technical White Paper, Duane Nickul, ed. www.oasis.org.

One should not, for example, have to provide redundantly the same personal information to open an online checking, savings or IRA account, and further, the interfaces one interacts with should have the same look and feel and use the same level and type of input data validation. Building all applications from the same pool of services makes achieving this goal much easier and more deployable to affiliate companies. An example of this might be interacting with a rental car company's reservation system even though you are doing so from an airline's reservation system.

Figure 3.3 – Wealth Management Service-Oriented Architecture

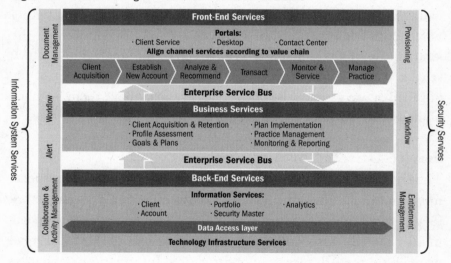

Source: Capgemini analysis.

MELDING INFORMATION TECHNOLOGY AND CULTURE

Building the ultimate adaptive private banking capability calls for more than the right strategies, business processes, technologies and infrastructures. It also requires adaptable people and a culture that supports change. Wealth management providers must establish and nurture cultures that foster experimentation, set clear targets at all levels and reward employees who are truly motivated to put clients first. In the absence of such a backdrop, the potential value of all IT investments can never be fully realized.

In today's hyper-competitive marketplace, private banks must develop online channels to better serve their clients and increase their own top and bottom lines. But banks should not settle for commoditized functions such as online trading; they need to push themselves to focus on innovative tools centered on collaboration between advisor and client. The online channel is a great source of potential value for private banks—but they need the foresight and fortitude to tap this resource. Furthermore, banks must confront the indisputable fact that future generations of high-net-worth individuals and households will demand the best IT services available, or quite justifiably take their assets and liabilities elsewhere. And as we will see in the next chapter, providing clients with appropriate levels of conveniently accessed user-friendly technology is just one facet of a larger challenge: the development of a full-scale and comprehensive holistic wealth management model.

CHAPTER 4

Holistic Wealth Management

MOVING BEYOND INVESTMENTS TO A BROADER RANGE OF SERVICES

Rooted in the industry-wide transition from stock brokering to wealth preservation, the rise of Holistic Wealth Management (HWM) dials up the medley of services offered by advisors to include virtually every aspect of an individual or household's financial life. Investments, risk management, insurance, tax, trust and estate planning, retirement planning, credit and cash management—all fall loosely under the broad umbrella of HWM. And all, not surprisingly, are rendered exponentially more complex when the individual or household fits into the HNWI or UHNWI category.

A gentleman exceedingly well versed in all aspects of HWM is Dómhnal Slattery, co-founder of International Aviation Management Group (IAMG)—a firm he sold in 2001 to the Royal Bank of Scotland for what we can safely assume was a price tag sufficient to make all future labor strictly voluntary. Yet he remains an exceptionally busy person at this stage of his life. Through Dublin-based Claret Capital, he manages his own family fortune along with the assets of three other families, and has participated in some of the world's largest private equity transactions.

While Slattery is a professed fan of the concept of HWM and regards it as the coming thing in the field, he cautions that it's critical to draw a firm distinction between HWM and schmoozing (or, for that matter, the unctuous provision of what some in the field refer to—frequently in hushed tones—as "concierge services"). Financial advisors, he strongly cautions, should not fancy themselves glorified butlers.

"There's this belief that ultra-high-net-worth individuals need to be looked after and loved," Slattery indignantly states. "There's this belief that high-net-worth individuals are always demanding free opera tickets from their financial advisors. But in my experience, it's simply not true. Most of my colleagues consider such events a chore and a bore. If I want to go to the opera, I'll go with my wife!"

Merrill Lynch Managing Director Michael Sullivan, co-head of a newly minted Cross Organizational Client Coverage Initiative that aims to drive greater synergies between the investment banking and wealth management side of the business, heartily concurs with Slattery. "Concierge services?" he asks. His team's clients, he insists, "want their money run the way they run their companies. They want spreadsheets, they want goals and objectives, they want projections, they want rigor and accountability from their FAs just as they demand it from their senior executives. If they're looking for tickets to a Knicks game, they'll go to Ticketmaster." A lesson for aspiring HNWIs is that although these tickets and services appear to be icing on the cake, it is probably more likely that the cost of these services is bundled elsewhere.

Sullivan, similarly to Joseph Lam, insists that what HNWIs must want and deserve is to feel valued by their financial advisors, with their needs understood and acted upon. And they quite rightly demand and require a broader and deeper range of service than the traditional private banks have historically offered. Meeting these demands is where the opportunity for new entrants, such as brokerage houses and banks building capabilities for the HNW, lies. Today, many HNWIs prefer to draw on the intellectual resources of a large institution with a global footprint combined with the intimacy of a boutique.

According to Sullivan, the four things all high-net-worth clients reasonably demand from their advisors, at the end of the day, are simply expressed.

1. Performance;

2. Service;

3. Proactive solutions;

4. Trust.

"They want performance against their game plan and performance against the markets. They want the best possible financial guidance and advice—bar none. They want the best information we can provide on a proactive basis, with solutions based on an open architecture platform. But what they want above all is trust—because without that, all the rest fades into insignificance."

Concierge services aside, HNWIs who can clearly afford tickets to cultural events may be eager to seek advice on tax, family wealth, estate and philanthropic issues, along with a whole host of other ancillary services for clients and households with over US$10 million in investible assets, including, for example, the aforementioned financial boot camps for their kids.

HNWIs want advisors to arrange access to some of the world's largest and most well-respected investment experts. They want ideas, strategies and products that are special and novel to the marketplace. In short, they want what Merrill Lynch's Private Banking and Investment Group (PBIG) aims to provide—high-end, high-touch services—by constantly endeavoring to deliver the "whole firm" to clients. If that means referring a client to another division within the firm, John Thiel, head of PBIG, insists that it's all about sharing knowledge among Merrill's various businesses.

Early on in his career as an FA, Thiel was often shocked to run into other FAs "who didn't regard it as somehow appropriate to ask a client how much money they had. I used to ask them why not. They'd get these befuddled expressions on their faces and say they just didn't think it was any of their business." In those early days, Thiel recalls, "I met a lot of good people, but the business was all about pushing product and not about determining clients' unmet needs, aspirations and long-term financial goals. If the number one rule of salesmanship is 'know your customer,' the simple answer was that we didn't." Conversely, clients should be willing to be open in sharing information with their financial advisors, given the FA has built the trust and credibility mentioned above. This information can often assist the FA in better understanding options and preparing proposals for how to best manage assets, either internally or externally.

Starting out in the nineties, the stirrings of HWM emerged at Merrill Lynch under John L. "Launny" Steffens, who insisted that financial advisors deliver Financial Foundation reports—comprehensive financial plans based on extensive personal surveys expressly designed to elicit and define clients' long-range financial goals and objectives—for all of their clients or pay the consequences in reduced compensation. Although that initially onerous mandate made Steffens one of the least popular people at the firm for a number of years—because in its early phases the shift from a transaction-based account to an asset-and-fee-based account can generate less profit—the advent of the Financial Foundation provided was the underpinning of what would come to be dubbed HWM.

As Steffens repeatedly stressed, a critical facet of HWM is the high value placed on a client's willingness to entrust all or at least most of their total assets *and* liabilities (loans, mortgages and the like) to the care of a single financial advisor or team domiciled at a single firm. Since it is not uncommon for high-net-worth individuals and households to spread their assets among a number of advisors and firms, the theory of HWM is that not unlike romance, fidelity is the key to enduring success.

By the mid-nineties, the rise of the Internet placed the full-service financial industry under an ominous cloud of perceived obsolescence. The whole notion of the trusted advisor was in genuine jeopardy. Why not just go buy an index fund? What was the point of managed money? Since managers didn't do any better, on average, than the *Wall Street Journal*'s notorious dartboard, why bother? The critics weren't totally off base, because it can be hard, statistically speaking, for even the best money managers to consistently beat the market.

The answer for both firm and client turned out to be a wholesale adoption of a broader outlook encompassing the provision of a full range of legal, accounting, insurance and financial advisory services, rolled up into a collaborative effort potentially drawing on the expertise of outside attorneys, independent money managers, possibly even a family office, and possibly a team of private equity specialists, derivatives designers or investment bankers.

Ultra-HNWIs might seek referrals from their financial advisor to commission such services as family security or even property management. In the best-case scenario, the client would have a primary and, ideally, sole point of contact at the firm capable of arranging and brokering these ancillary services with third-party providers. The financial advisor would perform like a financial maestro, orchestrating the variety of instruments required to play the client's concert. Ultimately, the role of the wealth advisor would be to simplify a wealthy client's financial life; in an era of growing complexity, streamlining can command a steep premium.

If a HNWI desires information and insight into foreign markets and exotic asset classes, a global institution might provide specialist wealth strategy teams spanning the globe and equipped with multiple specialties. A select number of wealth management providers employ this business model on a micro level, providing product specialists serving a narrow geographic range. Companies such as

Northern Trust employ an informal network to service clients' requirements regardless of source. In order to be truly effective, the specialist team approach must be accompanied by rigorous training for the relationship manager, who needs to be on familiar terms with all of the firm's global offerings or know whom to call upon elsewhere in the firm to tap the expertise required.

This team-based approach is typically most effective in advisory areas apart from investing. Some relationship managers may leverage groups of specialists prepared to advise clients on wealth transfer and other family and legacy issues, philanthropy and business ownership matters. Teams might commission attorneys and business analysts for tax and estate planning, in addition to ancillary services such as business evaluation.

Some clients may place a high value on the advice a financial advisor provides on the perennially anxiety-provoking topic of adequately planning for long-term health care expenses. Frequently, high-networth clients are concerned more about their aging parents than their own financial futures. Some clients are asking for—and receiving from financial advisors—dedicated health care financing services, including the evaluation of a range of health care options, and/or putting their clients in touch with relevant outside experts in the field.

M&A Reshapes Private Banking

The private banking business is beginning to display a barbell appearance—on the one end, large institutions with a global footprint and deep pockets, and on the other end, boutique shops with fewer resources and an emphasis on high-touch customer service. The middle ground is thinning out rapidly as mergers reshape the industry. For HNWIs, the decision of where to place their money between the two poles can pose some tough choices.

This dilemma was thrown into sharp relief in late 2006 when Bank of America (BofA) announced its acquisition of U.S. Trust, the private banking arm of Charles Schwab, for US$3.3 billion. Then in early 2007, Merrill Lynch announced it would buy San Francisco-based First Republic Bank for US$1.8

billion in cash and stock. With assets of US$10.7 billion, First Republic provides investment services including trust banking and luxury home lending through over forty-three branch offices in the United States.

BofA's rationale is to join the top tier of private banking—and asset-wise the deal will accomplish precisely that. JPMorgan has about US$230 billion in client accounts and Citi Private Bank has approximately US$220 billion, while the new private banking arm of BofA will have roughly US$260 billion. BofA officials insist that they are intent on maintaining the kind of top-notch service that U.S. Trust clients are accustomed to, but as with all acquisitions and ensuing integrations, how well the ambition and anticipated value add to clients and shareholders is implemented remains to be seen. Based on a SECOR Consulting analysis of over 2000 deals globally, included in a submission to the Canadian Federal Department of Finance on Shareholder Value Created and Destroyed in Financial Services Mergers, it was validated that acquisitions across all industries are better served through a related diversification strategy (i.e., bank–investment bank), rather than a consolidation (i.e., bank–bank) strategy. What is true in general holds true for Financial Services. Only 34 percent of the bank–bank mergers in the US and Europe from 1990 have been successful in adding shareholder value. However, related diversification deals have performed better, with bank–investment bank deals being successful for the acquirer 55 percent of the time.[1]

If lessons from this research and other post merger integrations hold true, the rationale for the BofA/US Trust deal stands. The two cultures—a mass-market retail culture on the BofA side and an exclusive, catering mindset on the U.S. Trust side—will not be so easy to fold together, and will require care, attention and time. Indeed, immediately after the announcement, BofA defended its planned cost efficiencies by assuring analysts that cuts would not target front-line customer services. Subsequently, a few months after the announcement, Peter Scaturro (CEO of US Trust) departed the company despite previous statements regarding his necessity to the integration.

---

1. SECOR Consulting Submission to the Canadian Federal Department of Finance on Shareholder Value Created and Destroyed in Financial Services Mergers: Dec 22, 2003.

The big private banking players argue, not surprisingly, that they can and do deliver top-notch customer service. Plus, they say, their strong balance sheets support loan underwriting, while they can bring the global resources and clout to bear to get HNWIs into coveted hedge and private equity funds. Boutiques, for their part, maintain that they provide superior personal service, and that big banks tend to push their own products, while boutiques are more likely to design best-of-breed solutions tailored to HNWIs' needs. As for breadth of products and services, boutiques are improving thanks to an ironic twist: they are outsourcing some products and services, such as loans, to the big banks.

Meanwhile, the middle ground, which some HNWIs argue has the best of both worlds—an institutional focus on wealth management, solid resources and personalized service—is occupied by fewer and fewer players. In December of 2006, Bank of New York (BoNY) announced its intention to buy Mellon Financial for US$16.5 billion. The union will unite BoNY's US$60 billion wealth management group with Mellon's US$92 billion group, combining two mid-tier players. By the end of 2006, the remaining mid-tier firms were a lonely group. Bessemer Trust, with US$47 billion in client accounts, and Northern Trust Corp., with approximately US$128 billion, both still profess an intention to remain independent. But the dynamics of the industry may overtake them.

When a HNWI's wealth management provider is undergoing a merger, it may take some extra vocalizing to ensure that he or she continues to receive the attention they deserve. A merger is a time of transition for the employees, who may shift jobs and firms, as well as for the clients, who must adjust to the new corporate culture being forged. HNWIs may not need to search for a new wealth provider in the event of a merger or sale, but that said, it may not be the time for HNWIs to put their wealth management on autopilot either.

EXPECTING MORE EXTENSIVE FINANCIAL ADVICE

Yet for all the emphasis placed in some reports on ancillary services and the wide variety of other fringe benefits increasingly provided by financial firms seeking to broaden their share of the HNWI market, the fact remains that the service most HNWIs seek from their financial advisor is precisely what their professional name implies: financial advice.

Clients will always demand that the advice provided by their advisors be objective, candid and solution-oriented as opposed to product-oriented. The most sophisticated clients are not impressed by products and services being "sold" to them, particularly if the prime motivation might be to generate a steady stream of fees for the firm. In this day and age, if a HNWI senses any untoward bias towards a particular family of products, it's likely the relationship with the financial institution will conclude fast. "The business model for most global banks hasn't changed much from just selling the product of the week," Dómhnal Slattery avers. Entrepreneurs like him have a sixth sense when they are being sold, and a marked aversion to being sold to.

When HNWIs are interested in buying in-house products it's often because the products are innovative vehicles specifically structured in-house and tailored to meet their needs. Ultra-HNWIs don't stay ahead of the curve by reverting to the mean; they demand products not available to the average Joe. HNWIs typically demand value added that's outside the mainstream—very likely an investment that is complex and illiquid. Which brings us to the greatest conundrum of holistic wealth management: *wealth advisors are being asked to add complexity to the high-net-worth investment portfolio at the same time that they're being asked to manage its growing complexities.*

Yet as previously noted, a holistic approach amounts to much more than traditional financial advice—no matter how brilliantly conceived. One key differentiator is the quality of the advice and strategies offered in support of non-financial assets. Increasingly, HNWIs are demanding that art, collectibles and other "investments of passion" be treated similarly to more common and liquid financial investments. Globalization has impacted philanthropy, with affluent philanthropists allocating a substantial portion of their assets abroad, slowly bringing philanthropy to the global stage. Lifestyle, legacy and philanthropic guidance are not traditionally core offerings for providers but, as is the case with financial investments, such issues require careful asset allocation and portfolio attention—subjects all treated in greater depth elsewhere in the book.

"The advice needs to be complete," contends Paula Polito, head of strategic brand marketing and management for Merrill Lynch's Wealth Management division. "High-end clients require a high order of benefits, and they demand a personal relationship. They want someone who knows how many children and grandchildren they're sending to private school."

"Money is always personal," Polito observes. "Financial institutions would do well to acknowledge that fact as a critical component of any holistic strategy. High-net-worth individuals have a right to, and should expect a partner they can trust—a desire that, not surprisingly, transcends age and geographic borders."

Of course, for the majority of HNWIs, money may be *so* personal that it can be challenging to view one's own needs, goals and requirements with an impartial or critical eye. One approach employed by some savvy FAs to overcome perfectly natural human biases is to encourage HNWIs to view their wealth no differently than how they might view their businesses or jobs. Few businesspeople feel comfortable making a significant decision regarding one part of their business without considering its possible impact on other aspects of their business. A similar approach may be effective when mulling specific asset allocations, charitable donations, estate planning or other investment strategies. Applying simple business management techniques to wealth management often helps HNWIs view certain personal decisions a bit more dispassionately and with a clearer head.

To bring even more context to the HNWIs' financial pictures—and to encourage them to be even more holistic in their approach—some advisors are pushing into actual business owner services. Business ownership has become the leading source of HNWIs' wealth across the globe. Often, business owners and the operations of those businesses are intricately entwined, so there is a growing need for increased convergence between commercial, private and investment banking. At most firms the traditional wealth manager is not equipped to serve at the crossroad between personal and business opportunity. This disconnect is a prime example of how wealth advisors are hamstrung by old technologies and business practices that divide their institutional view into accounts instead of clients—even as they profess to offer holistic services.

Clients understandably view themselves as having one relationship and one master account with each organization; hence, they would like to see different cuts, slices and groupings based on their distinctive needs. There should be one risk profile and one strategy governing an entire relationship, but unfortunately this has historically not been the case at many large global institutions. This is a frustration voiced by many clients who maintain multiple points of contact across departments of a financial services provider. Clients who are looking to grow wealth want to have access to multiple products regardless of the manufacturer. Some of the leading financial services providers are responding and are working to overcome this gap. For business owners, this is clearly something to consider when selecting your primary financial advisor.

USING DEBT TO BUILD WEALTH

One of the foundations of HWM is that for financial advice to be comprehensive, it needs to take a client's entire range of needs into account. In addition to asset management, skilled liability management can be critical to a client's broader financial health and well-being. And as investor sophistication increases, advisors and clients alike realize that a comprehensive approach demands leveraging liabilities as a way of preserving and even gaining wealth.

The key concept here is opportunity cost—for many sophisticated investors, taking on a liability in one area of the portfolio produces an asset in another. This is why, according to a Federal Reserve Board survey of Consumer Finance,[2] the nation's richest 1 percent took on US$342 billion in new debt between 1998 and 2004. That 1 percent now holds 7 percent of the nation's debt, with a total of US$650 billion, up from 5 percent in 1998. In other words, debt for this top group grew 150 percent in those six years, while debt for Americans in the fiftieth to ninetieth percentile range grew 100 percent in those years.

So does this growth mean that HNWIs have lost their financial discipline? Not by a long shot. For many HNWIs, debt is a financial tool, a way to allocate resources to the most high-yielding investments. Which is better, paying cash for a US$10 million ranch, or taking out a 6.5 percent mortgage and plowing that US$10 million into a private equity fund that's expected to yield 20 percent? The math is really pretty simple.

Non-HNWIs, on the other hand, typically don't have that kind of cash to redirect, and thus aren't targeting investments to offset the interest payments they are taking on. Interest payments on home equity lines of credit and credit cards detract from their wealth, while HNWIs take on debt specifically to *expand* their wealth. What's more, the high dollar amount of debt being taken on by HNWIs can be a bit deceiving. True, HNWI debt is increasing, but debt for the top 1 percent still represents only 3.7 percent of their total wealth. For those in the fiftieth to ninetieth percentile, debt represents 24 percent of their total wealth.

Marcus Mitchell, managing director for Americas Lending in Merrill Lynch's Global Bank Group, sees four broad ways that HNWIs are using debt to manage their portfolios. The first is leveraging their investment to diversify or enhance returns. He

2. "Recent Changes in U.S. Family Finances," Brian K. Bucks, Author B. Kennickell, and Kevin B. Moore, *Federal Reserve Bulletin*, Vol. 92 (Fall 2006), pp. A1–A38.

observes this often with private equity and hedge fund managers who are sitting on large, long-term positions tied to their own funds. By pledging their limited partner or general partner interest in the funds, they can borrow money from the bank and invest elsewhere.

Yet another frequent use of debt is for asset acquisition. Sometimes this takes the form of financing aircraft and boats; sometimes it's more of an equity injection into a new business funded by borrowing against a large block of stock. Other times, borrowing is performed to create a liquidity cushion available to purchase other assets or in case there's a sudden cash crunch.

Finally, borrowing is frequently employed in conjunction with an estate plan or generational-transfer strategy. Life insurance may be purchased by HNWIs to help heirs pay estate taxes; the dilemma then becomes how to pay for the hefty premiums. The answer: by pledging marketable securities along with the cash value of the life insurance policy, the HNWI can borrow against the policy to fund the premiums, eliminating out-of-pocket expenses.

"Why do wealthy people borrow when they've got the money?" Mitchell rhetorically asks before replying as follows: "Let's say I want to finance an aircraft or diversify my assets. It's all about the power of leverage—a concept that has transformed investment banking in recent decades. Just as companies seek to strike a balance between debt and equity, so do wealthy individuals, many of whom are used to thinking this way from running businesses, so it doesn't scare them to assume the risk as long as it's accompanied by a reward."

As an example, the senior partners in a hedge fund may be required to invest their own money in a deal, but their funds are already tied up in other deals. They borrow that money as an alternative to liquidating other assets, fully confident that they can repay the loan out of the proceeds of the deal. Of course, as Mitchell cautions, only individuals and households deemed qualified and capable of shouldering such leverage need apply; it takes investment savvy and sophistication to benefit from a prudent program of enhanced liabilities.

For advisors, HNWIs' attitude toward debt presents a number of significant business opportunities. Not only can advisors offer counsel on the wisest uses of debt and leverage for their clients, but they can also make attractive loans available to their clients through the financial institution—a product and service that in combination help to deepen the HNWI relationship.

DEFINING THE ROLE OF FAMILY OFFICES WITHIN WEALTH MANAGEMENT

Individual family offices, where a wealthy family (with at least US$100 million in assets) employs a full-time staff of financial advisors and other experts to see to it that every conceivable planning need will be met, obviously provide the ultimate in holistic service. Multiple family offices, serving a comparatively small number of often affiliated families, represent the second tier. Often unfettered by legacy systems, such organizations may more effectively manage the holistic total view and maintain personal relationships. However, their access to global resources in an era when such access is regarded as increasingly critical tends to be inferior to the major financial institutions.

The majority of family offices have four primary functions:

1. Centralization of records (all financial statements, bill paying, tax planning);

2. Business management (purchase and sale of business holdings, distribution of financial information, administration of tangible assets such as real estate and yachts);

3. Family management (family governance, education, philanthropy, wealth transfer planning);

4. Investment-related functions (investment policy setting, asset allocation, monitoring).

Figure 4.1 – Traditional Financial Services Institution Model Approach vs.
Family Office Model Approach

Characteristics	Traditional FSI* Approach	Family Office Model
Wealth Management Methodology	· Product-oriented; · Investment-management focused; · Advice centered on "in-house" portfolio only; · Little or no coordination/collaboration with third-party providers; · Service oriented toward individual mid-tier millionaires.	· Product neutral; · Investments are managed in the context of the family "balance sheet"; · Advice reflects a full view of client's assets; · Coordinates/collaborates with all providers to develop an integrated wealth strategy; · Service focuses on the mid-tier millionaire family "entity."
Products & Pricing	· Transaction-based pricing now moving towards assets under management or "by service" fee-based model; · Ad-hoc investment process; reacts to market conditions; · Portfolio reviews based on standard templates.	· Historically AUM-based pricing; · Investment process is often documented and standardized, according to agreed-upon investment policy; · Portfolio reviews are regularly scheduled and customized, according to client's needs and preferences.

Products & Services	· Advice & Planning to develop personalized wealth management plan:
	  – Set Objectives;
	  – Develop Strategy;
	  – Implement solutions;
	  – Review progress.
	· Banking Service:
	  – Direct deposit, check writing, funds transfer, etc.
	· Business Financial Services:
	  – Integrated cash management, business banking, etc.
	· Credit & Lending:
	  – Home, personal, investment and business financing.
	· Estate Planning:
	  – Trust services, tax assessments, etc.
	· Investment Management;
	· Retirement Planning.
		· Chief Advisor: Oversees relationships with all product and service providers, external counselors/advisors; provides personalized service, technical expertise and creative business leadership;
		· Investment Manager: Manages, analyzes and reviews family's financial capital, including investment policy, manager selection/review, asset monitoring/review and due diligence;
		· Financial Administrator: Ensures asset allocation mirrors client's investment philosophy, tax compliance, financial control, project management, and financial reporting;
		· Trustee: Educates and mentors: adminsters family trusts, ensures timely communications; and oversees philanthropic management;
		· Back Office Manager: Provides investment and partnership accounting, client reporting, internal controls and technology support.

* Financial Services Institution

Source: John Carrol, "The Functions of a Family Office," *The Journal of Wealth Management*, 4, no.2 (Fall 2001).

Dómhnal Slattery notes that typically even large, well-run and well-equipped family offices do not operate in a vacuum. They want the services and resources of big global banks if only those global banks could break down silos—or at least build bridges between them—and give family offices access to the services of the firm. Mr. Slattery recalls a business opportunity he recently had that required aggressive financing. His private bankers balked and the opportunity passed. The very next month, while meeting with that same bank's investment bankers, he was told: "Of course we could have done that—why didn't you bring it to us?"

Disheartening as this occurrence was for Mr. Slattery, he remains optimistic that large global banks will improve their holistic offerings to family offices, if for no other reason than that the hybrid model of his family office—part individual, part institutional, highly aggressive, with assets north of US$200 million—is a huge growth area. "There will be lots and lots of these opportunities in the next decade. Banks will want to find the next Blackstone and the next MSD Capital (Michael Dell's family office) and grow with them."

Slattery predicts that ten years from now, global firms prepared to make a strong commitment to these kinds of clients and this kind of service will attain and maintain a dominant position with regard to this incalculably valuable client group. To create loyalty among these hybrids (or "instividuals"—institutions providing individual service) he believes banks should allow clients to invest alongside the global bank. "Co-investing with the firm is the sweet spot, in my opinion. That engenders a lot of loyalty. That alignment of interest is the key to building a bond."

EXPECTING CLEAR REPORTING

There is no single aspect of holistic wealth management more critical to long-term investment success than clear, comprehensive and timely reporting of the ever-changing position of client portfolios.

The higher net worth the individual or household, the more emphasis tends to be paid to providing a broad view of the portfolio position that can—if the client desires—be easily drilled down into to achieve ever greater levels of detail—all rendered seamlessly by the latest portfolio management software.

This is the essence of the wealth management platform, and the place where the rubber meets the road when it comes to client service. Institutions that fail to provide clear reporting can never compensate for that failure by offering top-notch personal service or financial advice. One high-profile issue is that some global institutions, as well as regional banks and brokerages, may be constrained by the limitations of legacy back-end and account-based processes, as noted in the previous chapter on technology. Historically, many providers lack visibility from one account to another due to disordered back-ends. Accounts held in different countries add to the disarray. A full 78 percent of relationship managers surveyed for the 2006 *WWR* said reports have become more complex even as HNWIs increasingly clamor for greater simplicity and clarity.

Until fairly recently, HNWIs have grudgingly tolerated awkward reporting, but the impact of globalization on client portfolio complexity is triggering a call to action. In fact, HNWIs' inability to view asset holdings coherently is one of the biggest reasons cited by HNWIs for wanting to change firms or add independent advisors. According to the relationship manager survey for the 2006 *WWR*, only 50 percent of HNWIs are satisfied with current reporting. In addition, investors stated that clear and aggregated reporting was a leading reason why they would potentially switch financial service providers. That's a pretty frightening statistic for financial services providers and a powerful incentive to supply simplified one-stop reporting.

In any wealth management relationship, four pillars of reporting must be addressed.

1. Quality: Diversified investing requires reporting that is accurate and complete. As HNWIs shift out of their traditional comfort zones and invest in more complex instruments, many denominated in different currencies or linked to businesses operating in different time zones, they demand greater transparency. Providing timely tracking of shifts in country and multi-currency breakdowns, for example, is critical to meeting HNWIs' goal of maintaining tight control of global positions.

2. Customization: Not all HNWIs want the same reporting formats. The ability to provide desired detail and to include performance reports according to preferences lies at the very heart of maintaining a successful relationship. HNWIs expect recommendations to be positioned in the context of their total net worth and overall asset allocation, and when reviewing their ongoing relationship with their advisor they will consider how well this was done.

3. Simplification: Providing accurate positions, balances and information in line with a client's preferences or requests does not necessarily bring satisfaction. Finding a way to represent this information in an easily understandable format that aligns back to their overall financial plan and wealth strategies will become a higher priority as HNWIs diversify into new products and regions.

4. Cost containment and clarity: In the past, fees have been layered into services and products in ways that have made the costs of those products and services obtuse and difficult to examine individually or compare. This is no longer acceptable practice. Today, HNWIs demand reports that show exactly how much they are paying and for what. Firms should not fear this disclosure. Far from it. The *WWR* surveys show that while HNWIs are willing to pay a premium for good service, they want to see what they are paying. Clarity and transparency promote trust and in the end provide another way to strengthen the bond between advisor and HNWI.

The good news for advisors is that by working toward a more holistic approach, by reducing complexities, by offering comprehensive products and services, and by clearly reporting costs, a firm can establish and ensure its role as the family's trusted financial advisor. Indeed, as portfolios become increasingly global in scope, holistic wealth management will become increasingly in demand by HNWIs. Firms that can deliver will be in an excellent position to establish deep, long-term relationships. The more indispensable a firm makes itself to a high-net-worth family, the more likely it will be to retain those assets in the wake of a generational transfer.

DEMANDING PRIVACY

Many HNWIs experience a degree of tension between the seemingly conflicting needs for *comprehensive reporting* and *privacy*. In a perfect world, not only HNWIs but everyone would prefer a single, easy-to-read report encompassing all assets held by all providers—domestically and internationally. In real life, however, any of a number of issues can hamper this goal.

On the more prosaic side, some HNWIs understandably hesitate to share all their financial information with any one entity out of fear that their privacy will be compromised. For aggregated reporting a client must pick a trusted provider to manage information from all of their outside providers and third parties, and some HNWIs worry that that is too much information for any one advisor to have. Such information might, for instance, entice an FA to focus on luring those assets to his or her firm instead of focusing on advice and performance.

Such reluctance to share information for fear of being oversold is merely the tip of the iceberg. In reality, people may have multiple reasons not to want to pull all their financials together to provide a single, unified, easy-to-read view. A nasty divorce, estrangement between relatives, or murky business arrangements may require what some might regard as a dubious level of discretion. How people want financial information combined varies enormously from person to person and household to household; even if a bank already maintains many different accounts under an individual's name, in some jurisdictions it may be actually illegal to combine these accounts into a single report in the absence of the client's consent.

In some areas of the world, privacy needs to be guarded to avoid confiscation of assets by governments, or even the prospect of actual physical harm. In describing visits to clients in Latin America, relationship managers recall being told not to bring documents, a laptop or even business cards, out of fear that their family's security might be compromised if the level of their wealth were to be exposed. Many HNWIs in insecure regions or countries have very real reason to fear increased prospects of them and/or their family members being kidnapped the more people know about their total net worth.

In Africa, the Middle East and some parts of Asia, the wealthy are known for their obsession with discretion. There, too, it's not uncommon for all forms of bank-initiated correspondence to be discouraged. A commonly used term, HAM (hold all mail), is often used. Regulatory reasons dictate that some correspondence needs to be sent. In Switzerland, meanwhile, it remains culturally acceptable to fax information. But financial institutions dare not try this in many developing countries or they run the risk of losing a client due to confidentiality issues.

Any act that may be construed by relevant regulatory and law enforcement authorities as an attempt to conceal assets from their government tends to create complicated legal trails—and travails—for wealthy individuals. A favorite for Latin American HNWIs are private investments corporations (PICs) and trusts, frequently set up in the United States to shield their names behind seemingly unaffiliated legal entities. These are perfectly legal strategies, and can make it a challenge to follow the legal trail. But they also make it very hard to have a full view of the customer and provide holistic wealth management.

Fortunately, most HNWIs need not go to such lengths to protect their assets and loved ones, but these issues do exist for a sizable population of HNWIs. The lesson here is that global financial institutions must remain flexible when catering to their international clientele and never assume to impose any single approach, even an apparently advantageous holistic one.

Clearly, HWM is a multi-faceted discipline, incorporating asset and liability management, framed within exceptional service and alternative service methods and assurance of privacy. Applying the doctrine of asset allocation requires paying exquisite attention to cultivating a portfolio's overall balance, risk-adjusted for the long term. An appropriate analogy may be to artistic gardening—a similarly sophisticated discipline, part art and part science, in which the most talented landscape architects grasp at a deep level how best to mix hardy perennials with annuals to achieve a climatically balanced long-term effect. All of which rests firmly on a theoretical and conceptual foundation known as Modern Portfolio Theory (MPT).

CHAPTER 5

The Doctrine of Asset Allocation

ENHANCING RETURNS WITH MODERN PORTFOLIO THEORY (MPT)

One day in 1951, Harry Markowitz, a graduate student in mathematics at the University of Chicago, was sitting outside his thesis advisor's office waiting to discuss the subject of his doctoral dissertation. His field of research was linear programming, a discipline that employs complex mathematical models to maximize output for a given level of cost or to minimize cost for a given level of output. One of the most common applications of linear programming is a mathematical equation by which auto manufacturers seek to determine how many cars should optimally be built when constrained by specific amounts of materials and worker hours.[1]

Fortunately for the future development of the fine art of risk management, the mathematics professor was not immediately free to see Markowitz. While cooling his heels in the waiting room, Markowitz struck up a conversation with a stockbroker also waiting to see one of the professors in the department. Strictly to kill time, the broker asked Markowitz to describe his field of research. After listening intently for a few minutes, the broker casually observed that a promising application of linear programming might be for a young mathematician to tackle the

---

1. Story derived from *Against the Gods: The Remarkable Story of Risk* by Peter L. Bernstein (Wiley, 1996), 250.

challenges inherent in forecasting and tracking fluctuations in financial portfolios.

And so, the discipline of asset allocation—the most critical conceptual component of the now-widely-accepted doctrine known as Modern Portfolio Theory (MPT)—was born. Intellectually stimulated by the notion of applying his arcane tool kit to such a hitherto virgin field of research, Markowitz began by drawing what turned out to be a stunningly fruitful analogy between desired output as a manufacturer might define the term and desired output as an investor might define it. For investors, the desired output of a well-managed portfolio would be an above-average rate of return over time. In his linear analysis, Markowitz defined costs as the level of volatility to which any particular portfolio might be exposed in order to generate an above-average rate of return.[2] With regard to risk, Markowitz worked forward from the not unreasonable proposition that most investors' primary goal would be to reduce it or—if practically possible—to avoid it whenever possible.

The key to MPT, which Markowitz formally unveiled in the *Journal of Finance*[3] less than two years after his seminal and random conversation with the stockbroker, was the notion that optimal portfolio diversification could be obtained by drawing precise relationships between three forms of data: 1) the expected *return* of each component in the portfolio; 2) the expected *volatility* of each component's return; and 3) the expected *correlation* of each component with each of the other components.[4]

A well-balanced and diversified portfolio, Markowitz's theory strongly suggested, is one that combines a number of assets whose market fluctuations are not naturally well correlated with

2. Markowitz's definition of costs as a function of volatility has since generated some controversy, as critics have argued that a more accurate measure of the costs related to managing a portfolio would be some quantifiable level of risk.

3. Harry Markowitz, "Portfolio Selection," *Journal of Finance* (March 1952).

4. The Brandes Institute, a division of Brandes Investment Partners, "The Past, The Future, and Modern Portfolio Theory," 1998–2004, www.brandes.com.

each other. For example, if the phenomenon noted by economists that emerging-markets economies appear to be "decoupling" from those in developed markets continues to hold true, a degree of diversification could be derived by constructing a portfolio containing a number of "non-correlated" assets drawn from developed and developing economies.

What made Markowitz's MPT so revolutionary was that it turned the traditional advice doled out to investors—to construct a portfolio containing as many securities as possible that could reasonably be expected to increase in value over time—virtually on its head. After Markowitz, investors and advisors who subscribed to the power of "asset allocation" favored portfolios assembled on the premise that a key predictor of long-term investment potential was the degree to which any particular basket of assets contained a sufficient number of components whose anticipated returns could be presumed to be non-correlated with each other. The point was not just to pick good stocks, but rather to pick the right *combination* of stocks that promises optimal diversification. Investors, Markowitz argued, reasonably expect and deserve to be compensated for taking on any level of risk above that of a Treasury Bill—a level of compensation formally referred to as the "risk premium" attached to an asset.

By 1964, William Sharpe (destined to share the Nobel Prize in Economics with Merton Miller and Markowitz for their joint development of MPT) improved upon Markowitz's methods of evaluating assets, and continued to further refine the methods of risk assessment and management employed by the majority of asset managers today. Although it took a few decades to embed itself thoroughly into the investment universe and to gain widespread acceptance among the intellectually conservative brokerage community, by the eighties many more (although by no means a majority) of financial advisors had embraced the notion that traditional stock picking was not as effective a means of portfolio construction as one in which investments are evaluated on a statistical basis in terms of their long-term rate of return potential and expected short-term volatility. By some estimates, up to 90 percent of a portfolio's long-term positive performance could be ascribed to the quality of the asset allocation strategy employed, and less than 10 percent to the accuracy of the forecasts related to individual stocks in the portfolio.

The effects of MPT on wealth and asset management best practices were nothing less than profound. If stock picking—the traditional pursuit of the portfolio manager—was less critical to a portfolio's long-term performance than asset allocation and diversification, such an assumption only reinforced the industry's gathering trend toward redefining the role of an FA as a *relationship manager*: one who comprehends the entirety and complexity of a client's financial picture and aspirations, as opposed to one who can claim to have a pretty decent idea of which securities are likely to rise or fall in value over time.

MPT also strongly reinforced the notion that for an advisor to achieve the optimal asset allocation of a client's portfolio, a comprehensive approach to balancing the client's long-term goals and objectives was virtually a prerequisite. For financial services providers and asset managers, the overwhelming internal logic of MPT reinforced the argument that an asset allocation strategy was only effective if a majority—if not a totality—of client assets were maintained under one roof at a single financial institution. Otherwise, it would be impossible for any single money manager to see the entire household portfolio comprehensively.

So even if most HNWIs are not particularly comfortable computing Sharpe ratios, standard deviations and other arcane calculi of risk, today's widespread embrace of MPT reflects the nearly universal appreciation of the fact that asset diversification and allocation are critical components of any financial plan. Most investors, of course, intuitively grasp the notion that it is important not to put all of one's eggs in one basket. It's not unreasonable to conclude that the essence of Markowitz and Sharpe's achievement has been to mathematically codify and refine what really amounts to a modicum of common sense.

UNCOVERING THE PREFERRED ASSET ALLOCATIONS OF THE WEALTHY AND ULTRA-WEALTHY

The basic building blocks—otherwise known as asset classes—of any portfolio are:

• Equities (stocks in companies);

• Fixed income (bonds issued by companies or government agencies);

• Cash/Deposits;

• Real estate (either direct investment or through real estate investment trusts, known as REITs);

• Alternative investments, a growing category consisting of an eclectic product mix, that may include structured products, hedge funds, foreign currency, commodities and private equity to be dealt with in greater detail in the next chapter.

The asset mix of any portfolio will typically include a percentage of some or all of the above, although alternative investments remain primarily the province of HNWIs. As history and *WWR* surveys have repeatedly demonstrated, the wealthy display a heightened sensitivity to the economic environment and tend to reallocate portfolios in accordance with current and impending economic conditions. In 2002, for example, HNWIs adopted defensive allocations of their assets as a means of weathering a recession and a period of poor market performance. A market recovery a year later prompted these same wealthy individuals to reallocate assets to equities and alternative investments, which offered higher return potential.

Figure 5.1 – HNWI Assets by Investment Class, 2004–2008F

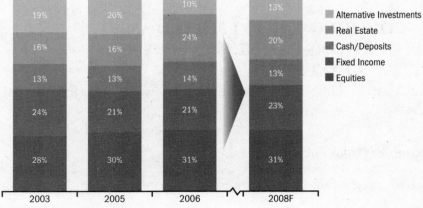

Source: Capgemini/Merrill Lynch Relationship Manager Survey, 2007.

In 2004, following exceptionally high returns in 2003, HNWIs adopted a conservative and diversified approach to their portfolios, increasing their allocations to fixed income and cash/deposits to combat market volatility. In 2005, HNWIs adopted even more aggressive strategies than in 2004. They increased their allocations to equities and alternative investments and, anticipating interest rate hikes, shifted funds away from fixed income. In 2006, HNWIs shifted away from alternative investments and toward real estate (as illustrated in Figure 5.1).

While clearly everyone would love to have an "ideal" portfolio—a Holy Grail typically defined as one promising a high potential return on investment unburdened by anything other than reasonable risk—in reality, investors understand that they must accept a certain level of risk to attain an expected level of reward; just like everything else in life, there are inevitably going to be trade-offs between the two. And how much risk the investor will be comfortably willing to take involves a medley of factors, including age, goals, time horizon and liquidity requirements.

Ultra-HNWIs Take the Lead

Over the years, the *WWR* has consistently shown that ultra-HNWIs—individuals with more than US$30 million in net financial assets—tend to make investing decisions ahead of market trends. Ultra-HNWIs account for 1 percent of the global HNWI population and about a third of its financial wealth, and tend to be more sophisticated and better informed than other HNWI investors when it comes to managing their assets. In many ways, ultra-HNWIs are thought leaders whose behaviors and attitudes about wealth management hold important lessons for HNWIs and other investors alike.

Ultra-wealthy portfolios tend not only to be more diversified than those of the mass affluent, they are also more aggressively invested than those of individuals in lower wealth bands. Overall, ultra-HNWIs allocate a greater percentage of their assets to alternative investments than do average HNWIs—24 percent compared to 20 percent, respectively, according to the 2006 *WWR* survey. The use of alternative investments demonstrates ultra-HNWIs' "tax intelligence," as many of these investments allow them to minimize or defer taxes. While ultra-HNWIs allocate a smaller portion of their portfolios to equities than do HNWIs, they exhibit a taste for more complex investment products such as hedge funds, private equity/venture capital, structured products and investments in their own businesses. Furthermore, ultra-HNWIs hold a significantly lower share of their assets in fixed income and cash, while allocating more of their wealth to real estate, than the average HNWI. The rationale is that they have more wealth to distribute, and history shows that real estate over the long term may be a relatively safer investment.

Ultra-HNWIs also tend to be more aware of how wealth is managed internationally, according to the professionals who help manage their portfolios. They tend to tolerate greater exposure to international markets and have more geographically diversified portfolios than their HNWI counterparts. They allocate a lower percentage of assets to North America in favor of regions with a higher number of emerging markets, such as Asia-Pacific and Latin America. In fact, in the survey, ultra-HNWIs say they believe that this movement of investment funds out of mature economies, such as the United States, and into attractive growth economies in other parts of the world is likely to pick up steam.

Since a large percentage of ultra-HNWIs are creating physical and financial presences in international locations, it's hardly surprising that more than 25 percent of HNWIs maintain both homes and relationship managers in countries other than their primary residence. For ultra-HNWIs, such personal and household globalization has become even more pronounced in recent years. More than half maintain residences and financial accounts located outside the nation in which they are officially domiciled, while 45 percent have wealth managers located beyond the borders of the nation they claim as a primary residence.

Overall, ultra-HNWIs' sophisticated asset allocation and risk management strategies help to explain how they have achieved and maintained their elite status on the world stage. Given their proven power to move markets, we anticipate that ultra-HNWIs' behavior will prompt HNWIs to consider embracing more sophisticated and diverse investment vehicles in developed and emerging economies when suitable.

Unexpectedly low returns, or unexpectedly high returns, are evidence that an investor's asset allocation may be unbalanced. The investment mix might be too conservative or too risky, but truly unexpected returns would typically reflect the fact that the original risk parameters are not well defined. Of course, human nature being what it is, when returns are surprisingly strong it can be particularly difficult to question risk/return objectives—but the problem with achieving unexpectedly high returns during one point in time is that it tends to indicate that the level of risk being taken offers the promise of unexpectedly lower returns at some point in the future. Figure 5.2 lays out a number of risk factors to be taken into consideration.

While it may be tempting to bask in the heady illusion that the rules of investing have been suspended for one fortunate individual or period, or that a manager has simply and brilliantly outmaneuvered the market, the latter is sadly hardly ever the case while the former has been proven well near impossible. An obvious example of this fact is the rise and fall of the Internet bubble in the late nineties, when dot-com companies were viewed by many investors as a risk-free way to earn enormous returns; ultimately, of course, these investments proved risky indeed and cost many their life savings.

Figure 5.2 – Typical Risk Factors that a Wealthy Family Should Be Aware Of

"Personal" Risk Do not jeopardize basic standard of living	"Market" Risk Maintain lifestyle	"Aspirational" Risk Enhance lifestyle
Protective Assets	**Market Assets**	**Aspirational Assets**
· Outliving your assets (longevity risk); · Interest rates; · Loss of purchasing power (inflation risk); · Disability; · Death; · Catastrophic illness (medical expenses); · Lawsuits; · Lack of liquidity; · Higher taxation or change in tax laws.	· Portfolio volatility; · Sustained market downturn; · Market shocks; · Geopolitical conditions; · Interest rates; · Fluctuation in relative value of local currency; · Higher taxation or change in tax laws.	· Asset concentration (concentrated stock or business ownership); · Loss of principal; · Loss of liquidity; · Higher taxation or change in tax laws.

Larry Fink, founder and CEO of asset management firm BlackRock, cites the recent example of commodities hedge fund Amaranth, based in Greenwich, Conn., a self-styled multi-strategy "market neutral" hedge fund that advertised itself as being able to maintain a perpetually low risk profile by quickly shifting in and out of different markets as opportunities wax and wane. Amaranth's wrong-way bets in the energy market in 2006 triggered roughly US$6.4 billion in losses, or 70 percent of its assets, forcing it to liquidate its investments to pay investors. Nine months before Amaranth ran aground, BlackRock began to question the risks the fund was taking because the return for 2005, about 30 percent, seemed too good. "When you see aberrant success, you have to ask, 'Did I take too much risk?'" Larry Fink asks. BlackRock began probing Amaranth to understand how it achieved those returns if it was still hewing to its stated investment strategy. After receiving unsatisfactory explanations, BlackRock decided Amaranth must be deviating from its multi-strategy in some way and taking on more risk than BlackRock wanted to be exposed to. Ultimately, it paid a 3 percent early redemption fee to exit the Amaranth fund, and when the fund abruptly disintegrated a few months later he was happy to have done so.

Fink's lesson is a valuable one for advisors and HNWIs constantly searching for new financial products that will generate the potential for high yields. The search for the next hot thing is hardly unreasonable. After all, the first investors into an effective investment strategy—whether it's a hedge fund or private equity—are almost always the ones who make the largest returns. As other investors see the results, more money floods in, driving up demand and reducing potential returns. HNWIs and their FAs must then move on once more if they want to stand any chance of consistently beating the market. In other words, the investment universe is populated by a continuous search for a higher, greener pasture in which to graze before the rest of the herd arrives. Yet being always in the vanguard carries risks that may be difficult to measure precisely, because they are new.

MOVING BEYOND MODERN PORTFOLIO THEORY

One practical problem with MPT and its lessons regarding the value of asset allocation and diversification is that most HNWIs, particularly self-made ones, have accumulated their wealth by defying precisely what MPT preaches. They tend to be exceedingly concentrated in one investment—typically their own business. The old belief that you get rich through concentration and stay rich through diversification may be pretty well understood, but it can be a pretty tough pill to swallow for HNWIs who for a variety of reasons are not well diversified and like it that way.

Diversification typically means reversion to average returns; HNWIs have not gotten rich by accepting average returns as the norm. "Most have become wealthy thanks to one or two success stories—not asset allocation," says Mr. Rothenberg of Capital Research and Management. "But once you have a certain amount of wealth you need to stop worrying about enhancing it, and start worrying about protecting it."

HNWIs cite emotional ties to their businesses as what makes the transition from concentration to diversification a difficult one. There's also the fact that these HNWIs really do know more about a business that has made them wealthy than any other investment they might make. As one HNWI says, "I'm confident I can grow my business by 15 percent. There's nothing out there I know of that can do as well. I know I'm unbelievably undiversified, but why should I sell to buy the S&P 500?"

There are still other reasons it can be difficult and not always advisable for HNWIs to follow conventional advice and diversify. For top executives at a public company who may have a huge amount of wealth tied up in company stock, selling a large block of stock can be a politically sensitive issue. Investors don't like to see management sell their stakes; they consider it a lack of confidence in the future of the business; no end of explanations about personal portfolio rebalancing and asset allocation is likely to fully assuage their concerns.

Also, there may be tax implications associated with liquidating a long-held position, which makes adopting a standard strategy of diversification difficult or ill-advised. Most investors do not want to liquidate positions to reinvest elsewhere unless they are compelled to do so. Of course, if you're lucky to be tapped for government service, then you can have your entire tax bill forgiven. Robert Rubin and Henry Paulson were both tapped to be Treasury secretaries while leading Goldman Sachs. In Paulson's case, he owned 3.23 million Goldman shares worth about US$485 million today, according to regulatory filings. He agreed to sell other investments, including a stake in China's largest bank, for a reported US$800 million. At a 15 percent capital gains rate, that's a tax savings on the Goldman shares of at least US$73 million and total savings of about US$120 million. Most other HNWIs, however, will have to find other ways to pay tax efficiently and diversify their assets.

In "Beyond Markowitz: A Comprehensive Wealth Allocation Framework (WAF) for Individual Investors," a paper published in *The Journal of Wealth Management*[5] by Ashvin Chhabra, Merrill Lynch's former chief of Wealth Management Strategies and Analytics, a number of HNWIs are profiled who have profited enormously by defying MPT's asset allocation provisions. Examples of their profitable defiance include:

1. Investors who took out substantial mortgages on real estate that doubled or tripled in value in just a few years, racking up above-average returns on their initial investment, which was the down payment on the property.

2. Corporate executives who hung on to their original stock options and grants in firms whose equity value doubled or tripled, far above the market.

3. Entrepreneurs who invested substantial amounts of financial and intellectual capital in their own business, whose value rose steeply over a comparatively short period of time.

The primary question posed by the paper: were these individuals taking foolhardy or unnecessary risk, or behaving in some way irrationally? The answer is clearly not the former but rather the latter. Certain individuals, particularly those blessed with special insight or knowledge of the value of certain assets (such as an entrepreneur's insight into the likely growth rate of their own businesses) might well achieve above-average returns based on

5. Ashvin B. Chhabra, "Beyond Markowitz," *The Journal of Wealth Management* 7, no. 4 (Spring 2005).

a risk-reward profile that is, if not impossible, certainly difficult to quantify.

Yet another aspect of risk that Chhabra's Wealth Allocation Framework addresses is the notion of *aspirational* risk. In general, one requires a lot of money (relative to what you have) in order to increase your wealth percentile. For example, for a household to move from the 40th to the 60th wealth percentile, its net worth would need to approximately *triple.* In order to move up in the wealth pantheon, one must acquire substantially, as opposed to incrementally, greater wealth. One cannot meet such an aspirational goal without taking on substantial risk—hence the term "aspirational risk." On the surface, taking such a degree of risk would seem to be at odds with the imperative to protect oneself and one's family from falling into a lower wealth percentile. It would seem reasonable to assume that most investors in this situation would pass up the opportunity for improvement in favor of the certainty of the status quo. However, human behavior frequently defies this assumption—particularly when we're speaking about the behavior of HNWIs and those who aspire to be like them and to invest like them.

At virtually all economic levels, aspirational risk-taking is a common phenomenon. Examples range from the frequent buying of lottery tickets to more mainstream financial investments, such as the substantial purchase of a single stock, investment in real estate, or small business startup. Every time a member of the peer group succeeds in his aspirational risk-taking, the difficulty of remaining in the same peer group is raised for those who passed on the opportunity. Consider how hard it is to improve or even maintain one's position on the Forbes 400 list. The net worth required to be the 400th richest American has increased by a factor of ten since the early eighties, to US$1 billion from US$100 million.

The conventional MPT framework lacks the flexibility to accommodate the dual demands of safety and aspiration, Chhabra contends. The WAF represents an important step toward incorporating these aspects of safety and aspiration while building upon the foundation of MPT. A HNWI's portfolio should allow him or her the opportunity to achieve the following:

• Protection from anxiety and poverty;

• Ability to maintain his or her living standards;

• Provide an opportunity to increase wealth substantially or meet aspirational goals.

Figure 5.3 – Personal Risk, Market Risk and Aspirational Risk

"Personal" Risk Do not jeopardize basic standard of living	"Market" Risk Maintain lifestyle	"Aspirational" Risk Enhance lifestyle
Protective Assets	**Market Assets**	**Aspirational Assets**

· Cash;
· Home and mortgage;
· Partially protected investments:
  - Traditional annuities;
  - Hedging through puts/calls;
  - Insurance;
  - Human capital.
	· Equities;
	· Fixed income;
	· Strategic investments:
	  - Funds of funds;
	  - Liquid "non-traditional";
	    investments, e.g., commodities.
		· Alternative investments:
		  - Private equity;
		  - Hedge funds.
		· Investment real estate;
		· Small business;
		· Concentrated stock and stock
		  option positions.

Low Risk/Return   Risk/Return Spectrum   High Risk/Return

For all the strengths of MPT, its essential weakness is that it only recognizes market risk and seeks to minimize it through optimal asset allocation. In contrast, the WAF identifies three very different risk dimensions and optimizes all three of them simultaneously. The fundamental idea is to create a financial strategy that organizes and allocates all of a HNWI's assets and liabilities into 1) a protective (low-risk) bucket, 2) a market (market-level risk) bucket and 3) a riskier aspirational bucket. According to Chhabra, successful HNWIs pay as much attention to *risk allocation* as they do to *asset allocation*. According to Chhabra, these are not—as some MPT theorists would have it—"deviations from rational investing" but investment decisions whose logic lies outside and beyond the rather limited confines of MPT as traditionally conceived.

COMMENTING EXPERTLY ON ASSET ALLOCATION

Merrill Lynch Chief Investment Strategist Richard Bernstein points out that the true test of a good asset allocation is the degree to which a client's portfolio is appropriately matched not just to a client's assets but also to his or her liabilities. "What even sophisticated investors tend to forget when exclusively focused on rate of return is that returns must be adjusted and expressed in the context of a client's *liabilities*," Bernstein observes. "Let's say a client has three kids heading off to college and he wants to retire while they're still in school." Bernstein points out that "In such a case, the liability side is going to be paramount."

Fully comprehending the liability side is the really tough trick, Bernstein contends. In fact, it is what separates the wheat from the chaff in the investment advisory business. "You can download a pretty decent asset allocation model from the Internet for free," he observes, emphasizing yet another area in which investment advisory services have been commoditized. "That model will do an OK job of telling you about sectors and weightings and even factor in a comparatively unsophisticated risk profile."

But the area in which a truly talented FA will outshine the computer model (in a way reminiscent of world chess champion Gary Kasparov beating IBM's Deep Blue) is by presenting a client with the full menu of possibilities and products designed to meet, mitigate and offset the needs on both the asset and liability side—an act of empathy that typically takes a human perspective to comprehend. According to Bernstein, a client's risk tolerance level is never simply a function of the size of his or her portfolio. "Someone with four billion dollars might rather die than lose one billion dollars, even if they still have three billion left over…a twenty-three-year-old un-married male with two hundred thousand dollars might have a far more aggressive style than a billionaire, because he—in both senses of the term—has considerably less to lose."

Accurately defining and where appropriate *extending* a client's time horizon, Bernstein maintains, is the key to long-term superior performance. "We conducted a study that persuasively demonstrated that the [farther away] a client sets their time horizon, the higher [the] probability exists of attaining higher long-term returns." The reason day traders are so rarely successful over the long term, he suggests, is that by shortening their time horizon to a matter of hours and days, they reduce their probability of making money to practically zero. On the flip side, a client willing to take a much longer view—possibly extending out decades—will vastly improve his or her chances of achieving superior performance over time.

Asset Allocations Vary Regionally

Asset allocation for specific HNWIs is affected by the maturity and pace of development of their local markets. The question is not just what a HNWI should invest in, but what is literally available from market to market. For instance, the Merrill Lynch Capgemini 2007 *Asia-Pacific Wealth Report* found that in 2006, Asia-Pacific's allocations to cash/deposits, a traditionally "safe" asset class, were significantly higher (24 percent) than the global average (14 percent), driven by wealthy investors in places like South Korea, Japan and China. The high cash allocation in South Korea and China reflected both a lack of alternative products and a lack of sophistication in the WM market. Meanwhile, Japanese HNWIs also had a limited availability of international product but, more significantly, were the most focused on wealth preservation, as opposed to wealth accumulation, which led them to allocate much of their assets to cash/deposits.

In addition to their cash/deposits, South Korean HNWIs allocated a quarter of their assets to fixed income, much higher than elsewhere in the region—again because a narrow range of products limited their investment options. HNWIs in Indonesia, on the other hand, had among the smallest allocation (about 13 percent) to fixed income, chiefly because they had limited access to fixed income products. In fact, Indonesia's local-currency bond market is among the smallest in the region: it is less than one-tenth the size of South Korea's local-currency bond market. (To spur its bond market, the Indonesian government in 2006 was considering refashioning its bond market's trading system along the lines of South Korea's.)

Observing these differences closely can be valuable for HNWIs and their advisors alike. On the one hand, HNWIs can see investment patterns in more developed markets and thus try to position themselves better. Advisors, for their part, get a hint of what new products and services clients might yearn for as the WM market develops. Clearly, for instance, there is a strong correlation between a high allocation to alternative investments and the maturity of the WM market.

The 2007 *Asia-Pacific Wealth Report* also studied Asia-Pacific HNWIs' allocations to alternative investments, and found that the allocations were highest in Singapore (10 percent). Considering that market experts view Singapore as one of the most mature and sophisticated WM markets in the region, it was not surprising to find that HNWIs there had the highest allocation to alternative investments.

HNWIs in China (one of the least mature markets in the region) also tended to allocate one of the larger percentages toward alternative investments (9 percent). Why? The most likely explanation is that Chinese high-net-worth individuals have a strong interest in personal business and private equity, a trend largely ascribable to the fact that the vast majority of Chinese HNWIs are self-made entrepreneurs. In contrast, HNWIs in South Korea, where the WM market is relatively immature, had the lowest exposure to alternative investments.

As WM in Asia's other developing markets matures and becomes more sophisticated, one can expect HNWIs outside today's leading WM markets to adopt the more diversified and aggressive investment strategies now found in places like Singapore and Taiwan. Alternative investments will gain favor and real estate will grow even more popular across the region as securitization of properties becomes more established. Savvy HNWIs and advisors have already begun to position themselves and their clients for this evolution.

Even with the modifications, questions, revisions and refinements suggested by theorists from Chhabra to Bernstein that improve on the original theories proposed by Markowitz, Sharpe and the other pioneering Modern Portfolio proponents, the greatest and most enduring accomplishment of the doctrine of asset allocation is that it has allowed individual investors to become more sophisticated, because it has encouraged them—via the ongoing imperative to diversify—to look beyond investments that were deemed safe strictly because they were familiar. Redefining risk has encouraged investors to seek a more diversified portfolio by investing in such ostensibly non-correlated assets as emerging-markets securities and alternative investments dependent on more flexible mandates than the traditional "long-only" strategies employed by garden-variety mutual funds. By stressing the link between volatility and reward, wealthy investors have developed a more sophisticated risk appetite, displaying a taste for adventurously moving beyond the financial equivalent of macaroni and cheese or a ham sandwich to the global grazing associated with eclectic nouvelle cuisine.

CHAPTER 6

Alternative Investment Strategies

THE APPEAL OF ALTERNATIVE INVESTMENTS

So many different kinds of investments tend to be lumped together under the "alternative" tag—including structured products, derivatives, hedge funds, private equity, foreign exchange, commodities and even so-called investments of passion—that the term threatens to be rendered meaningless. Just the same, items in the last category, including fine art, classic cars and sports memorabilia, require a significant cash outlay, and the wealthy are taking an increasingly sophisticated approach to vetting these purchases. In response, a number of high-end advisors are offering consulting services around art acquisition, prompting Bijan Khezri, CEO of the London-based Artist Pension Trust, to proclaim fine art "a new asset class" in the op-ed pages of the *Wall Street Journal*.[1]

Art

The art market is a notoriously boom-and-bust affair, frequently jumping during strong economic conditions and declining when the economic winds turn less favorable. Even so, interest in art as an investment has maintained its high pitch even in the face of a turbulent economy. During the last Gilded Age, fine art was primarily purchased by HNWIs as status symbols and as a sign that the collector had arrived, not that he or she was looking to make money

---

1. Khezri, Bijan, "The New Art of Art Finance," *Wall Street Journal,* September 19, 2007, D10.

on their acquisitions. Collectors have always hoped that their purchases had lasting value, of course, but today's focus on future returns when considering an art purchase is unprecedented.

Apart from the vagaries of the economy at large, the art market is (not surprisingly) strongly affected by changing tastes, as artists fall in and out of favor, insuring that pricing information is zealously guarded by auction houses and that liquidity (the ability to sell art for what it was bought) can, at times, be as murky as some collectibles' provenance. Thanks to the Internet, the art market is possibly more transparent than ever, yet it remains a market that is positively opaque by virtually any standards of investing.

Nevertheless, more and more investors continue to rush in. In 2006, Sotheby's Holdings sold US$3.6 billion of art, up a third from 2005. In the fall of 2006 alone, Sotheby's and Christie's International, the other major auction house, sold US$1 billion of Impressionist, modern and contemporary art. Christie's reports that the 2006 sales of Impressionist art were up 81 percent, while postwar and contemporary art were up 58 percent, from 2005. Sales of contemporary Asian art, most of it Chinese, zoomed to US$190 million in 2006 from US$22 million in 2004.

A number of factors would appear to be fueling this surge. First is the amount of wealth still sloshing around the globe despite the depredations of the 2007–08 credit crisis, turning the trend truly international. In 2006, a Hong Kong investor paid US$17.3 million for Andy Warhol's "Mao," a record for the artist. In the United States, at least up until the fall of 2007, hedge fund managers were shelling out huge sums to hastily assemble prominent collections, while many were becoming significant art patrons and board members of art institutions.

Another driver behind the surge in fine art is scarcity value. Despite the high volume of art on the market, big-name artists and indisputable fine work typically remains in short supply, making the search for second-tier and new artists more intense. All this has recently led to respectable returns for art and opportunities for huge returns. Michael Ovitz, co-founder of Creative Artists Agency, bought a painting by the relatively unknown Barnaby Furnas for about US$20,000 in 2003 and sold it for US$520,000 in 2006.

As art prices have surged, a more concerted effort has ensued on the part of academics to more accurately measure returns. New York University business professors Jianping Mei and Michael Moses compile an index that compares repeat auction sales of the same art objects over time—the Mei Moses All Art Index. Their index of postwar and contemporary art shows a compound annual return of 12.6 percent for the past decade, compared with a return of 9 percent for the Standard & Poor's 500 stock index. Meanwhile, to bring greater pricing transparency to the realm of art investing, Artnet tallies fine art auction sales involving 180,000 international artists. The database represents auction records from more than 500 international auction houses since 1985 and covers more than 2.9 million auction sales.

Yet the reliability of such measurements, given the tight-lipped nature of art sellers and buyers, can be difficult to gauge. Sotheby's and Christie's International are the biggest auction houses and the most obvious source of pricing information. But they often do not disclose terms of sales or even the identity of sellers or buyers. It's even more difficult, if not virtually impossible, to obtain accurate and timely information on art gallery sales. The art market is, as mentioned earlier, an opaque one, even with the advent of Internet auction sites such as eBay. It is also an unregulated market.

Still, art is more than just a numbers game—and always will be. Great returns tend to accrue to those with a great eye—the art investor's equivalent of having a sharp nose for business evaluation. Good, old-fashioned art appreciation (the non-financial kind) will help steer collectors. Former Microsoft executive and Russian space tourist Charles Simonyi vows that he will never sell his collection of works by pop artist Roy Lichtenstein or op art pioneer Victor Vasarely, but he also ascribes his success as an art investor to self-education, by which he has enhanced his personal understanding of the context of art both within the scope of art history and within the personal development of the artist. (It's also helpful, according to Simonyi, to become friendly with artists, both established and aspiring, and, if possible, to become something of a fixture on the art scene, as would be the case with just about any investing landscape.)

> Combine an interest in art collecting, the hefty sums involved, and the opaque nature of the market, and we've got a corner of WM that's a tailor-made opportunity for highly specialized wealth advisors. Some financial institutions already offer loans to make art purchases and some provide advice and market research on fine art. Whether the current art market is peaking is hard to say, but art collecting itself is timeless, a passion shared from the Caesars to the Medicis to the hedge funds managers of today.

Just how dramatic has the recent rise in alternative investments been? From 2002 to 2006, HNWIs more than doubled their allocations to alternative investments, boosting the share of the average HNW portfolio to 22 percent from 10, mainly at the expense of cash and bonds. By 2006, however, the wealthy and ultra-wealthy, possibly collectively sensing a negative shift in the class' risk profile, had slightly shifted their allocations out of traditional alternatives and into real estate.

One reason for this shift may be that alternative investments opportunistically capitalize on highly volatile markets; the 2007 *WWR* suggests that in 2006, a sharp reduction in the Volatility Index (VIX) could be presumed responsible for a discernible bias away from hedge funds toward more tangible assets—including investments of passion such as high-end collectibles.

Yet this shift in allocation is viewed as likely to be short-lived, because "a majority of investors simply don't find the expected return versus risk in the public stock and bond markets compelling," maintains Ralph Schlosstein, the recently retired co-founder of BlackRock. "They see alternative investments as a way to preserve wealth through absolute returns—which means seeking positive returns in both bull and bear markets while not being tied down to traditional performance benchmarks like the S&P 500 Index."

According to Daniel Sontag, head of Merrill Lynch's Global Wealth Management division for the Americas, the remarkable rise in interest in alternative investments on the part of high-net-worth clients has conferred at least one additional and little-noted benefit to portfolio managers: many alternative asset classes have historically been negatively or non-correlated with traditional asset classes, providing a classic MPT allocation balance. Particularly during periods in which stocks and bonds—which have historically moved in opposite directions—fluctuate roughly in tandem, a basket of non-correlated assets including alternative investments typically imparts added value while enhancing portfolio principal protection.

Real Estate

Real estate would appear to straddle the line between an alternative investment and its own discrete asset class. HNWIs can be invested in real estate in numerous ways: primary residence, vacation homes domestically and abroad, direct investment in residential and commercial real estate, or investment through REITs or other partnerships. And certain kinds of real estate—such as industrial warehouses that often have long leases—tend to hold up well in a down economy.

Notably, despite the headline grabbing nature of the sector, in which every interest rate move and inventory report seems to make the front page, HNWIs had been consistent with their allocation to real estate, holding steady at 15 or 16 percent for most of this decade.

Such faith has by and large been amply rewarded, although risks remain. The subprime mortgage meltdown in the United States beginning in early 2007 through 2008 battered the stocks of many mortgage companies and REITs. Residential real estate as an asset class suffered severely in many parts of the U.S. in 2008 albeit with some compelling exceptions, particularly at the ultra-high-end and in the most desirable neighborhoods.

It's important to bear in mind that the real estate market includes various types of assets, and that the major real estate categories do not necessarily move in lockstep, which can help to diversify a portfolio. The net result is that while the real estate market tends to be referred to in aggregate, sweeping generalizations about the direction of the market are difficult given the range of real estate and the idiosyncrasies of individual markets.

One indication of just how bipolar the market has become is that in early 2007, as single-home prices continued to decline in much of the United States and inventories increased, a pitched battle broke out between two prominent private equity investment consortia to purchase Sam Zell's Equity Office Properties Trust, a commercial REIT that owns directly or through partnerships about 600 office buildings in twenty-five markets, making it the country's largest office landlord.

James Marrelli, National Association of Realtors vice president of commercial real estate, notes that in 2006, a record amount of capital flowed into commercial real estate. "Institutional investors, pension funds and foreign investors have focused on commercial grade properties to diversify portfolio assets, with expectations of solid long-term gains." Outside of the hotel sector, more than US$236 billion in commercial real estate transaction volume was recorded in the first ten months of 2006, up from US$231.9 billion in the same period of 2005, not including properties valued at less than US$5 million.[2]

As the scope of real estate investing grows, so does the opportunity for both HNWIs and their advisors. More than ever, HNWIs can take on a view of real estate markets around the world, cashing in on a reliable wealth-creating asset. Increasingly, investors in commercial real estate are looking globally, beyond the United States and Europe to Russia, Turkey, China, India and Japan.

For advisors, perceived expertise in the more exotic markets is bound to matter more than ever in this age of increased investor sophistication and connoisseurship. If the question is whether to invest in a shopping center in Russia (or more likely a fund that specializes in such investments), advisors will need to deeply understand and be able to explain in plain language the pros and cons of such an investment, or have the resources to obtain such expertise. Every different corner of the real estate market has its own particular drivers; the health of each type of real estate varies greatly from city to city, much less country to country.

---

2. Interview with the authors.

STRUCTURED PRODUCTS FOR INDIVIDUALS

Stephen Bodurtha, a senior vice president and vice chairman of Merrill Lynch's Global Wealth Management division, has led teams that create innovative investment solutions tailored to the tastes of high-net-worth individuals. Bodurtha, who has self-described roots as "a financial products engineer," and his team try to "take some of the innovation sweeping the financial markets and adapt it prudently to the private client universe."

The critical differences between individual and institutional clients in the structured products world, Bodurtha explains, are the limits that clients place on risk tolerance and time horizon. "Individual investors typically have a hard time taking comfort in the fact that, if their portfolio value drops 20 percent in a year, sticking to the right asset allocation strategy will have a good chance of swinging the portfolio into the positive in the next cycle."

So how do advisors address the crying need on the part of people who have acquired great wealth to gain access to some of the more compelling opportunities available to investors in the marketplace without threatening a loss of principal? Starting out in the mid-nineties, Market Index Target-Term Securities (MITTs) were among the first protected equity-linked notes (PENs)—the private-client version of proprietary products employed by institutional clients as investment vehicles to manage risk by guaranteeing a protection of principal. The twist was that the issuer of these notes, in this case Merrill Lynch, was able to structure the products so that the client traded off a set amount of the notes' upside profit potential in exchange for minimizing downside risk. For comparatively risk-averse clients whose primary interest was principal protection, these notes became attractive components of their overall asset allocation and risk management strategy.

Yet another twist that further increased client demand for products that offered principal protection combined with a growth potential somewhat better than a Treasury note or a savings account was that the ongoing boom in the equity markets was producing ever-greater equity-related wealth. Much of this wealth was being captured in vehicles ranging from Employee Stock Option Plans (ESOPs) to the proceeds from Initial Public Offerings (IPOs). "A number of senior and highly compensated executives," Bodurtha observes, "would suddenly find themselves the proud possessors of material amounts of wealth concentrated in a very small number of stock positions."

What those clients needed to do was diversify their holdings. The essence of the wealth protection strategy achieved by the next generation of proprietary products (known as "collars") was to hedge the client's highly concentrated portfolio by permitting the client to 1) hang onto the stock while 2) permitting the client to shed some of the stock's downside risk by transferring some of the upside opportunity to a third party. "From a risk management standpoint," Bodurtha explains, "what these collars did was to insure the portfolio against the risk of a drop in a single stock that would unduly affect the value of the entire portfolio."

These products amounted to the first wave of a trend that Bodurtha characterizes as "a customization of risk," or what might be better termed "investor-centric innovation." "One of the most critical challenges when creating these products and tailoring them to individual client needs," Bodurtha stresses, "is persuading investors to clearly articulate their investment and risk parameters. Then it becomes our challenge to convey to them the fact that these goals— some of which might appear to be in conflict—might actually not be irreconcilable. That's where the innovation and ingenuity come in."

As Bodurtha points out, twenty years ago who would have believed that exchange traded funds (ETFs), introduced by The American Stock Exchange in the nineties, could be a viable product for private clients? But now these ETFs allow investors to own whole sectors, countries or asset classes with a single purchase. Another output of innovative financial engineering includes products permitting HNWIs to take a view on real estate markets in individual cities, thanks to the 2006 launch by the CME of future and option contracts on the housing markets in ten different U.S. cities.

Kevin Waldron, an FA with Merrill Lynch in Bala Cynwyd, Pennsylvania, has been helping clients plan for retirement using structured "bear notes" designed to protect clients with concentrated positions in certain sectors. Recently, such customized products have enabled clients to hedge against expected shocks from prospective housing market declines. "That market was so out-of-whack, we wanted to turn to [notes]," Waldron recently observed,[3] recalling that Merrill provided similar portfolio protection to clients in the technology industry before the tech meltdown in the spring of 2000.

Many of Waldron's HNW clients have accumulated substantial wealth through leverage or concentrated positions in certain industries, and viscerally resist "walking away from the way that they made their wealth." But many are finding an appealing hedge in housing-oriented structured bear notes, tied to the Philadelphia Housing Index, which are engineered to benefit from the negative environment in the housing industry. Some notes are structured so that even if the housing index rises, the client doesn't risk losing principal.

The list of innovative products migrating to the public markets goes on and on. For a quick lesson on the advantages and risks of a new alternative investment, consider the wave of catastrophe bonds issued since Hurricane Katrina. In 2006, hedge funds, pension funds and other money managers invested more than US$9.2 billion— more than double from 2004—in disaster-related investments. If a hurricane or some other disaster hits, the investors are on the hook, but if no damage occurs the gains can be substantial.

Advisors have been busy tailoring all sorts of tweaks, such as "wind risk," to these bonds, opening more opportunities for investors to make money and for sellers to obviate risk. One of the great

---

3. Elizabeth Wine, "Revamping Retirement," *On Wall Street*, September 2007, http://www.onwallstreet.com.

advantages of these new investments is they are not correlated with other investments. But, as with any new, successful strategy, the window to enjoy big gains can close quickly as other investors rush in. In the case of hurricane risk, for instance, recent yields of 10 percent may start to attract too many followers, inevitably pushing up prices, lowering returns and, perhaps, encouraging investors to take on excessive risk.

A Tycoon's Tale

Joseph Lam is in the billionaire business. Born and raised in Hong Kong and educated first as a nuclear engineer at Texas A&M and then in business at the University of Chicago, the former Goldman Sachs private banker who decamped to Merrill Lynch in 2000 did so because "Merrill was very strong in the mass-affluent category but not yet strong in wealth management." Offered an opportunity to build up Merrill Lynch's HNW practice in Hong Kong, Lam leapt (with his team of nine FAs, three senior partners, analysts, associates and support staff) to the burgeoning Pac-Rim operation, bringing with him approximately a billion dollars in assets under management (comprised of about twenty household and client relationships) and a longstanding focus, as he modestly puts it, "on serving best-of-class, highly sophisticated investment products to tycoons."

"Tycoons have no interest in plain-vanilla products," Joseph Lam states, commenting that for big-league clients of his, including major Hong Kong property developer Dr. Lee Shau Kee, "mutual funds are just not [their] bowl of soup. That's a commodity business," he states bluntly, "because anyone can do that—today, you don't even need an FA to do it."

What Lam's billionaire clients—he handles just a small handful, but that is enough—want from him and his fellow members of Merrill Lynch's newly established Pac-Rim Private Investment Banking Group is to "become partners with Merrill on a wide range of proprietary investments and private equity arrangements."

"When one of my clients partners with us, it becomes a much more significant and deeper relationship than that of a passive investor. If we go into business together on whatever it might be—a shopping mall in China or a major proprietary deal—and come out together both making money, that's a classic win-win for both sides."

As Lam describes it, his client Dr. Lee is chairman of so many things it's nearly impossible to keep track of them, but probably the largest and best known of his entities is the Hong Kong-based Henderson Land Development. When Joseph Lam first took on managing wealth in 1994 for Dr. Lee, he was worth—give or take a few hundred million due to market fluctuations—something like US$16 billion, with a fortune based almost exclusively on the value of his extensive properties in Hong Kong.

But then, the nearly eighty-year-old Dr. Lee—"who still doesn't have to wear glasses," Lam approvingly observes—began reading up on Warren Buffett, and conceived of a late-life ambition to beat Mr. Buffett at his own game: value investing, except Dr. Lee was more interested in expanding his wealth in the comparative short term than in the long term.

Dr. Lee was at the time a classic candidate for asset allocation, as nearly all of his wealth was tied up in one asset category, which Dr. Lee frankly stated, might one day run out of steam for the simple reason that his traditional stomping ground, Hong Kong, was rapidly running out of developable land.

While sharply stepping up real estate development activities on the mainland (sometimes in private partnership with Merrill Lynch), Dr. Lee took on almost as a hobby the pursuit of Warren Buffett as a world-class investor. As Dr. Lee later put it, according to Lam, "he started out at a distinct advantage to Buffett, because the tax structure in the U.S. is much less favorable to wealth creation and preservation than it is in Hong Kong. So as Dr. Lee often told me, 'for every dollar Buffett makes he keeps fifty cents, whereas for every dollar I make, I get to keep eighty-five.'"

Dr. Lee resolved to more than double his fortune in two and a half years, aiming for a compound annualized rate of return well in excess of 30 percent. By 2007—not without the advice of Lam and his team—Lee had handily met his goal. He achieved this astonishing investment success by perfecting taking a logical approach to investing that reflected his knowledge and personal style.

He began by looking at China, Japan, the United States, Taiwan, Singapore and all of the countries he knew intimately and employing a macro-economic, analytic, "top-down" approach to choosing the countries he wanted to be in. He made his selection based on an impartial and dispassionate analysis of those countries' projected economic growth in the future.

He decided to invest the bulk of his funds in mainland China. Having done so, he analyzed the various industrial and commercial sectors and made a similar analysis of which sectors were most likely to prosper over the coming decade of massive economic expansion. He decided that if he was going to invest in China, he needed to rely on the best local expertise available.

He then bought a basket of three stocks culled from his personal macro-economic analysis—stocks that, as Joseph Lam puts it, "he already likes very much...he likes the country, he likes the sector, he likes the industry, and most importantly, he likes the companies."

He then purchased a note, custom-tailored by Lam and his team, keyed to a value set at two years in the future. At the end of his first year, he and Lam checked out the performance of the three selected stocks, and pruned his portfolio by selling the worst performers if their value declined to an agreed-upon percentage of their price at the time of purchase.

By employing this refined variant of Buffett-style value investing, Dr. Lee met his goal and remains not just one of the world's wealthiest men, but one of a handful of the mega-wealthy.

DEVELOPING NEW PRODUCTS BY LISTENING TO INVESTORS

According to Tom Sweeney, a managing director in Merrill Lynch's Private Banking and Investment group, a significant source of inspiration is often HNWIs themselves. Some of Merrill's best alternative investment ideas come from HNWIs through what he calls "reverse inquiry." Sweeney is seeing more and more reverse inquiry—a process by which a client need is so specific that the products virtually design themselves—around credit default swaps and foreign exchange, which lead them to customized solutions for HNWIs.

Credit default swaps (CDSs)—the most widely used credit derivatives—are designed to transfer the credit exposure of fixed income products between parties. Consider an ultra-HNWI who owns US$10 million worth of a five-year bond issued by a high-risk corporation. In order to manage the risk of losing money if the company defaults on its debt, the ultra-HNWI enters into a CDS. Though the protection payments reduce investment returns, the risk of loss in a default scenario is eliminated.

In the case of foreign exchange ("forex") investments, Sweeney has been getting an increasing number of requests from ultra-HNWIs with substantial overseas property and other assets about designing customized investment products to protect them against declines in the U.S. dollar. "There's an unending opportunity for creative solutions," Sweeney says.

Ideally, these new ideas for ultra-HNWIs can eventually be applied to lower bands of wealth. Less wealthy investors always want the products and services being offered to those just above them, and advisors have a vested interest in perfecting these new products and services and finding ways to bring them downstream in a cost-effective manner.

Michael Saadie of Australia's ANZ Private Bank notes that he's seen numerous instances of innovative financial products designed for the bank's ultra-HNW clients drifting down to the HNW band. A good example is a protected equity product originally designed to leverage a single stock exposure held by someone in the firm's top one hundred families. ANZ was able to take that structure and adapt it for the executive segment, whose members often have large equity positions in the companies for which they work. "We can roll out specific strategies for each segment and build specific product opportunities for each."

Developing Bespoke Products

John Barrett and Nancy Bello of a Merrill Lynch team based in New York recount the story of a wealthy client family that approached them for a solution to a problem many of us would like to have. They were holders of a US$50 million "long bond" that paid a comparatively low rate of interest. "It was a completely illiquid piece of paper," Barrett recalls, "which carried interest but whose value at any particular point in time was not necessarily easy to determine." Working with Merrill's Equity Derivatives Desk, Barrett and Bello began designing a completely customized derivative product with an option structure that Bello describes as "permitting the family to gain equity exposure without forgoing the security of the bond." The product combined a 60 percent link to the returns of the S&P, a 20 percent link to a basket of Asian equities, and a 20 percent link to European equities—a truly global synthetic product.

GRABBING HEADLINES: HEDGE FUNDS AND PRIVATE EQUITY

The two alternative investments that have grabbed the most headlines over the past decade have been 1) hedge funds and 2) private equity. Performance of these investments is listed in Figure 6.1.

Figure 6.1 - Greenwich-Van U.S. Hedge Fund Index vs. Thomson Financials'
U.S. Private Equity Performance Index, 2003–2005

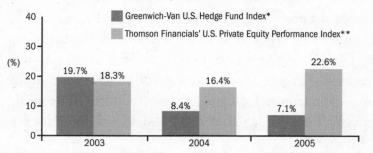

* The Greenwich-Van U.S. Hedge Fund Index is produced from the company's database of hedge funds, one of the world's largest collections of hedge fund data.
** Thomson Financials' U.S. Private Equity Performance Index is based on the latest quarterly statistics from Thomson Venture Economics' Private Equity Performance Database, and analyzes the cash flows and returns of over 1,814 U.S. venture capital and private equity partnerships with a combined capitalization of US$657 billion.

Hedge Funds

According to a report on the hedge fund industry recently issued by The Milken Institute,[4] the global hedge fund industry has experienced continuous and rapid growth (with the exception of a fleeting decline in the number of funds experienced during the first six months of 2006). From 1981 to June 2006, funds grew in number worldwide at an average annual rate of 30 percent. In a sure sign that the capitalist phenomenon of creative destruction is alive and well in the volatile hedge fund universe, as of June 2006, 100 funds with US$257 billion in total assets had exited the industry. Yet 6,445 funds remained in operation, commanding US$969 billion in total assets.

Net asset growth has expanded even more rapidly than the number of funds in absolute terms: hedge funds' average size has increased by more than 2,000 percent from 1981 to June 2006, from US$7 million to US$150 million. While funds with US$1 billion or more in assets account for only 3 percent of the total number of funds, they account for 35 percent of total assets. Conversely, those with US$100 million or less in total assets under management account for 70 percent of the number of funds but just 12 percent of total assets.

Of the 6,445 funds as of June 2006 slightly more than 50 percent, or 3,354, are domiciled in the United States. Of these, about half have their assets in the United States, with nearly all the remaining assets invested globally. Europe is second to the United States in terms of the number of domiciled funds, accounting for approximately 33 percent, or 2,153, of the total number of funds; of these only about 20 percent have their assets invested in Europe. The majority of the funds, 64 percent, have invested their assets globally. However, 76 percent of the funds with 75 percent of total fund assets still have their investments in U.S. dollar-denominated assets, regardless of where the assets are located.

---

4. James R. Barth, Tong Li, Triphon Phumiwasana and Glenn Yago, "Hedge Funds: Risks and Returns in Global Capital Markets," December 2006, The Milken Institute.

In the United States total hedge fund asset levels increased by 8 percent in the second quarter of 2007 to US$2.593 trillion, up from $2.401 trillion in the first quarter of 2007, according to the 2007 Hedge Fund Industry Asset Flow Report.[5] New allocations to the hedge fund industry increased total asset levels by an estimated US$339 billion through the first three quarters of 2007, but the reduction in assets from liquidations outpaced the increase from new fund launches in the second and third quarters.

Concern likewise abounded by year-end 2007 regarding the trendiness of certain hedge funds, a fashion only exacerbated by a tendency on the part of some managers to open funds simply to focus on a hot sector and sop up investment dollars. For instance, total assets in emerging market hedge funds reached an estimated US$299 billion in Q3 2007, an increase of US$48 billion through new allocations in the first nine months of the year. Emerging market equity focused fund assets are estimated at US$106.1 billion, widening the gap over EM debt fund assets estimated at US$77.3 billion.

Among other hot trends, China-focused hedge funds were the fastest growing sector of the hedge fund world in 2007, with total assets invested in hedge funds investing primarily in China reaching an estimated US$22.8 billion, up 89 percent over the previous year. Continuing on the hot theme, hedge funds investing in commodities and other natural resources grew to US$170 billion in assets under management in 2007, led by energy focused funds with US$133.8 billion. Energy sector hedge funds investing in equities returned 15.3 percent through September, but those investing directly in physical commodities did best during the volatile third quarter.

A key attraction of investing in distressed hedge funds for investors and advisors pursuing asset allocation and portfolio balancing strategies is that some—yet not all—hedge funds have remained historically uncorrelated to broad equity markets. As a result of this

5. Institutional Investor News and HedgeFund.net, "2008 Hedge Fund Asset Flows & Trends Report," November 29, 2007.

attractive non-correlation, distressed funds experienced double digit growth rates in 2007, attracting nearly US$10 billion in new allocations, bringing their grand total to just under US$200 billion.

Just as the hedge fund environment has changed, so too has the profile of the typical hedge fund investor: HNWI's have been largely supplanted by an influx of institutional investors. Some estimates suggest that today as much as 60 percent of hedge fund assets are institutional pension funds, endowments and other investment pools—which may over time alter hedge fund strategy, as these institutions tend to be more risk-averse and demand greater transparency.

At the same time, certain hedge fund strategies have become available even to registered investment companies. For instance, several dozen mutual funds now mimic certain hedge fund strategies although they remain subject to limitations not applicable to private funds. Essentially, these "long/short" mutual funds can bet either that a stock will rise or fall, while traditional funds only invest if managers believe a stock will rise.

Such funds are, however, limited in the amount of leverage they are permitted to employ and the degree to which they can be net short. In the first half of 2007, the broadest of all hedge fund strategies, long/short equity funds, attracted an estimated US$15.3 billion in new allocations. However, the majority of the total asset level rise came from fund performance, which added an additional US$39.3 billion, the second largest increase on record.

Funds of Funds

A popular hedge fund vehicle tailored to less wealthy investors[6] is the "fund of funds," which invests directly in traditional hedge funds rather than investing in individual securities. Total fund of fund assets, which are not double counted in the total industry figure, increased

---

6. Unless registered, individuals must be deemed qualified purchasers to invest in a fund of funds.

9.4 percent to an estimated US$1.250 trillion, including US$74.5 billion in new assets, the largest quarterly new allocation on record.[7]

Such entities held about US$500 billion at the end of September 2007, up 27 percent from a year earlier, according to Chicago-based Hedge Fund Research. Some investors who would be unable to invest in a hedge fund directly may be able to purchase shares of registered funds of hedge funds. In 2007, the hedge fund industry attracted a record US$194.5 billion in new capital, to US$1.87 trillion, according to HFR. Funds of funds saw net new inflows of US$59.2 billion for the year sending total assets invested in the category globally to US$498 billion.[8]

Private Equity

Although private equity (PE) is best known in its modern form pioneered by Kohlberg Kravis Roberts (KKR) in the early eighties, private equity's origins date back to 1901, after J.P. Morgan purchased the Carnegie Steel Company from Andrew Carnegie and Henry Phipps for US$480 million. With his share of the proceeds Phipps established the Bessemer Trust—the first "family office" in the U.S. A century later Bessemer continues to be a player in the private equity industry under Phipps' great grandson Stuart Janney.[9] Throughout much of its history, PE has largely been available only to institutional clients. PE firms—also known as "financial sponsors"—typically raise large pools of capital that they deploy to gain control of firms that they believe to be undervalued. PE investors typically control the firms they take over in hopes of significantly boosting their value—whether by installing superior management or aggressively cutting costs, including by performing controversial lay-offs and downsizing.

---

7. Ibid., James R. Barth, Tong Li, Triphon Phumiwasana and Glenn Yago, "Hedge Funds: Risks and Returns in Global Capital Markets," December 2006, The Milken Institute.

8. *Hedgeweek*, January 16, 2008.

9. www.bessamer.com

Financial sponsors do assume significant risks when they engineer such takeovers, but much of that risk is typically borne by the investors willing to place funds in their capital pools. With such significant sums involved, the game has historically been a preserve of large institutional clients. Yet many ultra-HNW individuals, eager to share in the often outsized profits of PE, are willing and eager participants in PE deals—obviously willing to shoulder the not-insignificant risk in the hope of gaining a not-insignificant reward.

According to Private Equity Intelligence, a London-based company that does research on the industry, private equity funds raised a record US$406 billion in 2006. More than 170 funds each holding US$1 billion or more in assets conducted US$475 billion in deals in 2006. While U.S. companies are leading the industry's continued expansion, Europe-based PE funds raised some £90 billion in 2006, up 25 percent from the prior year.[10] In yet another globalization trend, private equity firms from both continents are presently partnering to fund large trans-Atlantic deals.

The year 2007 also saw a number of prominent private equity firms moving to raise capital—somewhat ironically—in the public markets, beginning with the trend-setting US$4 billion IPO of Blackstone Group, followed by Carlyle Group's decision to sell a 7.5 percent share of itself to an investment group owned by the government of Abu Dhabi.

In 2006, PE fundraising reached new record levels, with data from Private Equity Intelligence showing that a total of 684 funds worldwide closed on US$432 billion in commitments. In the United States alone, PE firms raised US$215.4 billion, a record amount. This growth is best explained by the superior returns that these funds delivered in 2005. Indeed, the U.S. Private Equity Performance Index returned 22.6 percent in 2005, compared to 16.4 percent in 2004.

---

10. European Private Equity and Venture Capital Association (EVCA), www.evca.com.

While in 2006, leveraged buyout firms, a subset of PE focused on buying mature companies, raised about US$150 billion, half of that raised by only eight firms, including industry leaders Bain Capital, First Reserve Corp. and KKR. Yet, shortly thereafter, Blackstone Group announced that it was raising a US$20 billion fund, making it the largest PE fund ever. Blackstone won a bidding war to purchase Equity Office Properties Trust in a leveraged buyout for a record US$39 billion—a record soon topped by the proposed buyout of Dallas-based power producer TXU Corp. for US$45 billion. Yet by the second half of 2007, liquidity dried up and the psychology of the PE market abruptly shifted into reverse gear.

In fact, according to a late 2007 survey of more than 700 industry practitioners by *Financial News*,[11] "Private-equity firms expect markedly lower returns in 2008, with large buyout funds likely to suffer most," with three quarters of respondents reporting that they expected returns from large buyouts to be "somewhat lower" or "significantly lower" than last year, and with nearly a third of respondents expressing more pessimistic outlooks on their industry than at virtually any time during the first decade of the twenty-first century.

Because of the high investment minimums in the $5 million dollar range, PE, like hedge funds, has historically been available only to HNWIs. Unlike hedge funds, which may be subject to annual or quarterly redemptions, PE investors have typically been obliged to leave their money tied up for years in PE deals, making these extremely illiquid investments. BlackRock co-founder Ralph Schlosstein describes this illiquidity as the magic key to higher returns: "Giving up liquidity has been, at least up until recently, the most intelligent way to get good returns."

Schlosstein is convinced that PE's vaunted advantage is sustainable given the long-term nature of the investment and the growing costs of being a public company (thanks to legal fees and regulatory

---

11. "How Psychology Is Private Equity's Biggest Risk in 2008" *Financial News/Deal Journal,* December 17, 2007.

demands tied to Sarbanes-Oxley). According to Thomson Financial, the average annual returns on PE have topped 13 percent over the past two decades. Therefore, this vehicle should appeal to those with a long-term view and who are willing to trade liquidity for potential long-term gains.

Yet another key difference between PE and hedge funds is that hedge funds started with ultra-HNWIs and moved up to institutions and downstream to HNWIs. PE started with institutions and migrated down to ultra-HNWIs and now to HNWIs, with minimum investments in PE funds drifting from the millions down to US$250,000.

How far downstream PE may go remains to be seen. But yet another way that the mass affluent may be able to cash in on the PE wave is by purchasing shares in publicly owned PE companies.

In early 2007, Fortress Investment Group, which managed US$30 billion at the time, became the first PE and hedge fund manager to sell shares on U.S. markets. Indeed, while one of the hottest IPOs in years (closing the day up 68 percent from its initial price and making all five partners billionaires), by January 2008 Fortress shares dropped to record lows while the credit crunch continued to bite. By April 2007, Blackstone had also gone public like Fortress, but by January 2008, as private equity firms experienced unforseen challenges in obtaining financing and closing deals, Blackstone shares sank below US$20.

Despite such obstacles, Wall Street continues to flirt with methods of opening up the PE market to the less well heeled. PowerShares Listed Private Equity Portfolio, an exchange-traded fund launched in the fall of 2006, buys companies whose main business is investing in or lending money to private companies. There are also publicly traded "special purpose acquisition companies," or SPACs, that raise money specifically to purchase private companies. In 2006, SPAC IPOs raised US$2.6 billion, up from IPOs worth US$2 billion in 2005, according to Dealogic.

Another PE vehicle that might be of particular interest to HNWIs is a PE fund of funds, a format offered by several big Wall Street outfits including Lehman Brothers and Morgan Stanley. These funds pool money from HNWIs to invest in private equity funds. At about US$100,000, the investment minimum is lower than a typical single manager fund. Like investors in single PE manager funds, fund of funds investors should be prepared to hold onto their investment for years. That's because the PE investment life cycle—buy an ailing or undervalued company, turn it around, sell it—is rarely a rapid recipe.

One of the largest downsides of PE's outsized success is that the PE business has begun to draw the attention of regulators in the United States and Europe. A similar phenomenon occurred with hedge funds, much to the chagrin of the industry. In the U.S., the SEC at first tried to impose some rudimentary rules on hedge funds, such as requiring certain hedge funds with a specified number of investors to register with the Federal Securities Agency, a rule that was ultimately overturned by the courts. The SEC also voted to tighten anti-fraud rules regarding hedge funds.

FACING THE CHALLENGES AHEAD

Alternative assets provide a myriad of challenges and opportunities for HNWIs and their advisors. For HNWIs, certain alternative assets may provide a way to gain returns superior to the traditional stock and bond markets or to reduce a portfolio's overall volatility. They may also offer risk-distribution and mitigation characteristics, as many of these investments have historically demonstrated various levels of non-correlation both with other and with more conventional investments. This diversification has gained added importance during a period when stocks and bonds are more likely to rise and fall in unison.

But real risks remain. In a ceaseless search for the next new innovative product and higher returns, HNWIs must be prudent and vigilant against falling prey to the latest investment fad. They must bear in mind that past performance does not guarantee future returns and, as Mr. Fink of BlackRock warns, should be just as suspicious of unexpectedly high returns as they are dissatisfied with poor results. They must be willing but discriminating about tying up capital in an illiquid investment for several years, and never take management talent for granted. As sectors like hedge funds and private equity heat up and capital becomes plentiful, they should expect some marginally talented managers to jump into the fray. HNWIs, although tempted, may need to take a cautionary approach. They shouldn't jump in; rather, they should ensure that their risk appetite and time horizon can accommodate the anticipated returns.

To provide best-in-class advice to their clients about this complex and competitive investment category, wealth managers must be well-trained and highly knowledgeable as to the benefits and risks inherent in alternative investments and how to clearly explain their characteristics to clients; they need to offer a wide range of well-conceived alternative investment products, working seamlessly with their asset management and investment banking divisions and—if working in an open architecture or multimanager platform—with outside investment managers. Incentives must be well conceived and fully disclosed; and, finally, providers must improve transparency with HNWIs. As previously mentioned, consolidated reporting will become increasingly critical as HNWIs invest in a wider range of complex instruments manufactured by different parties. Responsiveness, communication and coordination are essential for alternative investments and form the basis of a good checklist for HNWIs to work from.

CHAPTER 7

Family Matters

FOSTERING FINANCIAL LITERACY, HNW STYLE

"At midnight," Johnson & Johnson heir Jamie Johnson observes in a bittersweet voice-over narration that kicks off his 2003 documentary *Born Rich*, "I'm going to inherit more money than most people can earn or spend in a lifetime. I've been waiting for this night for as long as I can remember. But the thing is, now that it's here, I'm not really sure what to make of it all."

For better or worse, he's not alone.

And almost surely for the better, help is on the way.

For parents and children alike, the challenges of preserving family wealth and passing it on to the next generation can be daunting, baffling and occasionally demoralizing. Self-made millionaires and billionaires worry (not without reason) that children born into great wealth will either personally lack, or fail to appreciate, the spunky entrepreneurial spirit that propelled their parents to their current position of status. Since their own self-esteem is often intimately connected with the cultivation of such a can-do spirit, it can be doubly difficult for them to empathize with their children's very different struggles with the issue.

Of course, if the offspring of every self-made entrepreneur were as entrepreneurial as the first in the line, multigenerational family wealth preservation would be a pretty straightforward affair. A case in point is that of the self-made millionaire Cornelius Vanderbilt, a one-time Staten Island ferry boat captain who upon his death in 1877 was worth more than US$100 million, making him the richest man of his generation in America. His son William, evidently something of a chip off the old block, doubled that fortune by the time of his own death in 1885. Yet less than a century later, when a family reunion at Vanderbilt University attracted more than one hundred and twenty descendents, not a single millionaire could be found among them. Obviously, somewhere after William the entrepreneurial spirit died out and was rarely, if ever, revived.

Though to be fair to the Vanderbilt family, a few wealthy Vanderbilts failed to attend that reunion, their saga of familial financial diminution nonetheless remains a dramatic example of how rapidly even the vastest family fortune can dissipate in a century, or over the span of four short generations. Of course, since family fortunes are typically divided among children, grandchildren and so on down the line, only the active presence of a major-league wealth creator among the immediate descendents is likely to keep the family fortune intact.

Yet math and time are only two reasons that family fortunes are so fragile; interpersonal dynamics also play a critical role. Apart from all the obvious causes—heirs feeling a sense of entitlement, or lacking the skills necessary to preserve the wealth they inherited or to create wealth of their own—the WM industry has traditionally offered a menu of solutions to these perennial dilemmas. One that appears to be rapidly falling out of favor is nevertheless adopted by many HNWIs by default, who with the very best of intentions attempt to shield their children as long as possible—often fruitlessly—from knowledge of the full extent of the family's wealth.

Such a strategy—akin to trying to keep Adam from taking a bite of the apple—can give rise to awkward scenes like one recounted by Jamie Johnson in *Born Rich*, in which he recalls a friend finding his father's name on the *Forbes* list of the wealthiest Americans and reading the citation aloud to his entire fifth grade class, much to his chagrin and embarrassment. Despite the fact that the information was obviously in the public domain, the ten-year-old Johnson heir experienced an odd sense of having committed a personal violation, as if he'd stumbled upon some awful skeleton in the family closet: "I felt I was learning a secret that I wasn't supposed to know."

Yet to wealthy parents hoping to raise "normal" kids, such discretion may seem like the better part of valor, as full disclosure might compromise their offspring's budding sense of self-worth or undermine any latent desire they might harbor to make it on their own in their own chosen field. On the other hand, trying to teach kids "the value of a buck" by avoiding facts often in plain sight may backfire if it leaves them woefully unprepared for the moment when they do in fact come into their handsome inheritance.

Stories abound of adults in their thirties and forties abruptly inheriting several million dollars and—after crying "Hallelujah"—quitting their jobs, making poor investments, or otherwise squandering the money in short order. It is widely assumed within the WM industry that such behaviors cannot necessarily be ascribed to lack of intelligence or character, but rather to the fact that the kids were ill-prepared, both by parents and society, to take on the responsibility of managing their own wealth for the future as opposed to the present.

"The real challenge," contends James Rothenberg, chairman and principal executive officer of Capital Research and Management, "is to try to educate children without their getting so focused on the amount of money that it obliterates their incentives. You need to talk to them and say, 'You must make your own way in the world and set this money aside.' You have lots of conversations like that."[1]

"If wealth is going to make them less passionate, that's a problem," insists BlackRock founder Larry Fink. "Personally, I don't care what they do, as long as they do it with passion." But the myriad difficulties surrounding open discussions of wealth between parents and children are often compounded by the fact that since every child

---

1. Interview with the authors.

is inherently different, it can be just about impossible for parents to adopt a unified approach to education, inheritance and other legacy issues. "It's not something you can read about in a book," Mr. Fink adds. "Each child interprets what I say differently. Each has different concerns and each has different probable financial outcomes based on the evolution of their careers."[2]

The methods and techniques a family adopts to advance their own wealth education as well as that of their children may vary dramatically depending upon circumstances. The greatest variance is perhaps produced by differences in the way the original family fortune was made. One HNWI, who for personal reasons prefers to remain anonymous, sympathetically observes that both of his immigrant parents worked hard all their lives and that his bartender father never made more than US$10,000 in any given year of his life, yet he contends that that apparent disadvantage is actually what encouraged his entrepreneurial spirit. "Each family's way of dealing with money is colored by the upbringing and childhood of the parents," he observes.

This particular HNWI remains anxious about the issue of motivating his children to be wealth creators as opposed to wealth dissipaters. He openly (if anonymously) agonizes over the possibility that if his children lack the motivational spur of poverty that he had as a child, they will never know the satisfaction of self-made success. In short, while many a HNWI wrestles with the possibility that their offspring will be irresponsible and squander their wealth, many more HNW parents display congruent angst about their kids squandering their lives and failing to live up to their full potential.

Patricia Angus, the managing director and head of Wealth Advisory Services at Shelterwood Financial Services (a multi-family office advisory firm providing investment management, family office, and business consulting services to high-net-worth families)

2. Interview with the authors.

observes that "even as recently as five or ten years ago, the common attitude was 'he's got to make a living.' But now many parents are starting to realize that maybe they don't; that the second generation's experience is just completely different."[3]

Yet another post-modern twist has been added to the centuries-old dilemma surrounding family financial privacy. Heightened transparency and greater disclosure of financial information required of companies with regard to compensation for senior executives has combined with a circus-like atmosphere of media attention paid to the lifestyles of the rich and famous, all of which has in some cases fatally compromised many a wealthy family's determined efforts to keep their financial lives out of the public domain. For example, keeping salaries and the value of stock options secret from today's tech savvy kids has become increasingly difficult—if not impossible. As T. Rowe Price CEO James Kennedy observes with disarming frankness, "All they've got to do is Google me."[4]

Yet the psychological upside of the financial information revolution is that it has forced a new level of frankness, openness and honesty about the complex issues surrounding wealth and its disconnects between generations. This occasionally means that, like it or not, some parents feel increasingly unfettered about being the bearers of (possibly) bad news. Some parents want children to understand in no uncertain terms that just because they are worth US$500 million, that doesn't mean the children are going to get it all—so they shouldn't plan on it. Warren Buffett famously summed up the view of many HNWIs when he said that he wanted to leave his children "enough to do anything, but not enough to do nothing."

Also, by loudly broadcasting the dysfunction found within some wealthy families, today's media may be doing at least a few wealthy families a real service by forcing some of the less salubrious aspects of

---

3. Interview with the authors.

4. Interview with the authors.

fortune and fame out into the open, confirming Chief Justice Louis Brandeis's celebrated admonition that "sunlight makes the best disinfectant." When the family feud between the son and grandson of New York society matriarch Brooke Astor broke out into the open in 2006, the whole sorry saga at least served as a cautionary tale regarding the potential divisiveness of money a bit more up-to-date than John Steinbeck's *The Pearl*. "So much more is being written than ten years ago, so there's an enormous amount of interest in working to prevent these problems and sustaining a healthy, productive family," notes Dr. Lee Hausner, a partner in IFF Advisors, a consulting firm created to enhance the human, intellectual, social and financial capitals of individual, family, foundation and non-profit clients.[5]

Doug Freeman, a prominent California-based tax attorney and Dr. Hausner's partner in IFF Advisors, advises the participants at the Merrill Lynch Financial Boot Camp at Wharton—and indirectly, all HNWI offspring. "Some people take pride in not knowing how much they're worth, believing they have more important things to think about than money. Others like to think that like celebrities and highly paid athletes, they can afford to hire business managers to keep track of all that stuff. But you can't plan where you want to go in your financial life if you don't know where you are. And you can't get there without a strategy. You're like a ship without a rudder."

Freeman drills his charges on the fundamentals: understanding how net worth—"the basic scorecard for financial condition"—is calculated, and "how by tracking it over time, you can measure the results of your financial decisions." He explains how the wealthy calculate and track their net worth, how to develop a cash flow statement, how to create a spending plan, and, in general, how to take control of their financial life. Maintaining a sense of control over these precious assets, Freeman insists, is not merely critical to preserving the wealth itself, but also their marriages, and above all, their sanity. Possessing great

5. Interview with the authors.

wealth in just about any form—but the inherited version perhaps most of all—can be inherently psychologically destabilizing.

Apart from information age wealth effects, there have been significant strides over the past quarter century around the science of behavioral finance. It is far more widely assumed today than in the past that many otherwise intelligent and rational people do not necessarily make rational decisions about and around money. In fact, deep-seated issues can lead people to make poor decisions over and over again. Danny Dunn, a Private Wealth Advisor with Merrill Lynch who is also a trained clinical psychologist, observes that "some investors are addicted to market timing and tend to chase returns to their detriment. I've had conversations with people whom I've told, 'Three times in a row you've missed a market turnaround,' which forces me to have to re-educate them once again about the dubious returns typically generated when trying to time the market."

Dunn also points out that on the less damaging end of the scale, a wealthy individual might become overly emotionally attached to a particular stock because their parents gave it to them, or because it was received from the sale of the family business. They might insist on not selling it even though for diversification purposes it's the correct course of action.

On the more damaging end of the scale is what Dunn describes as a "gap of thought"—or willful blindness to the emotionality of their decisions. The good news, however, is that as the concept of behavioral financial science has become better understood and accepted, the WM industry has reacted by adopting more subtle and nuanced positions regarding the emotional content of investment decisions.

Not surprisingly, Merrill Lynch, Citigroup, and JPMorgan Chase all provide versions of financial training for the children of HNWIs. Merrill Lynch's Financial Boot Camps provide lessons in portfolio management, asset allocation, transferring wealth to the next generation, estate planning and philanthropy management. Jeremy Arnold, head of Wealth Advisory at Barclays Wealth Management, advises that the best way to "work out your priorities…may be to sit down and write a family constitution. That requires a disciplined approach and might take six to nine months to do."[6] At the family office level, special consultants may be hired to lead family meetings and educational seminars. In all cases, the range of education is usually broad, encompassing investing basics as well as information on trusts, philanthropy and estate planning.

Franklin Templeton CEO Greg Johnson notes that marrying trusts, values and education can be a significant challenge. For him, the primary goal underlying his decision to set up trusts for his children was to find ways to encourage positive behavior over the long term. Tax considerations are often a lesser issue than parenting concerns. "How do you pass along values through the trust? That's where the wealth advisors can add huge value."[7]

PARTAKING IN VALUES RETREATS

Overwhelmingly, the greatest concern we hear from parents is "How can we prepare our children for wealth, and what impact will the inheritance have on my child?" says Stacy Allred, a vice president in Merrill Lynch's PBIG. Among the questions she typically fields from wealthy clients:

- How should I balance my assets between retaining what I need and sharing with my family and community?

- How can we make sure our children are informed about the family wealth, yet not give away too many details?

- How can we communicate with multiple generations while ensuring that each age group finds out just what it needs to know—and on their individual wavelengths?

---

6. Charles Batchelor, "Family Dynasties," *Financial Times*, July 8, 2007.

7. Interview with the authors.

• How can we set up a transfer of wealth so that future generations can benefit but also maintain the values so important to us?[8]

According to Karen Klein, a director in Merrill Lynch's Client Relationship Group, the first step toward achieving clarity around these legacy issues is to focus on creating a values-based multigeneration financial plan. PBIG assists clients through this process by inviting them to six-hour-long "values retreats" designed to help them get to the heart of the values that parents hope to pass on to their children, and possibly even to the generations to come.

Values retreats begin with a questionnaire that focuses on the emotional challenges and opportunities of possessing wealth. "It's like peeling back the layers of an onion to get to the core values of the family and then building a framework where they can use their shared values around earning, spending, saving and sharing of money to make financial decisions," observes Ms. Allred. At the end of the retreat, families are able to clarify their values and start the process of clearly communicating them to their children.

Such careful planning can help parents solve the often thorny riddle of when to begin transferring assets to heirs—and how much to give. If having motivated and productive children is a key goal, the family may collectively decide that delaying the transfer can be a powerful motivating tool. "When significant amounts are transferred during career-building years," comments Dr. Lee Hausner, "career building often stops. If adults in their twenties can make as much interest on the distribution from trusts as they can earn in their first job, there may be a temptation to choose not to become fully dedicated to building a career and to 'play' instead."

Some families are even turning to that tried-and-true staple of corporate life, the mission statement, for help in clarifying their

---

8. Merrill Lynch Private Banking and Investment Group, "Building Your Legacy: From One Generation to the Next, Families Can Pass On Wealth—and Values—as a Means of Inspiration"; The White Papers: Quarterly Intelligence for Informed Investors, Winter 2006.

financial-moral legacy goals. Charles Collier, Senior Philanthropic Adviser at Harvard University, observes that "the best result of this process is a sense of togetherness around a shared dream."

As an example of one family's mission statement, Collier offers the following partial citation:

> As members of this family we honor and respect our family's civic, social and corporate heritage by supporting our communities each in our own way, guided by principles of generosity, honesty and hard work to improve our lives and the lives of others. We shall act with care and integrity to inspire trust within our family and within our communities.[9]

ENABLING THE NEXT GENERATION OF WEALTHY THROUGH PEER NETWORKING

Peer networking may also provide useful knowledge. Simply talking with people in similar circumstances and sharing ideas can be invaluable. Some peer networks, such as TIGER 21, are focused on sharing investment insights, while others have a broader mission and are more geared to bringing HNW families together to discuss a variety of financial and non-financial topics. CCC Alliance is a group of successful families and individuals that collaborate regularly on wealth management and family office matters, drawing on a deep network to invite leading experts to speak on wealth management topics, including investments, philanthropy and family governance. Private investor George Russell's Threshold Group asks applicants to fill out detailed questionnaires on topics including family values. New York-based HNW peer network Synergos focuses on philanthropy. The Chicago-based Family Office Exchange runs a network of 350 families across twenty-two countries who meet annually. According to *Newsweek*, "the group's most popular service is its Listserv, where families query each other on things like estate planning and buying private jets."[10]

---

9. Interview with the authors.

10. Emily Vencat and Ginanne Brownell, "Ah, the Secluded Life; How the Superrich Are Finding New Ways to Set Themselves Apart," *Newsweek*. October 12, 2007.

Not surprisingly, members of the younger generation are often the more likely to join these peer groups, as HNW children often feel specific frustrations around their or their parents' wealth but may feel reluctant to express them among their non-wealthy peers, who might feel more resentful than sympathetic. As one advisor dryly comments in somewhat snide reference to the rising popularity of these peer networks. "The offspring can feel free to whine because everyone else at the table is in the same situation."

Albert Lee, Merrill Lynch's CEO for Taiwan and a veteran advisor to the HNW crowd of Asia, observes that he has seen peer networks spring up of their own accord from the educational seminars that Merrill Lynch has held for Asian HNWIs in Hong Kong. "These can serve as excellent networks of business contacts for young HNWIs more interested in creating their own wealth than simply living off their parents' accumulated assets."

Ultimately, every wealthy family must use education to develop its own intellectual wealth capital and partner it with financial capital. It has become more widely recognized that the WM industry needs to view wealth education in a more holistic way, and that its primary purpose is to enhance the well-being of the family members at every level—beyond just helping everyone to benefit from better or more stable financial returns.

The lesson for HNWIs is that educating their children around wealth is essential—and the result is more likely to be a family fortune that could endure for decades and perhaps even centuries. Ultimately, fears that knowledge of wealth will de-motivate children must be balanced with the need to prepare them for that wealth. What's more, hiding the truth of a family's circumstance rarely works for the long term, and can be counterproductive if children grow frustrated or resentful in the belief they are being kept in the dark.

PREPARING FOR GREAT WEALTH TRANSFER

In the coming decades, baby boomers in the United States are expected to both receive and bequeath huge sums of money, a transfer of assets that by 2053 is conservatively estimated to be US$41 trillion in the United States alone. In some regions of the world, shrinking populations will concentrate wealth. In China, it will not be uncommon for a set of four grandparents to share just one grandchild.

Make no mistake—the bulk of this wealth transfer is likely to go to family members. Even with the recent headlines surrounding the rise of philanthropy and the high-profile examples of Bill Gates and Warren Buffett, the tendency on the part of parents to leave their children the greater part of their assets is so well established in most cultures, if not in human nature at large, that prevailing patterns are unlikely to change dramatically within the foreseeable future. The 2006 *WWR* found that 84 percent of HNWIs are married, 83 percent of HNWIs have children, and that more than three-quarters of HNWIs' wealth is anticipated to go directly to their children.

Wealth transfer and estate planning, in other words, will be in high demand for the foreseeable future and there is much work for wealth managers to do. According to a survey of relationship managers for the 2007 *WWR*, 56 percent of HNWIs are considered inadequately prepared, while only 2 percent of HNWIs are believed to be completely prepared. Therefore, as individuals are planning their future, putting FAs to work on these topics now will begin to address future issues.

CREATING A WEALTH TRANSFER PLAN

According to IFF Financial Advisors, a number of key questions need to be answered by every wealthy family preparing for generational wealth transfer:

1. What are my goals for family members, and what are the resources available or needed?

2. What will be the impact of the planning I do?

3. How should funds be distributed while my child is still a minor or in school?

4. How should funds be distributed once my child is an adult and completes (or quits) school at a given age?

5. When should I start distributing principal outright to the child?

6. Who should be responsible for managing the trust assets of my children? (Parents? Siblings? Business associate? Friend? Bank? Financial advisor?)

7. Should I permit my child to become a trustee of his or her own trust?

8. Should I distribute my estate equally amongst my children?

9. How do I insulate my estate from risk—legal, financial, death, illness, incapacity, disasters and accidents?

10. Do I create a wealth management or distribution plan (either through a will or trust)?

Preparing to seize this opportunity, FAs must recognize that they are usually not the top choice among HNWIs for wealth transfer guidance. Trust and estate attorneys, tax attorneys and accountants have traditionally been the most sought-after wealth transfer specialists.

Merrill Lynch has developed dedicated awareness workshops on the subject of wealth transfer that have been implemented in all major regions—Latin America, North America, Europe and Asia-Pacific. Such seminars typically serve a dual purpose: 1) to build trust between HNWIs and FAs on the issues of wealth transfer and 2) to help advisors build rapport with the next generation, a critical step to retaining the family relationship after the transfer occurs.

Retention of inheritor accounts requires pulling off the hat trick of precisely balancing investment needs and motivations of both the current HNWI and the benefactor—not to mention the financial realities of the bank, which cannot afford to extend golden glove service to every heir. Michael Saadie's ANZ Bank segments clients into five categories:

• The top one hundred families;

• Business owners;

• Large investors/retirees

• Executives of the top one hundred listed companies;

• Professionals (partners of legal and accounting firms and medical).

In each case, the children of those clients are handled differently. If a child is a member of the firm's top one hundred families, all financial issues are handled by the private bank, no questions asked. In the case of an executive's son graduating from college, on the other hand, private bankers will arrange an introduction for the son with other financial professionals at ANZ outside the private bank.

To retain inheritors' business, advisors must prove to young HNWIs that they are not wedded to an "old school" investment philosophy and WM strategy. Financial advisors must realize that many younger HNWIs will approach investing differently and therefore have WM needs that may be dramatically different from those of their parents.

For example, the next generation of HNWIs will have a very international outlook, far more so than the previous generation. Advances in communication and international travel have become easier, spurring this trend. Family members, even those involved in the same business, live and work further away from one another, perhaps with residences in multiple jurisdictions. There's been a sort of HNWI diaspora that requires HNWIs and their advisors to manage wealth not just in relation to where they own their primary residence, but everywhere they do business, own homes, have family, or travel.

The next generation is already more technologically savvy and plugged in than their parents. This contributes to a more sophisticated outlook but also a greater degree of impatience with the level of service they are currently accorded by their advisors.

The next generation is less likely to be bound by tradition or custom to their parents' financial firms—whether a traditional private bank, a boutique, or a private-banking boutique incorporated within a firm with global reach.

Edward Bernard, a vice chairman at T. Rowe Price who joined the firm in 1988 and has been the director of the investment services division since 2006, asserts that the children of today's HNWIs are "growing up in a global context." He predicts that in the United States, more young professionals will begin to spend some of their career overseas, as has been the case for years among the British and Australians.

The Internet also de-emphasizes national boundaries, Mr. Bernard says, or at least makes them seem much less relevant when it comes to information gathering and investing. "A URL is a URL no matter what country the company is in. Over time, investment behavior will reflect this. If, in your daily life, you think globally, then your investment behavior will be global."[11]

RECOGNIZING REGIONAL DIVERSITY

The 2006 *WWR* found that 83 percent of wealth managers said inheritors will want increased exposure to international investments, and 76 percent said that inheritors will require the ability to be served in multiple geographies—a big potential advantage for global institutions. Underscoring this international trend is that 19 percent of HNWIs have children living abroad, making the international

11. Interview with the authors.

transfer and management of assets a certainty for a substantial number of future HNWIs.

These younger, more risk tolerant, globe-trotting HNWIs will force advisors and the institutions for which they work to have a global, integrated view, capable of fluid communication and coordination. The ability to tap several markets with a consolidated service model, rather than with multiple relationship managers, will be vital. It also seems likely these younger HNWIs will be more engaged in the investment process, pushing advisors to expand and innovate around international product offerings.

Victor Tan, market director of wealth management for Merrill Lynch in Hong Kong, notes that in Asia he's observed a growing trend: scions of wealthy businesspeople taking positions outside the family firm to gain a broader experience and perspective before returning home to roost. This career path gives the children a chance to prove themselves outside the safe haven of the family business and can boost confidence and decision-making skills. The net effect is that the children of wealth entrepreneurs are, in general, no longer having a difficult time assuming control of the family business; they have become more sophisticated and prepared, and these challenges may become opportunities, altering their investment approach to adopt a more fundamentally global perspective.

Darcie Burk, the Miami-based head of wealth management for Latin America at Merrill Lynch, says that wealth managers are closely observing the changes occurring in the southern hemisphere and are getting a hint of what's to come. The generational transfer is already under way there, with younger HNWIs, many of whom have received MBAs in North America and Europe and have returned with a far more aggressive approach to investing than their parents, starting to actively manage the family wealth. They're more comfortable with equities—an asset class shunned by their parents—and are generally more sophisticated and open-minded when it comes to innovative products.

Ten years ago, Ms. Burk notes, most Latin American HNWIs focused on preserving capital and were willing to accept lower returns in exchange for that guarantee of principal. That's changing fast as the next generation seeks to tap into the equity markets and structured products that contain some risk to principal but offer much more potential upside. Wealth *accumulation*, as opposed to *preservation*, has become their explicit objective.

APPRECIATING GENDER DIFFERENCES

To a significant degree, the gender differential trends shaping WM today reflect the specific priorities of wealthy women, from holistic management to an emphasis on education. "Education is absolutely critical," says Alyssa Moeder, a private wealth advisor at Merrill Lynch. "Women are willing to invest more time up front to understand what the financial advisor is doing, and once they get that comfort level they're usually willing to follow the advice pretty closely."

The profound influence of women on WM as a whole should not come as a huge surprise. According to TrendSight Group, by 2010, U.S. women will control 60 percent of the nation's wealth, or a whopping US$22 trillion. Meanwhile, women are starting new businesses at twice the rate of men (10 million business owners in the United States today are women), and 90 percent of women will have sole charge of their assets sometime in their lifetime. Little wonder their priorities are becoming the priorities of the industry.

While the percentages of wealthy women are highest in North America and Europe, their numbers are growing in Asia. According to the *2007 Asia-Pacific Wealth Report*, women account for 43 percent of HNWIs in Taiwan, 38 percent in China, 34 percent in Hong Kong, 27 percent in Japan, 22 percent in Singapore, 22 percent in Indonesia, 19 percent in South Korea, 15 percent in Australia and 12 percent in India.

Ms. Moeder notes that women are strong drivers behind the HWM trend. They tend to view wealth as a mechanism to achieve broader objectives and want their advisors to adopt a broad view of their entire personal, family and household circumstances. It's not so much that they want different products and services than men; they want a different service model. First, they want their lives made easier and so, in general, they are more open to a single, primary financial relationship than men; and, second, they value networking and finding various sorts of expertise through that primary relationship.

While women do not necessarily want different products and services than men do, it is true that their challenges are slightly different. The average age of widowhood in the United States is fifty-five, and women live an average of 5.4 years longer than men. So not only must women plan wisely so their investments can support their longer lives, they must also be prepared to manage their finances on their own and, more and more often, manage those of their parents, as well.

In light of the intensity of their drive to become more financially sophisticated, advisors may initially spend more time with a female HNWI than a male HNWI to get the relationship off the ground. The time spent may be well worth it, however, if it generates a more prolonged and stable advisor–client relationship. As is the case with many relationships, as a rule "women are less fickle than men, and are less concerned with the next hot thing," Ms. Moeder observes at the risk of stereotyping behavior. "It's a stereotype," she says, "but it's a correct stereotype. Women are more relationship-oriented; they value communication more."

Women also have a tendency to gather expertise from as many sources as possible. They want access to other individuals and institutions. In the past, the universe of advisors to a wealthy woman might be a financial advisor, an accountant and an attorney. But today women often seek out art experts, philanthropy advisors, consultants to help with their children's educations and entrance into colleges, even psychotherapists. "Women love to share best practices. They like to hear what others are experiencing."

PRESERVING THE FAMILY LEGACY

In general, wealthy families are increasingly conscious that the HWM concept permeates everything that they do relating to the issue of family and intergenerational wealth transfer. If wealthy families are doing a better job of educating their children as to the long-term impact of wealth on their lives—or are turning the job over to surrogates who are imparting such knowledge—clients are also gaining a new degree of sophistication regarding the rights, responsibilities, blessings and challenges enjoyed and suffered by the world's burgeoning HNW and ultra-HNW population. In no area of wealth management are these trends so pronounced as in the field of philanthropy, where issues of values, legacy, morality, social service and self-interest all come into play in a way that bears profound implications for the long-term evolution of our shared society.

CHAPTER 8

The New Philanthropy: Proactive Involvement

GIVING WITH PURPOSE

In 2007, the *WWR* detailed philanthropic donations for the first time, documenting a record US$285 billion donated to charities by high-net-worth individuals—an impressive sum, to be sure, yet one totaling a mere 1 percent of HNWIs' total US$37.2 trillion net worth. Amidst this comparative charitable cornucopia, the evidence was overwhelming that a new breed of high-net-worth benefactors, the vast majority of whom were self-made entrepreneurs, were eager to make their mark on philanthropy while demanding an unprecedented degree of accountability from grant recipients. Assets managed in donor-advised funds—which permit wealthy individuals to direct tax-free donations to good causes—rose 50 percent to US $4.9 billion from 2003 to 2005. Of this, a significant factor was a marked increase in the percentage of people worth more than US$30 million (17 percent) who donated more than 10 percent of their total wealth. (This trend was further confirmed by the *Chronicle of Philanthropy*, which noted that twenty-one Americans gave away at least $100 million last year, compared with eleven in 2005.) By 2006, this wave of contemporary philanthropists was giving record amounts to charities while insisting upon seeing "their money used wisely."[1]

---

1. Mark Cobley and Mike Foster, "Philanthropy Becomes an Investment Class," *Financial News*, July 16, 2007.

PHILANTHROPY LESSONS FROM ONE OF GREAT BRITAIN'S WEALTHIEST MEN

A leading light amongst this new class of "activist-entrepreneurs," the Duke of Westminster (who is not only one of Britain's wealthiest men but a lifelong and fiercely devoted philanthropist) comments approvingly on the relatively recent phenomenon that "donors on the whole are displaying a far greater interest in truly comprehending the uses to which their time, money and human as well as financial capital are being put."

Speaking from a modest office off a high-ceilinged corridor at the Eaton Estate Office, hub of an 11,000-acre estate near Chester in England that has been in the Grosvenor family since the late fifteenth century, the Duke is adamant about being characterized not as a "philanthropist" but as an individual privately yet intensely devoted to forging new and productive links between private industry and public social improvement.

The term that probably best describes his role as inspiration and motivator among this new breed of activist-entrepreneur-philanthropists is "social entrepreneur," although he is far too modest to apply the term to himself. His abiding interest in combining the best aspects of business and philanthropy is reflected in his description of his own efforts as "individual Corporate Social Responsibility." Today's heightened emphasis on accountability and efficiency of aid delivery can only be to the good, the Duke asserts, since this more energetic and engaged philanthropic style tends to make social work a more useful and productive force for the good of the entire society.

The origins of the vast and rapidly expanding business interests that form the Grosvenor Estate today are widely believed to be founded on the legacy of Gilbert Le Grosveneur—a name that loosely translates as "Chief Huntsman"—who loyally served William the Conqueror as Master of the Hunt. The Eaton Estate came into the family when Ralph Grosvenor married Joan, heiress to the estate, during the reign of Henry VI. But the bulk of the family fortune is the happy result of the Grosvenor ancestors' fortuitous ownership, timely development and long-term management of 300 acres of land it owned in London, which it smartly transformed into and maintains today as the fashionable neighborhoods of Mayfair and Belgravia.

Gerald Cavendish Grosvenor, the present-day and sixth Duke of Westminster, has famously followed in the philanthropic footsteps of his illustrious ancestor the first Duke of Westminister. In 1874, Hugh Lupus Grosvenor was elevated by Queen Victoria from Marquess of Westminster to Duke (the pinnacle of the peerage) in royal recognition of his outstanding career as one of his nation's non-profit pioneers. The First Duke had spent a great deal of time improving the lives of the less fortunate.

Today's Duke, following precedents set by previous generations of his lineage, artfully combines a tripartite role by being 1) one of the richest men in England, 2) a loyal soldier to the Crown (he has served as Assistant Chief of Defence Staff [Reserves and Cadets]) and 3) a devoted philanthropist. Unlike his ancestors, however, this twenty-first century aristocrat combines a deep personal commitment to philanthropy with an equally deep personal commitment to commerce. He not only serves as chairman of the Grosvenor Trustees, the shareholders of an extensive real estate investment and development portfolio in Britain, Ireland, Canada, the United States and Asia, but he also serves on the boards of dozens of charities, which he actively encourages to govern themselves along business lines.

While exuding a sense of relief at this trend toward greater accountability and rationality in the non-profit sector, the Duke ascribes the recent rise of philanthropy across the globe to the chronic inability on the part of municipal, regional and national governments (as well as multilateral institutions like the UN and the World Bank) to solve the world's often daunting social problems. Among the long litany of social woes on which he has personally expended significant amounts of social, human and personal financial capital are service charities (that benefit those who have served in Her Majesty's armed forces and their families), deeply embedded urban and rural poverty, violent crime, domestic child abuse, drug addition and substance abuse. The Duke personally applauds the recent entry into philanthropy of a number of self-made billionaire and millionaire philanthropists, because only when philanthropy is openly challenged by business to be more productive and more transparent does it stand a chance of evolving itself for the twenty-first century.

The most positive aspect of this development, Westminster believes, is that a welcome infusion of business ideas and ideals has revolutionized the hidebound world of philanthropy, leaving it far better prepared than it might otherwise have been to tackle tough problems in a new century that promises to be infinitely more complex than any before it. "Today's philanthropists," the Duke approvingly notes, "are able to take a long-term view, which governments either will not or cannot take. They have been able to both plan and act with an efficiency, agility and attention to issues of accountability that the State has either overlooked or been unwilling or incapable of addressing."

As recently as thirty years ago, he recalls, "too many philanthropists were content to simply write a check and be done with it." Not today, when taking a hands-off approach simply won't wash, in part because it does a disservice to the cause of charity and philanthropy itself. A prime example of this trend is the tough-love approach he took when asked to support a U.K.-based children's charity. Before providing any financial assistance of his own, he joined a chorus of voices insisting that the charity sell off its valuable headquarters property in London, thereby releasing considerable pent-up value that could be devoted to the needs of the children served by the charity.

A related and equally positive development, the Duke avers, is that he and a fair number of his fellow philanthropists, many with years of organizational training and experience under their belts, are offering—occasionally in lieu of but more often in addition to financial support—management and marketing expertise.

As for tendering advice to prospective philanthropists, the Duke suggests that above all, "people should support charities that mean something to them personally." Although, as a rule, he is not big on medical charities, he supports a national arthritis charity because his mother, a talented pianist, was personally afflicted by the disease. The Duke is a strong believer in private firms supporting their employees' philanthropic pursuits, approvingly citing as an example that of a property surveyor within the Grosvenor property group, who looks after the St. John Ambulance charity's property portfolio in his spare time because the charity could not afford to hire its own land surveyor. "Businesses need to take the lead in encouraging charitable work by their employees," Grosvenor insists, contending that HR departments should be made aware of what employees are doing in the philanthropic arenas and taking concrete steps to recognize such activities' value to the firm.

COMMITTING FUNDS AND DEMANDING ACCOUNTABILITY

The wealthiest of individuals, some of whom have never before shared their wealth with charitable organizations, are starting to do so in the current Age of Wealth. Many are demanding, contrary to custom, a more direct say in how the funds they contribute are allocated.

In 2007, even Carlos Slim Helu of Mexico, whose estimated US$68 billion telecom fortune is believed to have made him the world's richest man, reversed a previously poor philanthropic track record by announcing an admittedly belated commitment to set up a philanthropic foundation.

As one account notes:

> *In Europe, Jean Pierre Cuoni, chairman of private bank EFG International, has become a prominent supporter of The Right to Play, an organization that promotes sport and play programs for impoverished children in the emerging world. Belgian industrialist Baron Guy Ullens has been selling part of his art collection to fund humanitarian work, including an orphanage in Katmandu. Anil Agarwal, chairman of Vedanta Resources is putting US$1bn into an Indian university modeled on Harvard. [Activist-investor] Chris Hohn this month confirmed that his hedge fund, The Children's Investment Fund, donated US$460m to charity last year. Peter Cruddas, founder of finance group CMC Markets, plans to give US$200m to charities helping young people.[2]*

Many observers have noted that the trend hailed by Westminster and others of the billionaire band recalls the Victorian era of the present Duke's ancestor, the First Duke of Westminster, when vast sums generated by industry and trade were concentrated in the hands of a select few and state support for the disadvantaged was limited to nonexistent. This new breed of activist-philanthropists is ensuring that all funds dispensed for virtually any cause come with strings attached—and that these strings are, if not stronger than steel, at least as binding as polyester or nylon.

The Indianapolis-based Center for Excellence in Higher Education, an initiative established by a number of major philanthropists (including Home Depot co-founder Bernard Marcus and legendary investor Sir John Templeton), is dedicated to insuring that donors can attach legally enforceable conditions to their gifts, sharply curbing educational institutions' discretion in spending donors' contributions.[3]

COMPARING REGIONAL DIFFERENCES

According to a 2006 study by the Johns Hopkins Comparative Nonprofit Sector Project, the United States led all countries by giving

---

2. Ibid.

3. John Hechinger, "Big-Money Donors Move to Curb Colleges' Discretion to Spend Gifts," *Wall Street Journal*, September 18, 2007.

1.85 percent of total GDP from 1995 to 2002. By comparison, the U.K. gave 0.84 percent, Brazil 0.29 percent, Japan 0.22 percent, South Korea 0.18 percent and Germany 0.13 percent. In 2006, according to the 2007 *WWR*, North American HNWIs donated 7.6 percent of their portfolios, a more than 20 percent increase from 2005 levels, a boost largely ascribable to "a heightened sense of social responsibility among North American HNWIs."[4] By contrast, philanthropists in the Asia-Pacific region and the Middle East donated approximately 11.8 percent and 7.7 percent, respectively of their portfolios to charity. European HNWIs scored next to lowest on the regional list, allocating a mere 4.6 percent of their wealth to charity, while Latin America formed the philanthropic caboose, with HNWIs from the region giving approximately 3 percent to charitable causes.

In the United States, two big philanthropic themes have emerged: one is so-called "venture philanthropy" and the other is "giving while living." While clearly distinct trends, both share a number of key drivers, among them the fact that so many HNWIs are comparatively young by historical standards, and have ample money to give at a relatively tender age. Other self-made philanthropists are applying some of the principles that made them successful in business to their philanthropic pursuits, and have the time and energy to help actively drive—and in some cases define or refine—their charities' missions.

GLOBAL TREND 1: THE RISE OF VENTURE PHILANTHROPY

In 2006, the evolving concept of "venture philanthropy" was given a powerful boost when Bangladesh-based Muhammad Yunus was awarded the Nobel Peace Prize for his innovative method of alleviating poverty among the world's most desperately poor people. Through his Grameen Bank, Mr. Yunus has issued seven million "micro-loans" since 1983 to start small village businesses. The loans

---

4. Northern Trust, "Wealth In America 2007," January 2007; Capgemini Analysis.

are usually for \$100 or less, often to women, and there is a 99 percent repayment rate. What can \$100 do? A lot, it turns out, in countries where many people live on less than \$1 a day.

Although Yunus chafes at the term "venture philanthropy," he is willing to acknowledge its stated goal of eradicating poverty and evolving a more equitable society by advancing micro-loans mainly to poor rural women as a means of creating a culture of accountability and sustainability in regions of the world and swathes of society where such notions had never taken root.

Some observers of the foundation scene have gone so far as to claim that Yunus has thereby given rise to an entirely new institutional category—that of a "for-profit charity," a new hybrid entity forged by the marriage (or blurring of boundaries between) three traditional institutional categories: 1) government, 2) the for-profit sector, and 3) the not-for-profit sector.

Yet another comparatively recent trend in philanthropy is for non-profit organizations frequently founded by self-made entrepreneurs to blur the traditional boundaries between charity and commerce. In 2004, eBay co-founder Pierre Omidyar founded the Omidyar Network, which makes investments in both for-profit and non-profit ventures. He has, for instance, provided US\$4 million to the Grameen Foundation, and has supported Unitus, which develops microfinance institutions, and the International Development Law Institute, which develops law to support the growth of the microfinance industry. Last year he donated US\$100 million to his alma mater, Tufts University, stipulating that the funds be used exclusively to make micro-loans.

Yet another example of the increasingly blurry boundary between charity and commerce is Google.org, a for-profit entity founded last year to conduct charitable operations for Google. By forgoing non-profit status, Google can donate to what it believes are worthy causes and not worry about whether IRS considers it a charity. Richard Branson, for his part, is investing US\$3 billion of his personal fortune in the clean energy industry through what he calls his "hybrid venture capital unit," while also looking to tackle big issues like poverty and climate change. In an interview with the *New York Times*, Mr. Branson characterized the hybrid concept this way: "It may be giving, it may not be giving, depending on how things turn out…Although it's very risky capital, hopefully it won't be wasted."

In a speech delivered at the Tech Museum of Innovation in San Jose in early 2007, Microsoft chairman Bill Gates ventured that, "No foundation alone can solve the health problems of the developing world. We need businesses and governments as partners. That means we need to get these issues on the political agenda, and we need to tap into market forces to get the private sector involved. It means we all need to embrace a broader definition of responsibility. We must be willing to look at the failure of collective action and see how we can change it. Because these problems are so complex, government has to be involved in solving them."

Another prominent case in point is that of James Simons, the billionaire founder of Stony Brook, Long Island-based hedge fund Renaissance Technologies, whose Simons Foundation has committed US$38 million to autism research and has announced plans to spend another US$100 million in what is fast becoming the largest private investment in autism research in the world. While the outright sums are dwarfed by the billions donated to medical research by Bill Gates and Warren Buffett, the extraordinary degree of control that Simons personally asserts over where and how his money is spent makes his a case of venture philanthropy taken to the next level.

Simons, whose daughter suffers from autism, has provided DNA from his own family for research purposes, provided assistance in helping solve key mathematical research problems, and responded positively to a request from MIT (on whose board Simons serves) for brain research funding by expressly stipulating that the project focus exclusively on autism and that it put scientists of his selection on the payroll. And while some not-for-profit officials positively bristle at the idea of relinquishing even a degree of programmatic control to activist-donors, most realists are inclined to acknowledge that more emotionally engaged donors are likely to remain more deeply committed over the long haul.

So what does all this mean? The main driver behind this growing trend—as confirmed by the Duke of Westminster and others of his wealth and class, as well as self-made entrepreneurs who feel that the old ways of giving just aren't working—is talk about venture philanthropy and for-profit charity as a new form of sustainability, aimed at insuring that once the original infusion of capital is spent, a project can continue and remain self-sustaining.

Examples of this trend are the Acumen Fund, a non-profit charity that invests in companies that tackle global poverty and aims to provide the high-level management and entrepreneurial expertise more commonly found at venture capital funds. It has renounced making conventional grants in favor of loans and equity investments, finding that these create greater clarity of expectations and instill financial discipline. A recent success story is the Fund's substantial investment in International Development Enterprises in India, which manufactures drip irrigation systems that it sells to poor farmers for less than US$30. Acumen and others like it are non-profit organizations that engage in profit-making activities in order to decrease reliance on traditional, passive donors. Trappist monasteries in Belgium and elsewhere in Europe, which actively market their sought-after, original micro-brews and other spirits, represent the originals from whom these present-day models of fund-generating philanthropies derive.

According to Jacques Attali of PlaNet Finance, this more muscular and activist approach is especially well suited for today's young and wealthy entrepreneurs, because at a fundamental level, entrepreneur/philanthropists find the idea of funding fellow aspiring entrepreneurs around the globe to get themselves off the ground emotionally appealing, as to do so bestows a sense of connection, almost a kinship, or "an intertwining of interests."

GLOBAL TREND 2: GIVING WHILE LIVING

Both John D. Rockefeller Sr. and Andrew Carnegie famously gave away substantial proportions of their vast fortunes during their lifetimes. But Warren Buffett's 2006 decision to donate some US$37 billion of his fortune—US$31 billion to the Bill and Melinda Gates Foundation, and another US$6 billion to four family foundations—renewed interest in this approach among many HNWIs who in the past might have done most of their charitable giving through bequests at their death.

Not only tycoons and titans but other celebrities have gotten into the act. Of course, U2's Bono is probably the most widely known and admired entertainer-philanthropist, but actress Angelina Jolie is quickly becoming one of the most high-profile humanitarians of our time, putting her money and persona where her mouth is. Not only is she an ambassador for the United Nations, and an adoptive mother to children from underdeveloped nations, she is also responsible for building schools and improving communities. She takes her show on the road, both overseas and to Washington, where she regularly uses her star power to lobby for her favorite charities. "As much as I would love to never have to visit Washington, that's the way to move the ball," was how she put it to *Forbes*. Since giving birth to Shiloh, her third child, in May 2006—she adopted son Maddox in 2002 from Cambodia and daughter Zahara in 2005 from Ethiopia—she has adopted a child from Vietnam and promises more cameos on the Hill. "The more children I have, the more I feel it's my duty."

In early 2007, amidst predictable fanfare and the beneficent presence of Nelson Mandela, UHNWI Oprah Winfrey opened the Oprah Winfrey Leadership Academy for poor but talented girls in South Africa. A crowd of other celebrities joined Winfrey and Mandela at the opening day celebrations, including singers Tina Turner, Mary J. Blige and Mariah Carey, actors Sidney Poitier and Chris Tucker, and film director Spike Lee. Her decision to do her own thing was based in part, she maintained, on a sense of weariness with conventional philanthropy, passive donation and a desire to feel a more intimate connection to the people she was hoping to help.

While Oprah's rationale strikes a strong chord with many of her fellow HNWIs (for whom the most appealing aspect of donating money is enjoying the sense of well-being it bestows while still on the mortal plane), the satisfaction of managing one's philanthropic donations as actively as one might manage other assets is a deeply pragmatic emotion. Of course, other rationales may impinge on a number of these investment decisions, including the well-recognized tax advantages of philanthropy and the social engagement such activities bring.

David Ratcliffe, head of the Merrill Lynch Center for Philanthropy and Non-profit Management, insists that HNWIs are actively researching charities and keeping tabs on them through new online tools, such as GuideStar.org, CharityNavigator.org and CharityWatch.org, to make sure organizations are efficient and that gifts are being used correctly. "People have become more focusd on the measurement of success," Ratcliffe remarks. "They want the non-profit to be more accountable, to report back on how money has been used and how it's been effective." It's not unusual, he says, for a donor to tell a charity it must demonstrate progress, using certain metrics, within a certain time frame, or the HNWI will consider redirecting their charitable contributions to other organizations.

Some of this insistence upon greater accountability has simply been a heightened cynicism regarding the probity of large organizations in the wake of the Enron, WorldCom and Tyco corporate scandals of the late nineties. But non-profits also suffered some tarnishing of their own image when the American Red Cross raised US$564 million for the Liberty Fund, set up in response to 9/11, and then told donors it would use the majority of that money for other undefined purposes. Oral Suer, former chief executive of the United Way of the National Capital Area in Washington, was sentenced to more than two years in jail in 2004 for stealing about US$500,000 from the organization during his twenty-seven-year tenure.

A survey in 2006 by the Center on Philanthropy at Indiana University found that 75 percent of HNWIs would give more if less money was spent on administration, and nearly 60 percent said they would give more if they could determine the impact of their gifts. "These are highly competitive and performance-oriented people, and if they give money away they want it to be put to the best use," notes BlackRock co-founder Ralph Schlosstein. "These people worked hard to make their money, and they want as much impact as possible. I do believe there's a greater level of accountability of the non-profit sector than has historically been the case."

Yet Mr. Schlosstein also emphasizes that while he sees a tremendous drive among HNWIs to more precisely measure results, it comes from a tremendous desire to give. "The vast majority of people in my business believe they are working to benefit those more in need, because everything they make now is going to charity. There's an extremely strong sensation that we're incredibly fortunate and we need to give back to something we care about."

His comments were echoed by James Kennedy of T. Rowe Price, who cited his Jesuit upbringing as providing him with a sense of "obligation to turn around and help the ones behind you." James Rothenberg of Capital Research concurs: "I've got far more wealth than I will ever need or my family will ever need under any reasonable circumstance, so I look to philanthropy as a way not just to write a check but [to be] actively involved and engaged with helping people and helping an organization get better."

TAKING TAX CONSEQUENCES INTO ACCOUNT

A study recently conducted by the University of Indiana found that 52 percent of respondents would keep their giving levels the same even if they received no income-tax deduction whatsoever.

Thirty-eight percent said their donations would probably decrease somewhat, while only 7 percent said they would decrease
substantially.

Yet former Microsoft executive Charles Simonyi, who has already given away some US$85 million (most of it to a foundation he
created to fund the arts and sciences) cautions that it's easy to under-
estimate the degree to which the U.S. tax code—in stark contrast to
Europe's—encourages charitable giving. "Essentially, whenever you
make a donation you are making a challenge grant to Uncle Sam,
and every time he steps up to the plate. In Western Europe the idea
is that it's the government's duty, and I think this will accelerate."

One salutary effect of the U.S. tax code is that there are a multitude of tax rules to take into account when giving, depending on
the type of assets being donated and the type of charity. HNWIs are
educating themselves on the possibilities so they can make the best
decisions. David Ratcliffe notes that a general increase in investor
sophistication is having an effect on HNWIs' approach to philanthropy. "Donors are much more strategic in the way they think about
philanthropy. As financial services advisors, we spend a lot of time
educating them about effective and efficient planning to meet their
objectives, and that's spilling over into philanthropy."

Charitable gift annuities, charitable remainder trusts and pooled
income funds all allow donors to receive a cash flow even after making the gift. Oftentimes such vehicles are funded with appreciated
stock, real estate, the proceeds from the sale of a business or other assets that otherwise would be heavily taxed. Among the most
prominent of these vehicles are:

• Charitable remainder trusts: The donor transfers assets to an ir-
revocable trust and receives a regular payment stream, which is
taxable. At the end of the trust's term, what's left goes to a charity.
The donor receives an income-tax deduction for the amount estimated to end up with the charity.

• Charitable gift annuities: The donor gives money to a charity, which promises to pay him or her a fixed amount regularly for life. Although part of the annuity payments is taxable, the donor will also receive an upfront tax deduction for the amount estimated to end up with the charity.

• Pooled income funds: The donor gives money to a charity, which invests the money in a special fund and pays the donor his or her share of the fund's earnings. When the donor dies, whatever's left of the investments goes to the charity.

In addition, certain techniques, like Charitable Lead Trusts, provide donors with the ability to make current distributions to the charities of their choice and ultimately transfer the assets to other family members. These techniques allow for charitable contributions as well as "leveraged" transfer of assets to children or grandchildren with reduced gift and/or estate tax ramifications.

Consider the case of an American HNWI who had accumulated US$1 million of company stock via an employee stock-option purchase program. He wants that to generate an income stream of at least US$5,000 per month to help support his retirement costs. If he had sold his company stock outright, he would have had an upfront tax hit on all of the appreciation over the past twenty years. The capital gains tax rate at the time the HNWI was mulling his options was still 20 percent and the shares had appreciated by US$833,660, so the tax hit would have been US$166,732.

To avoid those taxes, the HNWI funds a charitable gift annuity contract in exchange for US$1 million in appreciated shares of stock. The Internal Revenue Service then applies a 53.73 percent charitable bargain-sale ratio to his gift, which effectively reduces the reportable capital gain to US$537,300 from US$833,660 and prorates the reporting over the donor's life expectancy of 13.2 years. Based on his current age, the donor qualifies for a 7.7 percent

annuity rate, which pays him US$77,000 per year, or monthly payments of US$6,417 in retirement.

MAKING A DIFFERENCE WITH FAMILY FOUNDATIONS AND DONOR-ADVISED FUNDS

Family foundations represent yet another preferred route to charitable giving that has grown greatly in popularity and numbers over the years—from 23,770 foundations in 1982 to 64,843 in 2002, according to Monitor Group. But there are signs that this explosive growth may be slowing thanks to increasingly complex taxes and regulations governing such foundations.

Not only do family foundations provide an effective means to pursue philanthropic goals, they frequently serve to unite families around a common mission and set of goals. For a family foundation to function properly, however, fundamental principles, policies and practices must be set in place. This is especially important as the foundations created over the last twenty-five years mature and the original family founders die. To handle this transition to the next generation, the governance of the foundation should be clear, or risk the intrusion of potentially dysfunctional family dynamics.

For some, a family foundation arguably begins to lose its luster; however, another grants management charitable structure is gaining momentum: the donor-advised fund. In 2005, the country's largest donor-advised funds held assets of US$15.5 billion, up 22 percent from the year before, according to the *Chronicle of Philanthropy*. Here's how they work: An individual contributes at least US$5,000 in cash, stocks or other assets and gets an immediate tax deduction for the contribution and retains the right to recommend how the money should be distributed to charitable organizations. The donor can postpone the actual distribution of the money for years and in the meantime choose from a menu of investment options to grow the pool of money.

Such funds are typically offered by charities set up by major financial institutions as well as community foundations, and provide a donor with many options in recommending disbursements of the funds. Technically, the fund managers are not bound by the donor's wishes since the donor's funds are owned by the charity, yet donors retain the right to name the charity and make disbursement "recommendations," and in practice those suggestions are typically honored once properly vetted by the managing charity. Donor-advised funds can be set up quickly and inexpensively, as opposed to family foundations, which can be cumbersome to set up and manage from a tax and regulatory standpoint.

Apart from their obvious tax, cost and management benefits, David Ratcliffe of Merrill Lynch observes that donor-advised funds, which permit HNWIs to recommend multiple grants over many years, provide investors in them both the capability and the right to carefully monitor the charities they choose to recommend and advise and redirect funding to other charities when they deem appropriate.

Donor-advised funds offer something else in great demand by today's HNWIs: *portability*. People are much more mobile than in the past. When living in, perhaps, the Northeast and raising their children, HNWIs may want to donate to local causes; but once their children are grown, they may spend more time in Palm Springs, California, or Naples, Florida, and wish to redirect charitable dollars to those areas. Donor-advised funds can move with the HNWIs, and help fund their changing priorities throughout their lives.

Due to the low threshold to open donor-advised funds—often just $5,000 to $10,000—such funds are increasingly being created by HNWIs who nominate their children or grandchildren as grant advisors. It's a way to help young adults engage a network of philanthropic interests, learn how to research their own charities and develop the skills necessary to be responsible stewards of capital. Thus, donor-advised funds dovetail nicely with HNWIs' use of philanthropy to develop their children's moral compass and to shape a life of purpose as well as privilege.

For wealth advisors, an additional benefit of donor-advised funds is to deepen an advisor's existing relationship with the HNWI while possibly establishing a rapport with the next generation. Some advisors argue that working closely with HNWIs on their philanthropy is the very best way to deepen a relationship since an advisor gains insight into HNWIs' personal priorities. This broader, more holistic view of the client can help the advisor tailor value-added, differentiated advice.

While the United States may lead the world in charitable giving, and Europe may continue to lag, HNWIs in other parts of the world are starting to give more openly and frequently than ever before. Michael Saadie of ANZ has seen a marked increase in the desire of HNWIs in Australia to give back to their society—mostly, he says, for the sheer joy of sharing their wealth and affecting change, but also to create a legacy and perhaps to assuage a touch of guilt. "The newer money is setting up more and more charitable trusts, many more than seven years ago."

A similar charitable awakening is also occurring elsewhere in Asia, where in the past donations have been made sparingly and with little publicity, in part due to a now-outdated reverence for the Confucian values of self-reliance and individual responsibility. In 2006, Li Ka-shing, the chairman of Hong Kong conglomerate Hutchison Whampoa Ltd. (and Asia's richest man, with a fortune estimated at US$30 billion plus) roiled the virtually nonexistent world of Mainland Chinese philanthropy by announcing plans to give a third of his fortune—a pledge estimated at more than US$10 billion—to his family Li Ka-shing Foundation.

According to the *Wall Street Journal*[5] Mr. Li's pioneering social entrepreneurial lead is being enthusiastically followed by Yang Lan, a prominent talk-show host frequently referred to as the Chinese

5. Kate Linebaugh and Jane Spencer, "The Revolution of Chairman Li—China's Richest Man Leads Others to Give, Bucking Nation's Taboos," *Wall Street Journal*, November 2, 2007.

Oprah Winfrey; Yu Pengnian, the eighty-five-year-old head of the Chinese luxury-hotel empire Shenzhen Pengnian Hotels, who has donated roughly 80 percent of his net worth to fund cataract operations for thousands in rural China; and Niu Gensheng, chief executive of Mengniu Dairy Group, who has donated shares in his firm valued at nearly US$600 million to a foundation devoted to agriculture, education and medical endeavors.

"In Asia, our traditional values encourage and even demand that wealth and means pass through lineage as an imperative duty," Mr. Li told the *Wall Street Journal*, exhorting his fellow Asians to "transcend this traditional belief." They, for the most part, are eagerly awaiting the announcement of a comprehensive law on charitable giving for China, an event predicted by Liu Youping, chief editor of *China Philanthropy Times*, published by China's Ministry of Civil Affairs.

For his part, Mr. Li has personally underwritten the construction of Shantou University, a regular hotbed of corporate social responsibility, where Starbucks Coffee Co. founder Howard Schultz has lectured on business ethics, former CNN correspondent Peter Arnett teaches journalism, and the pedagogical philosophy openly espouses the traditionally Western values of open discussion, transparency, creativity and freedom. As West and East meet in the world of philanthropy, trends toward a fusion of styles bode well for the evolution of an active non-profit sector in China.

In Hong Kong, Dr. Lee Shau Kee of Henderson Land Development has grown concerned with the growing disparity in wealth and prosperity between urban and rural China. He intends to train one million children of farmers to work in the city, where they will earn higher wages and thus be able to support their families back on the farm. "I want to help people to help themselves," Dr. Lee notes, "which is much more valuable for both sides than just making a donation. By training the child of a farmer you compound the value of that dollar spent on training since that child will now help their parents. This is the multiplier affect. There's no point in just feeding them or just giving them money."

Dr. Cheng Yu-Tung of New World Development—another client of Joseph Lam's—has interests in property, infrastructure, telecom, jewelry stores and casinos all around Asia. In the eighties, Dr. Cheng embarked on a program to train Chinese doctors in the United States. The problem was that the student doctors, once they landed in San Francisco, usually did not come back—in fact only about 20 percent did, a trend that worsened after Tiananmen Square. In response, Dr. Cheng began having students trained in Hong Kong where they couldn't seek political asylum. This is a good example of prudent business acumen being applied to philanthropy, and how corporations can bring some of their best practices to bear.

WITNESSING A DECLINE IN GIVING?

While philanthropy is unquestionably a force for good, in a world where the gap between the rich and poor is growing steadily, one unsettling trend cannot be ignored: in the United States at least, HNWIs as a group are giving less as a percentage of their net worth than ever before, while non-HNWIs are giving more. According to Internal Revenue Service data published by the *New York Times*, the richest individuals, worth US$20 million or more, left 20.8 percent of their estates to charity in 2004, down from 25.3 percent in 1995. Among taxpayers with US$1 million or more of income, the percentage of their income they gave away dropped to 3.6 percent in 2003 from 4.1 percent in 1995. Meanwhile, those with incomes of less than US$1 million became more generous, upping their donations to 3.5 percent of income from 2.8 percent in the same time frame.

Whether such numbers may be an anomaly, Jeff Sachs, special advisor to the United Nations secretary-general, told the *Financial Times* in early 2007 that wealthy philanthropists could do more to lift Africa out of poverty than could the Group of Eight leading nations. He exhorted the wealthy to follow the examples of Gates and Buffett and contribute to a new private sector foundation to help speed the elimination of diseases and tackle specific challenges.

As Sachs put it to the *Financial Times,* if the 950 billionaires whose wealth is estimated at US$3.5 trillion were to contribute an annual 5 percent "foundation" payout of their total net worth, that would provide US$175 billion per year to charitable causes. "We don't need the G8, but we do need the 950 people on the *Forbes* list…Maybe private philanthropists will champion solutions to individual problems rather than the G8."

EXPRESSING OPTIMISM FOR HNWIS' GRANDCHILDREN

In 1930, in the wake of the Roaring Twenties and at the outset of the worst economic depression the world had yet seen, British economist John Maynard Keynes published an upbeat essay entitled "Economic Possibilities for Our Grandchildren" in which he defied his disciples who predicted a semi-permanent depression and forecast instead a shining new world of a century hence, when steady but gradual technological progress accompanied by gradually compounding capital accumulation would produce—as he optimistically put it—"ever larger and larger classes and groups of people for whom problems of economic necessity have been practically removed."[6]

Although Keynes failed to live to see the coinage of the term HNWI (perhaps fortunately for him), he accurately forecast a period and even precisely enumerated the drivers of a new Gilded Age in which wealth would be far more greatly dispersed than at any other time in human history. This period would be one in which goods and services would become abundant and nearly cost-free, interest rates on capital would plummet to near zero, and

6. John Maynard Keynes, "Economic Possibilities for Our Grandchildren," *Essays in Persuasion* (New York: Harcourt, Brace & Co., 1932), 358–373.

the greatest challenges facing the wealthy class would be how to live a life of unlimited leisure that would also be filled with purpose and meaning.

While Keynes' financial future of nearly universally distributed wealth above and beyond the means of necessity has yet to come to pass, by the twenty-first century (not quite a hundred years from 1930) the world had indeed fulfilled Keynes' prophecy of producing a "standard of living in progressive countries one hundred years hence that will be between four and eight times as high as to-day."

In "Creating a Moral Biography of Wealth,"[7] Paul Schervish, the director of the Center on Wealth and Philanthropy at Boston College, ponders the social and even existential implications of the possibility that Keynes' era of nearly universal prosperity may one day soon be reality as opposed to fantasy. Among today's younger HNWIs, he has observed a propensity to search for a sense of ultimate meaning and higher purpose to life—that hitherto unimaginable luxury for many that the possession of great wealth confers.

One natural extension of portfolio management envisioned by Schervish is the creation of a "moral biography" of personal wealth in which its possessor employs total assets under management as tools to embark upon "a spiritual process of self-examination" that goes well beyond and far afield of any conventional process of portfolio analysis. It is the sort of adventure that Charles Simonyi embarked upon when, after accumulating great wealth, he decided to give nearly US$100 million of it away while gaining fame as one of the planet's pioneering space tourists. It is the sort of adventure that philanthropists like Bill Gates, Warren Buffett, Gerald Grosvenor, Dr. Lee and Dr. Cheng have embarked upon as they seek fulfillment in improving the lives of others, using the same analytical tools and skills that helped them first improve their own.

7. "Creating a Moral Biography of Wealth: A Conversation with Paul G. Schervish," The Whitepapers: Quarterly Intelligence for Informed Investors, Winter 2006, a publication of Merrill Lynch's Private Bank and Investment Group (PBIG).

As more and more HNWIs and non-HNWIs begin to look beyond mere wealth, and the period of acquisition and accumulation that produced it, to the next phase of their lives, they will—as John Maynard Keynes precisely predicted—"for the first time since creation...be faced with [the] real [and] permanent problem of how to use this freedom from pressing economic cares, how to occupy the leisure that science and compound interest will have won...to live wisely and agreeably and well."

This book represents one modest attempt to lead us to the place where a few of us will be prepared to ask—and even answer—such questions. As Keynes presciently wrote, "it will be those who can keep alive and cultivate into a fuller perfection the art of life itself and do not sell themselves for the means of life, who will be able to enjoy the [age of] abundance when it comes."

Cyclical credit crunches, market volatility and upheavals aside, the age of abundance is already here for many of us and a fair percentage seem to be striving to "live wisely and agreeably and well." As Winston Churchill, who certainly knew something about living wisely, agreeably and well, once said, "We make a *living* by what we get, but we make a *life* by what we give."

CHAPTER 9

The Future of Holistic Wealth Management

CREATING CONDITIONS TO BUILD AND PRESERVE WEALTH FOR THE FUTURE—THE MICHAEL LEE-CHIN WAY

The Daniel Libeskind-designed, aluminum-and-glass, 175,000-square-foot Michael Lee-Chin Crystal juts jarringly out over bustling Bloor Street West, a stylish and starkly contrasting modern addition to the neo-Byzantine façade of Toronto's Royal Ontario Museum (ROM). Yet striking as the structure is architecturally, perhaps its least likely aspect is that it is the fruit of a C\$32 million donation from prominent investor and financial celebrity Michael Lee-Chin, a Jamaican-born immigrant to Canada who in 2007 ranked number 618 on the *Forbes* list of the world's wealthiest individuals, with a net worth of US\$1.6 billion. It's least likely not because Mr. Lee-Chin isn't philanthropically minded—he's famously so—but because he's the son of a grocery-store-owning father in the rural backwater of Port Antonio, Jamaica, and of an entrepreneurially minded mother who sold Avon products door to door and worked long hours as a bookkeeper to make ends meet. He is also the author of a unique framework and philosophy of diversification and wealth accumulation and preservation that was proven highly successful for many long-term investors in AIC, the mutual fund company he established more than two decades ago.

So how on earth, Lee-Chin rhetorically asks while swiveling in a leather wing chair in the formally furnished boardroom of AIC, the Canadian mutual fund giant he organically grew from a tiny entity he acquired in 1987, could someone from his ostensibly disadvantaged background have made it on the annual *Forbes* list of the world's wealthiest individuals for six years running? The answer came to him in 2002 while sitting in the office of the Jamaican Minister of Finance in Kingston, writing a check to purchase a controlling 75 percent share of the National Commercial Bank of Jamaica.

"For me, buying the National Commercial Bank"—Jamaica's largest consumer bank—"would be tantamount to an American buying Citibank," he explains. "So as I was writing out that check, I thought to myself, 'How is this possible? How is it possible for the son of an orphan born of a teenaged mother to be writing a check to buy the National Commercial Bank?' Just before I wrote out the check, the question came to mind. Just *after* I wrote it, the answer came to mind."

For starters, he decided that he owed a fair part of his remarkable good fortune to the fact that he was born in a country and at a time when a poor boy (whose grandfathers were Hakka Chinese immigrants to Jamaica and whose grandmothers were Afro-Caribbean Jamaicans) was free to attend a good local high school and an excellent college, McMaster University in Hamilton, Ontario, where he studied civil engineering on a Jamaican government scholarship. After returning to Jamaica to work on a national highway project, he decided that civil engineering was not his cup of tea and made his way back to McMaster to pursue a graduate degree in business.

But he also would realize, some thirty years hence, that sheer happenstance had conspired with character and conditioning to propel him to the next stop on the road to riches. While working after hours as a bouncer in the campus pub, he encountered a former college classmate happily celebrating his $200-a-day take-home pay from selling mutual funds for Investors Group. With that pay scale comparing favorably to the $2.50 an hour he was taking home as a bouncer, Lee-Chin's otherwise neutral outlook on the financial services industry abruptly brightened from "hold" to "buy."

Despite failing the psychological test for prospective trainees, he talked his way into the sales training program at his friend's firm. Days after completing the course he found himself waiting at the Toronto airport for his mother's delayed flight from Miami. "That day," he recalled, "was a Sunday. I was feeling stressed out because I knew nothing about the financial world. My entire work experience had been as an engineer combined with a few months as a bar bouncer. I was twenty-six and all of my friends were broke. How on earth was I going to get clients to see Monday morning?"[1]

"So that Sunday afternoon after I heard my mum's flight was delayed I decided to get in my car and drive around the nearest neighborhood to get my thoughts together. As I drove around this very nice neighborhood I saw people outside tending their gardens. So I said to myself, 'Okay, Mike, here they are, they *really* want to see you.' I told myself that the next person I saw, I was just going to close my eyes, grit my teeth, put my foot on the brake, jump out of the car, and talk to my first real live prospect."

To every one of those real live prospects he posed precisely the same question. "Sir—or Madam—I'm here working with members of this community, showing them how to minimize their taxes and taking their tax receipts to create a substantial asset base. What time would be good for you to see me? Early next week or later on in the week?" Out of the six prospects he approached, he snagged five appointments and ended signing up his first clients that Monday morning.

It didn't take long for the consummate salesman to build up an enviable track record as a pitcher of mutual funds to mass-affluent

---

1. Interview with the authors.

clients. But only after stumbling across a brief biography of Warren Buffett did he experience the eureka moment that set him on the path to true prominence as an investor. "Warren's methodology to me made total sense. I felt I could replicate it. I didn't think I had the ability to prognosticate where markets were going, or prognosticate where interest rates were going, or where the economy was going. But I did think I could train myself to identify great businesses, which is the secret of Warren's success."

Lee-Chin's devotion to "The Buffett Way" extends to the AIC slogan/mission statement printed on his business card: "Buy. Hold. Prosper." Inspired by Buffett, he distilled his own investment philosophy to five cardinal rules:

1. Invest in a handful—"less than the fingers on your hand"—of high-quality firms;

2. Ensure that those firms are domiciled in long-term growth industries;

3. Understand those firms and industries comprehensively;

4. Invest for the long term and with discipline, focus and commitment, ignoring market fluctuations and pressure to sell in down cycles—also to maintain a high rate of return *after taxes*;

5. Use other people's money to leverage those investments.

In applying his five principles, Lee-Chin was well aware that he was single-mindedly defying one of the cardinal rules of his own industry: the gospel of diversification and broad-based asset allocation. Too many of the mutual funds he was advising clients to buy into, he decided, owned too many stocks for the fund managers to truly understand the firms and the industries at the deepest level. Relying on analysts to conduct due diligence didn't strike him as a sound strategy. Instead, he decided to move aggressively "beyond Markowitz" and put all of his eggs into one (he believed) promising basket.

In 1983, he used his diversified portfolio of stocks as collateral to borrow C$500,000—considerably more than his net worth at the time—from the Continental Bank of Canada to buy 500,000 shares of financial services firm Mackenzie Group at C$1.00 a share. He arrived at this momentous and obviously risky decision by using the following thought process: "I asked myself the question, which industry do I best understand? Remember that I'm a financial advisor. So [for] which industry do I best understand the regulatory environment? The competitive nature of the landscape? Who the competitors are? Margins pertaining to the different products? The long-term nature of the industry? I answered that question in the following way: 'The industry I'm in—the wealth management industry!'"

As he plunged more deeply into his analysis of the long-term future of the WM industry, he found that it met his long-term growth-and-value criteria like a glove. "In the early eighties, the wealth management industry wasn't nearly as developed as it is today. So I worked my way down the list one by one. 1) If I had to narrow down my investment choices to a handful of industries, what would one be? 2) Is it an industry I understand? 3) Is it predicated on other people's money? 4) Is it domiciled in a strong, stable, long-term growth industry? 5) Will it stay strong and stable over the long run?"

In five years, Lee-Chin's faith in the future of the financial services industry in general and in Mackenzie in particular was validated as his bucket of shares soared in value to C$3.5 million. Not only was his theory vindicated, but the run-up provided him with sufficient personal credit with his banker in 1987 to enable him to borrow more funds to finance the purchase of a small, local firm of financial advisors. At the time, AIC had a mere C$800,000 under management. Within the decade, AIC had blossomed into a mutual fund behemoth, with over C$14 billion under management throughout the period its flagship Advantage Fund, which had become a darling of the Canadian mutual fund industry, rigidly adhered to the Michael Lee-Chin philosophy by holding fewer than twenty stocks in its bulging portfolio.

Yet over the years, and particularly during periods of heightened speculation and bubble mania, AIC has suffered its fair share of redemptions as Lee-Chin's steadfast commitment to "Buy. Hold. Prosper." has been sorely tested by his firm refusal to ride the roller-coaster into tech stocks or plunge into other fashionable investments. Regardless of what's going on in his business life, though, Lee-Chin has remained both a UHNWI *par excellence* and a proverbially generous man. With his personal wealth, Lee-Chin has underwritten business institutes in and around Toronto, donated heavily to the ROM, and aggressively invested in his native Jamaica and elsewhere in the Caribbean—places and sectors he both understands and to whose often fragile economies he wants to "give back." Using Portland Holdings, his privately held investment vehicle, he has been snapping up land, real estate holdings including office buildings, telecom firms and, of course, banks and other financial firms.

Asked about the future trends of high-net-worth investment, Lee-Chin emphasizes that no advances in technology, social changes or innovative products are likely to undermine the fundamentals of value investing. That said, he is a firm believer in—and a product of—the continuation of the relentless globalization that will continue to drive WM across borders to service increasingly globe-trotting HNW clients. He firmly believes that access to markets will become more transparent and that global consolidation of industries is likely to drive global diversification of assets. The HNWI population shifting funds in and out of alternative investments such as hedge funds, derivatives or structured products into real estate, or demanding concierge services or plunging into "investments of passion" will not and cannot, in his opinion, fundamentally alter the competitive landscape of the WM industry or shift the essential dynamics of long-term investment.

In this view, he concurs with fellow Buffett disciple the Hong Kong billionaire Dr. Lee Shau Kee that at the end of the day all consistently successful long-term investors follow precisely the same rules. In the timeless world of the long-term value investor, the future is likely to look very much like the past.

IDENTIFYING FUTURE TRENDS TO TAKE INTO CONSIDERATION

As we continue with our conclusion of *Wealth*, and taking Michael's philosophy into consideration, we believe there are a number of trends that will continue to shape the Wealth Management Industry moving forward. Some of them are evident today and others are still emerging. Regardless, individuals and their FAs will do well to consider the wide-ranging impacts of these trends when investing their considerable assets.

1. Products designed for the HNWI market will continue to become more complex, sophisticated and international in nature and scope supported by the continuing globalization of services;

2. Technological advances will drive down the WM barriers to entry, enabling one-stop shopping. This will further cement the fact that the ultimate differentiating factor will be the quality of the relationship between client and advisor. The quality of this relationship will be driven by the client, versus the advisor;

3. The Asia-Pacific region will continue to become the dominant source of wealth creation;

4. Intergenerational wealth transfer will drive a focus back to capital growth as a source of wealth creation, complementing the current dominant source of wealth creation from business ownership to capital growth;

5. Industries that will remain attractive and dominant for the long-term include financial services and agriculture;

6. The devaluation of the U.S. dollar will further drive global investment to Europe and Asia, as well as increase foreign investment in the United States.

What remains clear is that the Wealth Management Industry will remain buoyant and attractive, regardless of economic ups and downs and the inherently cyclical nature of financial services.

INCREASING WEALTH ACROSS THE GLOBE

Despite the unsettling credit crunch of 2007–08—and barring the development of unforeseen economic reversals in the form of a global recession or depression—the most influential and seemingly resilient secular trend affecting the burgeoning population of HNWIs of the world is that the ongoing spread of global capitalism is producing pools of ever-more consolidated and concentrated wealth. In absolute terms, according to the 2007 *WWR*, the worldwide number of HNWIs with portfolios of more than US$1 million rose by 8 percent in 2006, while the total assets of the wealthy grew by 11 percent.

Bolstered by buoyant equity and real estate markets, the ranks of the wealthy worldwide have swelled by significant percentages throughout the first decade of the twenty-first century, nearly doubling in less than a decade to 9.6 million from 5.2 million. The ongoing globalization of wealth means that regionally, while wealth continues to be unevenly concentrated in North America and Europe, in Latin America, Asia and the Middle East (regions long home to the world's greatest inequalities) the growth in wealth has been nothing short of breathtaking. According to the 2007 *WWR*:

• Of the 9.6 million HNWIs in 2006, 49 percent lived in North America;

- Latin America boasts 14 percent of the world's wealth, while harboring just 5 percent of HNWIs;

- Asia is home to roughly a quarter of the world's HNWIs, of which approximately one-fifth are mainland Chinese;

- Mainland China is home to 320,000 HNWIs, who collectively possess US$1.59 trillion of assets and boast an average net worth of roughly US$5 million. Approximately 4,540 ultra-HNWIs in China control assets upwards of US$30 million;

- The HNWIs of Hong Kong are collectively worth around US$460 billion, an astounding example of wealth concentration in a city of roughly seven million people;

- Out of a population of nearly 1.3 billion, India's HNWIs, by contrast, control some US$350 billion (India's 150,000 expatriate millionaires contribute to the explosive economy);

- Japan, the world's second-largest economy, is home to nearly half of Asia's millionaires, yet its longstanding lead as a haven of the wealthy is rapidly giving ground to China;

- Singapore, with its venerable tradition of independence and legal and political stability—and strong legal protections of financial privacy—has become a haven of offshore and private banking for Asia's mega-affluent;

- While the total net worth of Asia's HNWIs rose 10.5 percent to US$8.4 trillion in 2006, private bankers in Hong Kong and Singapore—where the bulk of Asia's private banking industry is concentrated—managed a total of US$600 billion;

- Taiwan, Thailand, Indonesia and Malaysia are home to rapidly growing HNWI populations;

- In the Middle East, high oil prices and widespread financial reforms—particularly in the financial centers of Abu Dhabi and the

UAE—have contributed to a culture of wealth creation and preservation that contrasts with the free-spending seventies in that more indigenous wealth is being invested within the region.

• Africa, once the world's economic basket case, is enjoying a wave of wealth creation unseen on the continent since the late Middle Ages. According to the IMF, since 2001 African economies have grown on average by 5 percent annually, a pace that the IMF predicts will quicken over the next five years to a robust 5.6 percent (compared to 4.8 percent elsewhere).

The seemingly irreversible globalization of wealth means that in order to not merely survive but thrive in the twenty-first century, the WM industry must go where the money is—which it is, with a predictable vengeance. In 2007, the Bank of China embarked on a potentially profitable partnership with the Royal Bank of Scotland (RBS) to provide financial-planning expertise to the local HNWI population. The Bank of China now boasts only one hundred to two hundred private-banking clients, with average investible assets of US$655,000, an amount one private banker estimates represents at best a tiny fraction of their individual and household net worth.[2]

Yet opportunities for growth remain considerable, if for no other reason than as the *Financial Times* reports, less than half of all wealth managers today hold more than 40 percent of their clients' investible wealth. "Over the next three years, this proportion is expected to increase dramatically so that 80 per cent of wealth managers hold 40 per cent of a client's wealth."[3]

What this worldwide wave of wealth means for the WM industry is that if it is successful in gaining ever-greater advisory influence

---

2. Jason Leow, "China's Rich Get Catering—Private Bankers Tap a Rising Wealth Pool," *Wall Street Journal*, June 5, 2007.

3. Jane Croft, "Private Banks Set for Boom Period," *Financial Times,* June 27, 2007.

over ever-greater proportions of HNWIs' assets, the already fierce competition among a comparatively small number of brand-name providers for high-quality service will only increase at every conceivable level, from breadth, range and quality of products to quality of human relationships to quality of technology.

Among the surging ranks of the ultra-affluent, levels of sophisticated service, guidance and advice hitherto reserved for the fortunate few will need to be provided to the comparatively many. Stand-alone private banks, independent wealth advisory services, and private banking organizations cradled within larger organizations will all be competing with the *ne plus ultra* of mega-wealth preservation, the family office.

At the same time, as the wealth of the world is created and ideally preserved by an historically unprecedented number of households and individuals in absolute terms—yet proportionally far fewer in percentage terms—the level of client sophistication and expectations will only relentlessly rise over time. As access to vast flows of undiluted information is enhanced by ever-more nuanced and powerful technology, the degree of importance accorded by clients to the human factors (trust, empathy, comprehension of the "whole picture") will also climb exponentially.

This has only increased the tendency for competition in the industry to give rise to consolidation. Brokerages, banks, fund companies, and independent money advisors are falling over themselves seeking an ever-greater share of the HNWI pie by offering an ever-broadening array of advisory services, ranging from the mere management of money (clearly number one on a relative scale of importance yet largely viewed as a given by the average discerning HNWI) to the more discretionary and therefore differentiating factors of handling tax and estate issues, guiding philanthropic endeavors, arranging private equity participation deals, providing access to exotic instruments and hedge funds, and even planning exotic vacations down to the most minor detail or counseling wayward children on behavioral issues. The more they compete, the more likely they are to realize that by joining forces they can better serve their clients, and it's likely that HNWIs are well aware of this fact.

According to *Forbes,* the intensity of the competition gives rise, at some points, to a level of concierge service that may strike some as faintly laughable. Citigroup offers "equestrian management" services for clients who own horses. JPMorgan Chase counters with art advisory services.[4] Still, according to Sara Hamilton, founder and chief executive of Family Office Exchange (as quoted in *Forbes*), a resource network based in Chicago, 30 percent of the work conducted by private bankers serving the HNWI population is "devoted to accounting, filing taxes and keeping records in compliance, another 18 percent to 20 percent is devoted to investment management, and 12 percent to 15 percent to finance, tax and estate planning. Just 7 percent of the time is devoted to managing a wealthy client's 'lifestyle demands.'"

And while the establishment of family offices—replete with their own staff of lawyers, accountants and investment planners employed full time by the office—remains the *ne plus ultra* of WM, such high-maintenance entities are only deemed worthwhile and affordable for ultra-HNWI households, families or affiliations of families controlling liquid assets in excess of US$100 million. For the ever-increasing number of families that fall below that threshold yet command significant wealth, multi-family offices that combine the resources while divvying up the costs are seen as a coming trend.

EASING THE STRESS OF INTERGENERATIONAL WEALTH TRANSFER

It is widely agreed that the pending transfer of assets from the boomer generation to their children and grandchildren will collectively

---

4. Liz Moyer, "Where the Rich Bank Their Money," *Forbes,* October 11, 2007, http://www.forbes.com.

amount to the greatest intergenerational legacy the world has ever seen. A 2006 study conducted by Paul Schervish and John Havens of Boston College's Center on Wealth and Philanthropy estimates that between 2001 and 2055 some US$41 trillion will have changed hands in the United States alone.

What is also becoming clear is that while offspring may be in a position to inherit more wealth than at any point in history, parental attitudes toward wealth transfer may also be evolving as parents sort through a range of often conflicting concerns: their desire to support their offspring financially, and their legitimate anxieties regarding the depletion of motivation and a potential for the diminution of their personal happiness as their wealth saps satisfaction.

Nick Tucker, a managing director in the Global Wealth Management division of Merrill Lynch in the U.K., has observed an increase in the number of clients who express anxiety and discomfort about their children receiving large sums of money— particularly among self-made entrepreneurs. "Often entrepreneurs and wealth creators want their children to be like them," Tucker recently reported to the *Financial Times*.[5] "They want to give their children the same start they had and do feel that, if they give more than that, then they are depriving the children from doing what they have done."

The most promising and effective way for parents to resolve these issues, in Tucker's experience, is for them to more deeply engage their children in open discussions regarding family values with values-based retreats, promote their financial literacy, foster open dialogues around often sensitive issues through programs like boot camps, and in general boost transparency and candor between the generations regarding what is reasonable and equitable to expect from the impending transfer and what is not.

---

5. Sharlene Goff, "Parents Opting for Tough Love with the Family Fortune," *Financial Times*, October 27, 2007.

TRENDING TOWARD OPEN ARCHITECTURE AND UNBIASED ADVICE

The frequency and severity of equity market fluctuations since the dot-com crash of 2001 has directed the HNWI population worldwide toward a preference for alternative investments and assets classes, ranging from investments in real estate and other commercial property, private equity and hedge funds, and structured and derivative products, as investors and advisors alike seek to protect portfolios from sudden and unsettling equity market corrections.

Sophisticated investors' increasing appetite for alternative investments has only fueled the shift toward "open architecture," as the majority of WM firms recognize that it is nearly impossible to maintain all expertise inside the firm. The most client-centric approach will always be to maintain a continual search for "best in class" and "best of breed" fund managers and funds outside their own firm.

Some private banks, including Merrill Lynch, make a point of not allocating private investor money to their own funds under discretionary mandates. Sophisticated investors are also increasingly aware that a shift from a transaction-based to a fee-based model (in which the advisor does not gain financially from selling a product) is the only guarantor of true independence and impartiality.

This trend has further fueled an ongoing shift toward providing a wider range of ancillary services and the holistic approach, because advisors who might once have eschewed the provision of tax, estate, retirement, pension, and mortgage and debt planning now compete with each other to offer services that mimic or emulate institutional collaborations between divisions of the whole firm, as has been the case with the shift toward a systematic drawing on expertise from across the firm at some of the larger institutions like Merrill Lynch.

In the end, the aspirational phenomenon identified by Capgemini as "uptiering"—in which clients at virtually every rung on the net-worth spectrum aspire to the level of service provided to the tier above—combined with the inevitable march of technology strongly suggests that the preferences, objectives and expectations currently enjoyed by the wealthy and the ultra-wealthy will, over time, trickle down to an ever-greater share of society. At the same time, the seemingly irreversible tendency for essential financial services to be commoditized means that the high-net-worth-centric share of the business will provide leadership for some time to come.

So we conclude, appropriately enough, with the final paragraph of the introduction to our first (1997) *WWR*:

> *HNWIs not only demand a broader range of products, but also expect their financial advisors to be well-versed in these products and the global markets in which they are offered. Most of all, perhaps, they are seeking advisors with the wisdom to recommend investments that precisely meet their particular needs and objectives.*

A similarly timeless and universal sentiment was expressed in 1911 by the twenty-six-year-old Charles Edward Merrill in *Leslie's Illustrated Weekly*:

> *To select intelligently the investment securities best suited to the needs of each individual requires of the investment banker long experience, special training, and a thorough knowledge not only of the intrinsic merit of the securities that he recommends, but also of the investment situation of that particular individual...To make effective this personal service, the cooperation of the client is imperative.*

INDEX

A

Abu Dhabi, 71, 157, 216
Acadian Asset Management, 71
accountability, in philanthropy,
    187–88, 194–95
active performance-driven investors,
    xxvi
activist-philanthropists, 188, 191–92
Acumen Fund, 192
Advantage Fund, 212
advertising, 7
advisor-client relationships. *See* client-
    advisor relationships
advisor facing technology, 85, 88–89
Africa, 71
    frontier market, 70
    GDP, 25
    HNWIs in, 24
    local HNWI investment, 62–63
    wealth creation in, 216
Agarwal, Anil, 188
aggregated account information, 76,
    86, 117
aging populations, 44, 63
AIC, 207, 212
AKD Securities, 70–71
Allred, Stacy, 170
alternative investments, xxi, 69, 125,
    127, 213, 220
    appeal of, 139–43
    art, 139–42

    increased dependence on, xxviii–xxix
    real estate, 143–44
    regional differences, 137
    risks, 161
    structured products, xxi, xxiii–xxiv,
        125, 139, 145–48, 213, 220
Amaranth Advisors, 44, 129–30
American Institute of Certified Public
    Accountants (AICPA), 17
American Red Cross, 194
The American Stock Exchange, 146
Angus, Patricia, 166–67
anti-trade legislation, xxxii
ANZ Bank, 13, 151, 176
Arnett, Peter, 201
Arnold, Jeremy, 169–70
art, 139–42
Artist Pension Trust, 139
Artnet, 141
Asian Contagion (1997), 36, 44
Asia-Pacific, xxi, 26–27, 36, 47, 58, 213
    emerging markets in, xxix
    entrepreneurs, 39
    GDP, 25
    HNWIs in, 22, 24, 137, 215
    local investment, 62
    peer networks, 173
    philanthropy, 200–202
    private banking, 47–49, 215
    stock market growth, 67

Asia-Pacific Wealth Report (2007), 136, 137, 179

aspirational risk, 129, 133–34

asset acquisition, 111

asset allocation, xxviii, 9–10, 19, 48, 60, 74, 119, 122, 123, 134, 138
    defying, 132–33, 210
    meeting clients' needs, 135
    regional variations, 136–37
    see also Modern Portfolio Theory (MPT)

asset-backed securities (ABS), xxiii, xxiv

asset classes, 125

asset gathering, 9

asset management, 10

Astor, Brooke, 168

Attali, Jacques, 41–42, 192

auction houses, 140, 141

Australia, HNWIs in, 200

The Australia and New Zealand Banking Group (ANZ Bank). *See* ANZ Bank

B

Bain Capital, 158

Bangladesh, 70, 72

Bank of America (BofA), 104, 105

Bank of China, 216

Bank of New York (BoNY), 106

Barrett, John, 152

bear notes, 147

Becchi, Scott, 93

behavioral finance, 169

Bello, Nancy, 152

Berlin Wall, collapse of, xvii, 36, 40, 54

Bernard, Edward, 43, 177

Bernstein, Richard, 135, 136

bespoke products, 152

Bessemer Trust, 106, 156

"Beyond Markowitz" (Chhabra), 132

Bill and Melinda Gates Foundation, xxxi, 193

BlackRock, 37, 43, 58, 129–30, 142, 158, 161, 165, 195

Blackstone Group, 114, 157, 158, 159

Bodurtha, Stephen, 145, 146

Bombay Sensex, 68

Bono, 193

Born Rich (documentary), 163, 164–65

boutiques (financial services), xxv, 88, 89, 104, 106

Brandeis, Louis, 168

Branson, Richard, 190–91

Brazil, xxix, 25, 58–59, 67–68

BRIC nations, 25, 28

Britain, 42

Buffett, Warren, xxxi, 167, 174, 191, 203, 204
    influence on Michael Lee-Chin, 210

Bulgaria, 72

Burk, Darcie, 59, 60, 178, 179

business ownership, xix, 21–22, 23, 108–9

C

CAC 40 (France), 26

Calamander Group, 13

Canada, 67–68

Canton, James, xxxii

Capgemini, 15, 78, 91, 93, 221

Capital Investment, Inc., 35

capitalism, 41

Capital Research and Management Co., 41, 131, 165, 195

Caribbean private banks, xxi

Carlyle Group, 157

Carnegie, Andrew, 156, 193

Carnegie Steel Company, 156

Carroll, Christopher, 29–30

Carroll, Jon, 95

cash/deposits, 125, 136
catastrophe bonds, 147
CCC Alliance, 172
Cemex (Mexico), 73
Center for Excellence in Higher
    Education, 188
Center of Philanthropy, Indiana
    University, 195
Central Registration Depository
    (CRD), 17
certified financial planners (CFPs), 17
certified public accountants/personal
    financial specialists (CPAs/
    PFSs), 17
charitable gift annuities, 196, 197
Charitable Lead Trusts, 197
charitable reminder trusts, 196
chartered financial consultants
    (ChFCs), 17
Chavez, Hugo, 41
Cheng Yu-Tang, 14, 202, 204
Chhabra, Ashvin, 132, 133, 134, 138
Children of Paradise (Hausner), 2
children of wealthy people, 3, 163
    comfort with equities, 178
    financial education, xxx–xxxi,
        169–70, 173, 181
    global context of, 177
    keeping wealth a secret from,
        164–65, 173
    and philanthropy, 199
    preparing to inherit wealth,
        165–66, 170–72
    trusts, 170
China, 37, 44, 136
    cell phone users, 45
    factory to the world, 27
    fixed exchange rate, 46
    foreign trade and exports, 45
    GDP, 25, 45
    HNWIs in, 137, 215, 216
    and India, 50
    and Latin America, 27–28
    managed currency of, xxxii
    offshore investments, 46
    policy changes, 45–46
    political unrest in, 41
    trading partners, 27–28
    wealth management in, 46–47
The Children's Investment Fund, 188
Christie's International, 140, 141
Chronicle of Philanthropy, 183, 198
Churchill, Winston, 205
Citigroup, 169
    Citibank, 47
    Citi Private Bank, 105
client-advisor relationships
    technology and, 80–81, 89–93, 213
    women and, 180
Client Associates (CAs), 91
client facing technology, 85, 86–87
CMA (Cash Management Account),
    6, 8, 9
collars (proprietary products), 146
collateralized debt obligations
    (CDOs), xxiii, xxiv
Collier, Charles, 172
Committee on the Global Financial
    System (CGFS), xxi
commodities, 28, 71, 125, 139
communism, collapse of, 36
concierge services, 100, 101, 213, 218
confidentiality, 118
    see also privacy
consumer price index (CPI), 30
content management systems, 85
Cost of Living Extremely Well Index,
    29–30
Côte d'Ivoire, 70
Creative Artists Agency, 140
credit card fraud, 82
credit crisis (2007-2008), xxi, xxiii, 140

credit default swaps (CDSs), 151
crony capitalism, 39, 45
Cruddas, Peter, 188
cultural globalization, 38
Cuoni, Jean Pierre, 188
CVRD (Brazil), 36

D
DAX (Germany), 26
day traders, 136
debt, as a financial tool, 109–12
decoupling, 69, 74, 123
decumulation, xxxii
Deng Xiaoping, 44–45
deregulation, 6
derivatives, 139, 220
developing countries, 34, 57, 67
    see also emerging markets
DigiTAG device, 83
disaster-related investments, 147
disclosure, xxx, 167
discount brokers, 11
disintermediation, 89–90
distressed hedge funds, 154–55
diversification, xviii, 60, 74, 122–23,
    130–31, 138, 146, 210
    challenges of, 131–32
DLF (India), 54
donor-advised funds, xxxii, 183,
    198–200
dot-com crash of 2001, 128–29, 220
Dow Jones Indexes, 27
    China 88, 68
    World Stock Index, 67
Dubai, xxix, 62, 71
Dunn, Danny, 169

E
E.A. Pierce & Co., 8
Eaton Estate, 184–85
eBay, 141

economic slowdown (2004-2005), 20
e-IPOs, xxxiv
Ellison, Lawrence, 29–30
emerging markets, xxix–xxx, 27, 64, 67
    becoming mainstream, 68–69
    coining the term, 33–37
    declining returns, 69
    GDP growth in, 25
    hedge funds, 154
    HNWI/ultra-HNWI investment
      in, 27, 39, 44, 127
    mutual funds, 67
Emerging Markets Fund/Growth
    Fund, 35
Emerging Portfolio Fund Research, 67
emotionality of wealth, 169, 171
Employee Stock Option Plans
    (ESOPs), 146
energy sector hedge funds, 154
Enron, 56, 194
entrepreneurs, 21
    in emerging markets, 39
    invested in own businesses, 132
equities, 125, 146
Equity Office Properties Trust, 144,
    158
Estonia, 72
E*TRADE Securities, 90
Europe, 21–22, 26
    aging population/low birth rate, 55
    Eastern, 36
    GDP, 25
    and globalization, 54
    HNWIs in, 24
    wealthy lifestyles in, 30
European Central Bank, 54
European Union, 54–56
exchange traded funds (ETFs), 146
Extreme Future, The (Canton), xxxii

F

family balance sheets, 86, 88, 89, 113
family education, xix, xxx–xxxi
family foundations, 198
Family Office Exchange, 172, 218
Family Office Metrics, 95
family offices, xxv, 112–14, 156, 218
    primary functions of, 112
FDI (Foreign Direct Investment) in
        India, 51
Federal Reserve Board, 6
    survey of Consumer Finance, 110
Federal Securities Agency, 160
Fidelity Investments, 11, 71
financial advisors, xx, 13–15, 65, 103
    accreditation and designations, 17
    in Asia, 48
    changing role of, 11–13
    children of HNWIs, 178
    expectations of, xxvii, xxviii, 65,
        100–101, 106–9
    fee structure, 18
    and female HNWIs, 180
    finding, 16–19
    holistic approach to services, 220–21
    meeting client needs, 13
    performance benchmarks, 19
    philosophy and interests, 17
    recruiting and training, 13–15
    referrals to, 16
    relationships with clients, 14,
        15–16, 124
    remuneration, 17
    services offered, 18
    technology for, 88–89
    and wealth transfers, 175–77
financial boot camps, xxx–xxxi, 1–2, 4,
        168, 169–70, 219
financial education, xxx–xxxi
    boot camps, xxx–xxxi, 1–2, 4, 168,
        169–70, 219

and security, 83
financial globalization, 38
Financial Industry Regulation Author-
        ity (FINRA), 17
financial literacy, xxvii
Financial Planning Association (FPA),
        17
Financial Services Authority (FSA), 17
financial services industry
    advertising, 7
    and art purchases, 142
    automation, 11–12
    boutiques, xxv, 88, 89, 104, 106
    business ownership services, 108–9
    client satisfaction, 79, 80–81
    commission, 5
    competition, 12, 80, 89, 92, 97,
        217–18
    confidentiality, 82–83
    evolution of, xxiv, 11
    mergers and acquisitions, 104–6
    regulation, 6–7
    services for HNWIs and ultra-
        HNWIs, xxiii, 4, 12, 15–16
    and technology, 5, 79, 80–81,
        84–85, 90
    traditional approach, 113
    transitioning from transaction-based
        to wealth management, 5–7, 8
financial sponsors, 156
    see also private equity (PE)
Fink, Larry, 37, 43, 129–30, 161, 165,
        166
Finlay, Francis, 34
First Republic Bank, 104–5
First Reserve Corp, 158
fixed income, 125
Forbes 400, xxii, 133
foreign currency, 125
foreign exchange ("forex") investments,
        139, 151

for-profit charity, 189, 192
  see also venture philanthropy
Forrester Research, 84, 90
Fortress Investment Group, 159
Fox, Vincent, 60
France, 26
Franklin Resources, 66
Franklin Templeton Investments, 35,
    66, 71, 170
Freeman, Doug, 168
frontier markets, xxix, 70, 71–72, 74
funds of funds
    hedge funds, 155–56
    private equity, 160

G

Gallagher, Tommy, xxxiv
Gant, Chris, 93
gap of thought, 169
Gates, Bill, xxxi, 89, 90, 174, 191, 203,
    204
Gazprom (Russia), 36
gender, and wealth management,
    179–80
Gen X-ers, 13
Germany, 26
giving while living, xxxi–xxxii, 189,
    193–95
Glass-Steagall Act, 6, 7
global capitalism, xvii
    see also globalization
global economies, wealth creation in,
    67
globalization, xxi, xxiii, xxvii, 36, 74
    challenges for United States, 57
    detractors of, 40–41
    facets of, 38
    future of, xxxii–xxxiii
    impact on HNWIs, 37–44
    and investment opportunities,
      63–65

and local investing, 61–63
and philanthropy, 107–8
and private equity, 157
problems with, 42, 43
and reporting, 115
rise in international investing,
    xxix–xxx
and technology, 75–76
and ultra-HNWIs, 128
and wealth management, 212
Goldman Sachs, 28, 131
Google.org, 190
Grameen Bank, 42, 189
Grameen Foundation, 190
gross domestic product (GDP), 24–25
Grosvenor, Gerald Cavendish, 6th
    Duke of Westminster, 185, 204
Grosvenor, Hugh Lupus, 1st Duke of
    Westminster, 185
Grosvenor, Ralph, 184
Grupo Modelo (Mexico), 73

H

HAM (hold all mail), 118
Hamilton Bradshaw, 70–71
Hamilton, Sara, 218
Hartnett, Michael, 71
Hausner, Lee, 2–3, 168, 171
Havens, John, 219
Hawkamah, 61
health care expenses, 104
Hedge Fund Industry Asset Flow
    Report (2007), 154
hedge funds, xxxiii, 69, 111, 125, 139,
    152, 153–56, 159, 161, 213, 220
    distressed, 154–55
    emerging markets, 154
    energy sector, 154
    funds of funds, 155–56
    growth of, 153–54
    institutional investors, 155

and liquidity, 158
regulations, 160
Henderson Land Development, 149, 201
high-net-worth individuals (HNWIs), xx, xxiv, xxv–xxviii, xxxii, 11
  breakdown of regional assets, 23
  children living abroad, 177–78
  expectations for service, 76, 115–16
  gender, 179–80
  and globalization, 37–44
  growth of wealth, xxii–xxiii, xxxiv
  in insecure regions, 118
  international investing, 66, 68–69
  lifestyles of, 29–30
  local investments, xxx, 61, 62, 64
  next generation of, 176–77, 177–78, 204
  number of, xx, xxii–xxiii, xxxiv, 10, 24, 214
  preferred asset allocations, 125–30
  prime driver of wealth, 24–29
  regional differences in wealth, 24
  requirement for financial advisors, xxvii
  retirement, xxxii
  sources of wealth, 20–21
  talking to children about wealth, 3
HNWIs. *See* high-net-worth individuals (HNWIs)
Ho Chi Min Stock Index, 68
Hohn, Chris, 188
Holistic Wealth Management (HWM), 9, 99–100, 102
  clear reporting, 114–17
  finding an advisor, 16–19
  origins of, 102–3
  and specialist teams, 103–4
  using debt to build wealth, 109–12
Hong Kong, 48, 215
Hon Hai (Taiwan), 73

Hope Group, 44
Hurricane Katrina, 147
hurricane risk, 148
Hutchison Whampoa Ltd., 200
Hyundai (South Korea), 36

I
IFC Emerging Markets Index, 35
IFF Advisors, 2, 168, 174
Imara African Opportunities Fund, 71
Imara Asset Management, 71
income earners, 21, 22, 23
income gap, 22
income taxes, 22
India, 37, 44, 49–54, 68
  ADRs (American Depositary Receipts), 52
  and China, 50
  foreign direct investment policies, 51
  globalization, 49
  GDP, 25
  HNWIs in, 53, 215
  local investment, 62
  Non-Resident Indians (NRIs), 51–53
  outsourcing to, 28, 51
Indonesia, 27, 136–37, 216
industrial globalization, 38
informational globalization, 38
information gap, 76
information technology (IT), 85–89
  see also technology
inherited wealth, 21, 23
inheritor accounts, retaining, 176
Initial Public Offerings (IPOs), 26, 56, 57, 146
Institute for Private Investors, xxxiv
institutional investors
  and hedge funds, 155
"instividuals," 114

intergenerational wealth transfer, xxiii,
      4–5, 19, 111, 214, 219–20
   anxieties about, 219
   baby boomers', 174
   how wealth was originally made, 166
   and peer networking, 172–73
   regional diversity of, 177–79
   values-based plan, 171
   wealth transfer plan, 174–77
   when to transfer assets, 171
International Aviation Management
      Group (IAMG), 99
International Development Enter-
      prises, 192
International Development Law Insti-
      tute, 190
International Finance Corporation
      (IFC), 33, 70
international investing, xxix–xxx, 60,
      66, 74
International Monetary Fund (IMF),
      37
Internet, 42, 79, 177
   banking services, 77
   information available on, xxvii, xxx
   use by clients, 78–80
Internet bubble (1990s), 128–29
Investec, 71
investing
   fundamentals of, 64
   Lee-Chin's rules of, 210, 211
investments of passion, 107, 139, 213
investor-centric innovation, 146
investor sophistication, xviii, xxv, xxvii,
      75, 109, 135, 138, 144, 217
   and philanthropy, 196
Isle of Man, 39

J
Jamaica, 70
Janney, Stuart, 156

Japan, 136
   HNWIs in, 215
   markets, 26
Jianping Mei, 141
Johnson, Charles Bartlett, 66
Johnson, Gregory, 66, 68, 170
Johnson, Jamie, 163, 164–65
Jolie, Angelina, 193
JPMorganChase, 34, 48, 105, 169,
      218

K
Kennedy, James A.C., 77, 167, 195
Kenya, 70
Keynes, John Maynard, 203–4, 205
Khezri, Bijan, 139
Klein, Karen, 171
Kohlberg Kravis Roberts (KKR), 156,
      158
Kuwait, 62

L
Lam, Joseph, 14, 100, 148–49, 202
Latin America, xxi, 26, 36, 58–60
   entrepreneurs, 39
   GDP, 25
   hedge funds, 59
   HNWIs in, 24, 58, 179, 215
   local investment, 62
   trading with China, 27–28
Latvia, 72
Lavayssière, Bertrand, xvii, 15, 38, 58,
      91, 92
Lavin, Richard, xxxiv
Lee, Albert, 46, 47–49, 173
Lee-Chin, Michael, 207–13
   rules of investing, 210, 211
   Warren Buffett's influence on,
      210
Lee Shau-Kee, 14, 148–50, 201–2,
      204, 213

legacy systems, 85, 87–88, 115
Le Grosveneur, Gilbert, 184
leveraging investments, 110–11, 155
liabilities, 135
Liberty Fund, 194
life insurance, 111
Li Ka-Shing, 200–201
Li Ka-Shing Foundation, 200
linear programming, 121
liquidity, xxvii, 43
liquidity risk, 43–44
Lithuania, 72
Liu Youping, 201
local currencies, 29
London FTSE 100, 26
Luxembourg, 4, 39
luxury goods, 30
Lynch, Edward, 5, 7

M

Maastricht Treaty, 54
Mackenzie Group, 211
Malaysia, 216
Marcus, Bernard, 188
market capitalization, 26
Market Index Target-Term Securities (MITTs), 145
market risk, 129, 134
Markowitz, Harry, 121–23, 124, 138
Marrelli, James, 144
"mass-affluent" investors, xxxiv–xxxv, 10–11
mature economies, 67
Mayer, Martin, 8
McCann, Bob, xvii, 38
McLaughlin, Patricia, 54
Medallion Fund, 76–77
Mei Moses All Art Index, 141
Mellon Financial, 106
mergers and acquisitions, 104–6
Merrill, Charles Edward, 5, 7, 221

Merrill Lynch, 5, 12, 169, 220
    acquisition of First Republic Bank, 104–5
    in Asia, 49
    Financial Boot Camp, xxx–xxxi, 1–2, 168, 169
    "The Financial Foundation," 10, 102
    Holistic Wealth Management (HWM), 102
    in India, 53–54
    innovations by, 7–8
    in Latin America, 59
    Private Banking and Investment Group (PBIG), 11, 49, 101, 150, 171
    Private Wealth Advisors (PWAs), 15
    services for HNWIs and ultra-HNWIs, 10–11
    and technology, 90
    Trusted Global Advisor (TGA), 90–91
    wealth transfer workshops, 175
    Wealth Management Work Station, 91
Met Circle, xxxiv
Mexico, 67–68
    mortgage market, 60
    peso devaluation (1994), 36
Michael Lee-Chin Crystal, Royal Ontario Museum, 207
micro-lending programs, 41–42, 189
Middle East
    emerging markets in, xxix–xxx
    GDP, 25
    HNWIs in, 24, 216
    and investing in developed markets, 40
    local investing in, 61–62
    oil reserves, 28–29

middleware, 85

The Milken Institute, 153

Miller, Merton, 123

mission statements, for families, 171–72

Mitchell, Marcus, 110, 111

Mobius, Mark, 35

Modern Portfolio Theory (MPT), 119, 122–25
     effects on wealth management, 123, 124
     moving beyond, 130–35

Moeder, Alyssa, 179, 180

Morgan, J.P., 156

Morgan Stanley, 160
     Emerging Markets Index, 28, 70

mortgages, 60, 143

mortgage meltdown (2007-2008), 143

Moses, Michael, 141

MSCI AC Asia-Pacific Index, 67

MSCI Emerging Markets Index, 71, 73

multi-family offices, xxv
     see also family offices

mutual funds, 155

N

Namibia, 70

Nathu La Pass, 50

National Association for Personal Financial Advisors (NAPFA), 17

natural gas, 28

Niu Gensheng, 201

non-profits, and scandals, 194–95

Non-Resident Indians (NRIs), 51–53

North America
     foreign investment in, 57
     HNWIs in, 24
     and international investing, xxix
     sources of wealth, 22

Northern Trust Corp., 104, 106

NRI Portfolio Investment Scheme, 53

O

OASIS (Organization for the Advancement of Structured Information Standards), 95

offspring of wealthy people. *See* children of wealthy people

oil, 28–29, 61–62

Omidyar Network, 190

Omidyar, Pierre, xxxi, 190

O'Neal, Stan, 12

online private banking, 77–85

online security threats, 82–83

online trading, xxxiv, 97

open architecture, 86, 91–92, 101, 220

Oprah Winfrey Leadership Academy, 193–94

outsourcing technology functions, 51, 94–96

Ovitz, Michael, 140

P

Pakistan, 71

Paulson, Henry, 131–32

peer networking, xxxiv, 172–73

personal risk, 129, 134

philanthropy, xxxi–xxxii, 181, 183–205
     accountability, 187–88, 194–95
     celebrities, 193
     decline in, 202–3
     encouraging in employees, 187
     and globalization, 107–8
     infusion of business ideas into, 186–87
     measurable results, 195
     online tools, 194
     regional differences, 188–89, 200–202
     rise in, 174, 185–86
     tax implications, 195–98

Philadelphia Housing Index, 147
Philippines, 27
Phipps, Henry, 156
PlaNet Finance, 41, 192
Plano Real, 59
political globalization, 38
Polito, Paula, 108
pooled income funds, 196, 197
populism, 41
portfolios, ideal, 126
Portland Holdings, 212
PowerShares Listed Private Equity
    Portfolio, 159
prenuptial agreements, 2, 3
privacy, 117, 167
private banks, xxv, 4, 217, 220
    Asia, 47–49, 215
    high-touch versus technology,
        80–82
    mergers and acquisitions, 104–6
    Merrill Lynch, 11
    online, 77–85
    Switzerland, xxi, 4, 82
    traditional, xxi
Private Equity Intelligence, 157
private equity (PE), xxxiii, 125, 139,
    152, 156–60, 161, 220
    funds of funds, 160
    returns on, 157, 159
private investment corporations
    (PICs), 118
Private Wealth Advisors (PWAs), 15
products
    new, xviii, 150–52
    purchasing or selling, 107, 109
professional organizations, 17
proprietary technology, 76
protected equity-linked notes (PENs),
    145
provider facing technology, 85, 87–88
pure-play administrative specialists, 94

Q
Qatar, 71

R
Ratcliffe, David, 194, 196, 199
real estate, 125, 132, 143–44, 147, 213,
    220
Regan, Donald, 5, 6, 7
REITs (real estate investment trusts),
    125, 143, 144
Renaissance Technologies (Rentec), 76
reporting, 114–17
    four pillars of, 115–16
retirement, xxxii
reverse inquiries, 150
The Right to Play, 188
risk
    and alternative investments, xxix,
        161
    and diversification, 138
    global, 61
    and ideal portfolio, 126
    liquidity, 43–44
    private equity and, 157
    and structured products, 145, 146
    tolerance for, 135–36
    typical factors, 129
    unexpectedly high/low returns, 128
risk allocation, xxviii, 134
risk management, xxviii
    see also asset allocation
risk premium, 123
Rockefeller, John D., Sr., 193
Romania, 68, 72
Rothenberg, James, 41, 131, 165, 195
Royal Bank of Scotland (RBS), 216
Royal Dutch Shell, 44
Royal Ontario Museum, 212
    Michael Lee-Chin Crystal, 207
RTS Index (Russia), 26, 28, 68
Rubin, Robert, 131

Russell, George, 172
Russia, xxi, 26, 68
   commodities, 28
   GDP, 25
   sovereign debt default, 36, 44

S
Saadie, Michael, 13, 151, 176, 200
Sachs, Jeff, 202–3
Samsung Electronics (South Korea),
   36, 73
São Paulo Bovespa, 58
Sarbanes-Oxley (SOX), 56, 159
Sasol (South Africa), 36
Saudi Arabia, 62, 70
scandals, corporate, 194
Scaturro, Peter, 105
Schengen Agreement, 54
Schervish, Paul, 204, 219
Schlosstein, Ralph, 142, 158, 195
Schueneman, Diane, 91
Schultz, Howard, 201
Securities and Exchange Commission
   (SEC), 6, 17, 57
security (technology), 82–83
September 11, 2001, 39–40
Service-Oriented Architecture, 85, 94,
   95–96
Shanhai/Shenzhen market, 26
Sharpe ratios, 124
Sharpe, William, 123, 124, 138
Shelterwood Financial Services, 166
Shenzhen Pengnian Hotels, 201
Simons Foundation, 191
Simons, James, 76, 191
Simonyi, Charles, 76–77, 141, 196,
   204
Singapore, 37, 68, 137
   financial advisors in, 13
   HNWIs in, 215
   offshore banking in, 55

Singapore Wealth Management
   Institute, 14
Slattery, Dómhnal, 99–100, 107, 114
Slim Helu, Carlos, 37, 187
Slovakia, 72
Slovenia, 70, 72
social entrepreneurs, 184
socialism, 41
Sonnenfeldt, Michael, xxxiv
Sontag, Daniel, 142
Sotheby's Holdings, 140, 141
South Korea, 136, 137
Sovereign Wealth Products (SWPs),
   40
specialist teams, 103–4
special purpose acquisition companies
   (SPACs), 159
spending, 29–30
Standard & Poor's 500 Index, 26, 73,
   142
Standard & Poor's/IFC Frontier Index,
   70, 71, 72
Steffens, John L. "Launny," 8–9, 102
stock exchanges, regional, 24, 26
stocks and bonds, 143
Stony Brook, 191
structured products, xxi, xxiii–xxiv, 125,
   139, 145–48, 213, 220
   bear notes, 147
   individual versus institutional
      clients, 145
subprime mortgage meltdown (2007-
   2008), 143
Suer, Oral, 194–95
Sullivan, Michael, 100, 101
Sweeney, Tom, 150, 151
Switzerland, xxi, 4, 39, 55, 82, 118
Synergos, 172

T
Taiwan, 37, 46, 47, 73, 216

Tan, Victor, 14–15, 178
taxes
    income, 22
    and philanthropy, 195–98
    withholding tax (Switzerland), 55
tax havens, 39, 55
technology, 5, 75–97, 103, 213
    benefits for clients, 76
    client familiarity with, 78–80
    client satisfaction, 79, 80–81, 82
    and competition, 89, 92, 97
    cost of investment, 84–85
    and culture, 96–97
    and globalization, xxxii, 40
    outsourcing, 94–96
    and philanthropy, 194
    revenue growth, 82, 84
    security, 82–83
    and transparency, 83–84
    wealth made in, 10
    and workflow, 87
Templeton Emerging Markets Fund,
    35
Templeton, Sir John, 35, 188
Thailand, 36, 37, 44, 216
Thiel, John, 101–2
Third World Equity Fund, 33, 34–35
Threshold Group, 172
Tiffany, Paul, xxxii
TIGER 21, xxxiv, 172
time horizon, 136
transparency, 7, 39, 83–84, 116, 167
Trappist monasteries, 192
TrendSight Group, 179
Triple A strategic approach to wealth
    management, 9
Trusted Global Advisor (TGA), 90–91
trusts, 170
Tucker, Nick, 219
TXU Corp., 158
Tyco, 194

U

Ukraine, 70
Ullens, Baron Guy, 188
ultra-high-net-worth individuals
    (ultra-HNWIs), xx, 218
    and asset allocation, 125–30
    demands of, xxv–xxviii
    education of offspring, 1–2
    and emerging markets, 127
    and globalization, 128
    and Holistic Wealth Management
        (HWM), 103
    and new products, 151
ultra-HNWIs. *See* ultra-high-
    net-worth individuals
    (ultra-HNWIs)
United Arab Emirates, 68, 216
United States, 56–58
    falling dollar, 58, 214
    GDP, 25
    and globalization, 56
    income taxes, 22
    philanthropy, 188–89
    regulations, 56–57
Unitus, 190
uptiering, 93, 221
U.S. Private Equity Performance
    Index, 157
U.S. Trust, 104, 105

V

values retreats, 170–72, 219
van Agtmael, Antoine, 33–36, 39, 73
Vanderbilt, Cornelius, 163–64
Vanderbilt, William, 164
Vardy, Nicholas, 70
venture philanthropy, xxxi, 189–92
Vietnam, xxix, 68, 71, 72
Vietnam Stock Exchange, 70, 72
Virtual Service Networks, 94–95
Volatility Index (VIX), 142

W

Waldron, Kevin, 147
wealth, 214–18
  earned, 22, 23
  inherited, 23
  regional differences, 21–24, 214–16
  spending, 29–30
Wealth Allocation Framework (WAF),
    xxviii, 132, 133–35
wealth management, xxviii
  eight convictions about, xviii–xix
  four pillars of, 31
  future of, xxxii–xxxv, 213–14
  and globalization, 212
  holistic approach to, xxvi–xxvii
  impact of technology on, 75–97
  Service-Oriented Architecture, 96
wealth management firms, 4, 161
  see also financial services industry
wealth management framework,
    207–13
wealthy families
  dysfunction, 167–68
  emotionality of financial decisions,
    169
  mission statements, 171–72
  tracking net worth, 168
Westminster, Duke of, 184–87, 188, 192
wind risk, 147
Winfrey, Oprah, 193–94
withholding tax (Switzerland), 55
women, and wealth, 179–80
WorldCom, 56, 194
World War 1, 42
World Wealth Report, xxii, xxiii, xxiv,
    xxix, 30
  1997, xx, 221
  2000, 10
  2006, 20, 75, 115, 174, 177
  2007, 23, 52, 142, 174, 183, 214
Wriston, Walter, 7

Y

Yang Lan, 200–201
Yunus, Muhammad, 41–42, 189–90
Yu Pengnian, 201

Z

Zell, Sam, 144